Pit
Bull

Pit Bull

Lessons from Wall Street's Champion Trader

Martin "Buzzy" Schwartz
with Dave Morine
and Paul Flint

HarperBusiness
A Division of HarperCollinsPublishers

HarperCollins books may be purchased for educational, business, or sales promotional use. For information please write: Special Markets Department, HarperCollins Publishers, Inc., 10 East 53rd Street, New York, NY 10022.

FIRST EDITION

Designed by Nancy Singer Olaguera

Library of Congress Cataloging-in-Publication Data

Schwartz, Martin S.
    Pit bull : lessons from Wall Street's champion trader / Martin "Buzzy" Schwartz with Dave Morine and Paul Flint.
        p. cm.
    Includes index.
    ISBN 0-88730-876-7
    1. Floor traders (Finance) 2. Wall Street. I. Morine, Dave. II. Flint, Paul. III. Title.
HG4621.S295 1998
332.64'273—dc21   97-49931

98 99 00 01 02 ❖/RRD 10 9 8 7 6 5 4 3 2 1

*To all of my family, especially my wife, Audrey,
who embodies the essence of life*

"How long can you stay at the top?"

—Sir Edmund Hillary

Contents

Acknowledgments   xi

1 Trade or Fade   1
  Mashed Potatoes   *15*

2 The Plan   17
  The Grubstake   *30*

3 Paradise Island   33
  Viva Las Vegas   *47*

4 The Great Pyramid   49
  Inside Skinny   *67*

5 Auric Schwartz   69
  Going for the Gold I   *77*

6 Made to Trade   81
  Switch Hitting   *96*

7 Never Short a Republican   99
  The Losing Streak   *110*

8 Champion Trader   113
  Honor Thy Stop   *122*

9 Little Brown Bags   125
  To Thine Own Self Be True   *141*

10 Lots 204 and 207   143
  Big Shots Make Big Targets   *156*

11 Going for the Gold II   159
  Sitting Down by the Lake, Waiting
    for the Tidal Wave   172

12 Commodities Corp   175
  How I Read the Wall Street Journal   185

13 Sabrina Partners   189

14 How's My Money Doing?   203
  Sorry, Dad, You're Fired   212

15 Down the Tubes   215
  Two Lessons for Life   229

16 Night Fighting   233
  Money Talks, Bullshit Walks
    (aka Early in the Day, Early in the Week)   246

17 The Best Trade   249

The Pit Bull's Guide to Successful Trading   263
  My Typical Day   288

Index   295

Acknowledgments

I would like to thank my family for their universal support and encouragement throughout my life. To my parents who oftentimes sacrificed greatly to give me the best education and a loving and honest home. To my brother, Gerry, who spent many hours teaching me to be a better athlete and a better person. To Pappy Snyder who represented the epitome of optimism and left me with the legacy of his journal to continue the "story." To my wife, Audrey, who is the rock of the family and able to demonstrate great humanity and wisdom. To my children, Stacy and Bowie, who teach me how rewarding and challenging it is to be a good parent.

To Dave Morine who had the vision and skill to bring me through this project. To Ruth Morine for her constant cheerful encouragement. To Paul Flint for his marvelous intellect and good humor—once a Marine, always a Marine. Semper Fi. To Jim Levine, my agent, Amherst classmate, and friend, for his patient guidance and professional skills. To Morgan McKenney, my superb assistant, for her energy and drive in helping me finish the last chapter, "The Pit Bull's Guide to Successful Trading."

To all of the people at HarperBusiness for their help in bringing this project home—you are all first-class. To Adrian Zackheim for gambling on a first-time author and seeing the project through. To Dave Conti for his superb editorial skills—your suggestions made the book much better. To Lisa Berkowitz for her marketing skills and promotional contacts. To Janet Dery, Maureen Kelly, and Amy Lambo for making this project easier.

To all of those unnamed people who have taught me so much both good and bad along this journey that is called life.

Thanks,
Buzzy

Trade or Fade

Three Bid for Ten, Three Bid for Ten, Three Bid for Ten. I kept saying it over and over in my mind like a mantra. If Mesa Petroleum hit 62⅝, I was going to try and buy ten October 65 call options at $300 per option. Each option would give me the right to buy one hundred shares of Mesa stock at a "strike price" of $65 per share any time up until the third Friday in October, the expiration date of the call option. This was going to be my first trade from the floor of the American Stock Exchange and I was scared to death that I was going to screw it up, that I wasn't going to be able to hack it as a trader.

It was Monday morning, August 13, 1979, and Trinity Place was bustling with men in business suits heading to work. New York's financial world was preparing to start another day. I stopped outside the entrance of the building marked 86, took a deep breath, pulled out my badge, and for the first time walked through the door that said "Members Only." The guard looked at my badge, saw that it said "Martin Schwartz & Co., 945," nodded a good morning, and let me in.

I turned left down the stairs to the coatroom. Members were lined up at the counter, exchanging their sport jackets for their blue smocks, the official garb of the American Stock Exchange. Since it was my first day, I didn't have a blue smock, so I had to introduce myself to Joey Dee, the attendant, and give him my badge number, "945." I put on my smock, pinned on my badge, and checked to make sure that I had my pen. Men in blue smocks were sitting on benches all around me changing their shoes, putting on crepe soles and shoving their leather ones into the cubbyholes that lined the walls. I couldn't find a seat so I decided to change my shoes later. Having crepe soles was the least of my worries.

I went upstairs to the members' lounge to await the opening. Walking into the members' lounge of the American Stock Exchange was not like walking into the Harvard or Yale Club. The cloud of smoke that hung over the room came from cigarettes, not pipes; the furniture was covered in Naugahyde, not leather; and the members were mostly Irish, Italians, and Jews, not WASPs, or at least WASPs who had gone to the right schools. These guys were the B team of finance, the direct descendants of the Curb Exchange, the group of bootleg traders who ran their books on the streets outside the New York Exchange from the 1890s until 1921.

I made myself a cup of tea and walked out onto the floor. The morning light streamed through the enormous windows that take up almost the entire wall on the far side of the Exchange. It's a huge room, about three-quarters the size of a football field and easily five stories high. The floor was set up a lot like an indoor flea market. Specialists, guys named Chickie and Frannie and Donnie, the people who made the market on specific stocks and options, were perched on metal stools in front of horseshoe-shaped racks of pigeonholes going through their orders. There were different pigeonholes for different stocks, options, expiration dates, strike prices, day orders, market orders, whatever. The other members, the traders and brokers, were wandering around, pens and tickets in hand, getting ready to buy and sell.

Above, in the balcony, which was suspended over three sides of the floor, representatives from the brokerage houses sat in tiers, checking their phones and spotting their runners on the floor. Between them, on the near wall, spectators were beginning to file into the visitors' gallery. Holding everything up were huge Roman columns with bulls and bears sculpted on either side and binding it all together, like the ribbon around a huge box of candy, was the big Trans Lux ticker tape. The tape ran along the walls blinking out the prices of all the stocks while just above it the Dow Jones wire flashed the latest news. Even though the Exchange had yet to open, all eyes were darting around searching for quotes and other bits of information that might give them an edge.

Precisely at ten, the bell rang and everyone started moving.

They reminded me of horses breaking from the gate, except now *I* was part of the race. I galloped over to the far corner where Mesa options were traded. A noisy little crowd of blue smocks was gathering around Louis "Chickie" Miceli, the specialist. The specialists for stocks and options on the Amex were responsible for maintaining orderly markets. As the specialist for Mesa options, it was Chickie's job to facilitate buy and sell orders for other brokers and to trade for his own account, constantly adjusting the market price so that the supply matched the demand.

"Chickie!" shouted a broker from Merrill, "How are the Oct 65 Mesa calls, Chickie?" He was coming in from the edge of the crowd with a public order.

"Three to a quarter, fifty up," Chickie said. I had to work through in my mind just what they were saying. Chickie would buy up to fifty October 65 Mesa options at a price of 3 and sell up to fifty at a price of 3¼. Since an option represented one hundred shares of stock, that meant that at this moment I could buy up to fifty options for $325 per option. Each option would give me the right to buy one hundred shares of Mesa stock at a price of $65 per share at any time between now and the third Friday in October. I was betting that before then the price of Mesa would go up, making my options more valuable. But 3¼ was too much. I was willing to buy ten options at 3, for a total of $3,000. The mantra kept ringing in my head, "Three Bid for Ten, Three Bid for Ten."

"Three and an eighth bid for ten," barked Merrill.

"Sold," yelled a guy from Hutton. The Hutton broker had hit the bid from the floor. If he hadn't, Chickie, as the specialist for Mesa options, could have hit the bid at 3⅛, or could have placed it on his book. I wished that my ear was attuned to the language of the floor. That would come with time, I hoped.

I checked the quote screen above Chickie's head. Mesa had opened on the New York Stock Exchange at 62⅞. I nudged my way further into the crowd. Elbows dug into my ribs as other traders jockeyed for position. I wormed in as close as I could. Chickie had a phone cradled to his ear checking on how Mesa was running on the Big Board, the New York Stock Exchange (NYSE).

Tick. The quote above him changed to 62⅝.

The crowd started to come alive. Mesa was moving. "Three Bid for Ten, Three Bid for Ten," I mumbled to myself. I cleared my throat. "Hey, Chickie. How many Oct 65 calls offered at three?"

"Thirty offered at three, Newboy."

"Three bid for twenty," someone next to me yelled.

"SOLD! Twenty at three," Chickie said.

"How many now at three?" I said.

"Ten offered at three."

"Er, um, ah . . . "

"What'll it be, Newboy, trade or fade?"

This was it, trade or fade. Buying a seat on the American Stock Exchange was the keystone to the plan I'd formulated twelve months earlier. The plan had been the result of my marriage to Audrey Polokoff. Unlike most of the women I'd known, Audrey saw that I had some potential, but she also knew that I'd spent the last decade pissing it away. "You're thirty-four and you've always wanted to work for yourself," she'd told me. "Make that your goal and go do it. You've got a good education. That'll always stay with you. The worst that can happen is that you'll go bust and go back to doing what you're doing now, being a securities analyst."

The market was moving. People were crowding in closer, the noise level was beginning to rise. Chickie had the phone glued to his ear. He was getting ready to change the bid. If my information was right, he'd be moving it up. I was going to miss my trade.

"THREE BID FOR TEN!" I shrieked.

"SOLD! Ten at three."

The trade was in. I pulled out my order pads and my pen. "Black to buy, red to sell," I muttered to myself, "don't screw it up." I wrote out my order and looked for the clerk. His job was to take the order and process it. One copy for me, one copy for Bear Stearns, whom I was using for my clearing firm. Clearing firms are bean counters; they run trades through the Exchange accounting systems and provide traders with daily profit and loss statements.

I took out the pen with my seal taped to the top and stamped the ticket "945." There, it was official, my first trade was done. Then I eased out of the pack and waited for Mesa to start ticking up.

It was only 10:30, but my blue smock, starchy clean when I'd put it on an hour earlier, already had circles of sweat under both armpits. I felt exhausted, there was a pain in my lower back and my feet were starting to hurt. My leather soles felt like lead. I would have sat down, but there was no place to sit. That was one of the anomalies of buying a seat on the Exchange. You didn't get a seat. You got the right to wander around the floor, and as every old-timer knew, you did that in crepe-soled shoes.

The action on Mesa was heavy. Chickie was throwing out bids and offers were flying back and forth. I could hear them, but I couldn't understand them. I gazed up at the tape.

Tick. 62⅜.

Mesa was heading in the wrong direction. Audrey's words, "The worst that can happen is that you'll go bust and have to go back to what you were doing before," flashed through my mind. I didn't want to go back to doing what I was doing before. For nine years I'd lived on airplanes, bouncing from city to city, meeting with portfolio managers, giving them my views on stocks so they'd give their commissions to my firm, kissing ass. That's what securities analysts do. They work for the research departments of brokerage firms and spend their time traveling around visiting companies, interviewing managers, digging through financial reports, looking for hot stocks that their firms can recommend to their clients. I was sick of it. When you're twenty-five, flying around the country big-shotting it up with your friends from college courtesy of your company's credit card is pretty cool, but when you're closing in on thirty-five, it's gotten pretty stale. Your friends are too busy with their own lives, and your parents are beginning to wonder if there's something wrong with you. They're the ones who paid the tuition and now expect a return on their investment. They're the ones who keep asking, "Why aren't you married? Where are our legacies? When are you going to grow up and get a life?"

Tick. 62¼. Ah, fuck.

All the time I'd been working as a securities analyst, I'd been playing the markets, and all the time, I'd been losing. I was smart, I had a good education, I'd been a winner all my life, so how come I could never make any money playing the market? I couldn't figure it out. Neither could my family. I was the one that the bets had rode in on, and I was the one still running in last place. Was the Schwartz family history about to repeat itself? Was I about to go tapioca and spend the rest of my life being frustrated like my father?

Tick. 62⅛. Still heading south.

My father was the oldest of four children. His parents were immigrants whose families had fled to America to escape the pogroms of Eastern Europe. In the early 1900s, my grandfather became a tailor in New Haven, Connecticut. He stitched and saved, but he never amounted to much. It was my grandmother Rose who had the drive. She owned a candy store and was determined that my father should go to college, that he should become a professional. As the oldest, he was the chosen son, the Moses who would lead the Schwartzes to the promised land, the one who'd deliver the American Dream to all of us.

My father had given it his best shot, but he didn't have it. He was more like my grandfather than Rose. He'd gone to Syracuse University, but by the time he collected his sheepskin it was 1929 and the American Dream was about to turn into the American Nightmare, the Great Depression. My father, along with millions of other Americans, bounced around from job to job until 1938 when he married my mother. Then, the best job he could get was working for my other grandfather, Pappy Snyder, which was hardly the promised land. After that came the war, but due to his age and two kids, he never served. It wasn't until 1952 that he finally made his big move. Pappy had retired and my father was out of a job, so he took all of our money, got a second mortgage on our house, and bought a mom-and-pop grocery store on Whalley Avenue in Westville, a suburb of New Haven.

I was only seven, but even I knew it was a bad move. What my father refused to see was that his store was just four doors down from a big new shiny First National supermarket. How he ever thought he was going to compete with the largest super-market chain in New England was beyond all of us. I remember asking my mother when I was older how she could let him do something that stupid. All she said was, "He was so desperate. I had to give him the chance to fail. Even failure was better than doing nothing."

Tick. 61⅞.

At least my father had the Depression. I had no excuse. I had degrees from Amherst College and Columbia Business School. I had been in the marines. I had the experience. I had Audrey. I had it all. What the hell was going on here? Why was Mesa still going down, when I knew it should be going up?

Tick. 61⅞. Doublefuck.

What should I do? Should I get out? Should I buy more? It was time to call Zoellner. It was Zoellner who'd gotten me into Mesa.

Bob Zoellner was my mentor, the best trader I'd ever met. I'd run into Zoellner back in 1973 when I went to work for Edwards and Hanly, a small retail brokerage firm. That was right after I'd gone tapioca playing commodities. Right away I saw that Zoellner was a great, great trader. In 1974, when Edwards and Hanly was hemorrhaging money on its retail brokerage operations, he'd almost single-handedly kept the company afloat by shorting stocks and making millions in the firm's trading account. Going "short" means selling shares of stocks that you don't own now, but will have to buy back later, hopefully at a lower price. Nobody was better at it than Zoellner.

I grabbed one of the phones that are scattered around the floor of the Exchange. I dialed for an outside line; the operator asked for the number. Zoellner was over in Jersey. What the hell was his number? 201-something. My mind had gone blank. I mumbled some numbers and the phone rang.

"Vickie! Vickie! Is Bob in? I've gotta talk to him. It's Marty. . . . How you doing? . . . Right, everything's fine. Yeah, I'm on the floor now. New experience." Pause. "Bob. How you doing? What do you think of the market? Yeah, yeah, me too, I'm a little nervous about it. Tape looks a little tired. Listen, Bob, I just bought some options in Mesa, whaddya think?"

"I got a big position in Mesa, Marty. It looks good. Boone Pickens is gonna go forward with the restructuring; I think there's real good value, but the market, the Street, doesn't see it yet; I feel very strongly it's going up."

"You do, Bob, you do? Thanks, Bob. You pretty sure about this one, Bob? Uh, ah, you know, ah, I don't know whether to buy more or what the hell to do."

"It looks good, Marty."

"God, I hope you're right. I'll talk to you soon, thanks a lot, really appreciate it."

Talking with Zoellner was good. I summoned up some more courage and waded back into the crowd around Mesa.

Tick. 61½.

"Chickie! Chickie! Uh." I could hardly get the words out. "How are the Oct 65 calls, Chickie?"

"Newboy, for you, they're two and a half bid, offered at two and five-eighths."

"Two and nine for twenty, Chickie! Two and nine!" I was bidding to buy twenty more options, each for a hundred shares of Mesa, at a price of 2⁹⁄₁₆ per share, or $256.25 per option, for a total of $5,125.

"Sold! Two and nine-sixteenths for twenty."

My October calls were trading in sixteenths now. On the American Stock Exchange, when a stock option drops below 3, the minimum trading increments move from eighths to sixteenths, the infamous "s'teenths."

Tick. 61¼.

Fuck, I couldn't watch anymore. I was now "long" thirty Mesa October 65 call options. Oh, man, I didn't think it was going to be this tough. I had to get off the floor. The only reason to stay there was to keep my money moving, but I didn't have any more money to move. I'd been positive that Mesa Petroleum was going to be a gusher. My plan had been to sell it for a quick profit and to roll the proceeds into a bigger and better trade. Now it was going against me and I didn't have any money coming in. I began to think about how I was going to live without a salary. I had to get out of there.

I trudged up the stairs, pushed open the door, and stepped

out into the sunlight, still in my blue smock. I walked across the street and wandered into Trinity Church Burial Ground. I found a free bench on the far side of the church and sat down. It was hot. The burial ground was a refuge for drunks, bums, and all kinds of other losers. It was a place they could hang out without getting hassled. None of the permanent residents ever complained.

I noticed that I was sitting in front of Alexander Hamilton's grave. The inscription on the white monument read, "Alexander Hamilton. Died July 12, 1804. Aged 47." Here I was, thirty-four years old.

July 12 was the day after Alex was shot in a duel with Aaron Burr in Weehawken, New Jersey. Alex had written a scathing article about how corrupt Burr was and why he shouldn't be the governor of New York, so Burr had shot him dead. Alex was the first secretary of the treasury and the financial father of our country, but had been forced to resign in 1795 because of personal financial problems. I remembered reading this in my American Studies course at Amherst and wondering how anybody so smart could have gotten so screwed up. Now I was beginning to understand. I got up, brushed off my blue smock, and walked slowly back across Trinity Place to check on Mesa.

Tick. 60⅝.

I slumped over to Chickie's post. "Chickie. The Oct 65 Mesa calls, how are they now?"

Chickie grinned back at me. "Newboy, they're two and a quarter bid, offered at two and three-eighths."

Chickie. My God, Chickie. My Mesas were dropping like a stone. I'd bought ten at 3 ($3,000), and twenty more at 2⁹⁄₁₆ ($5,125). Now they were bidding 2¼ ($6,750). On paper, I was down $1,375, a 17 percent loss in a few hours. I couldn't take it anymore. I had to think. I had to go home.

The next day, Tuesday the fourteenth, I felt better. Audrey had calmed me down. She'd told me that I was the smartest guy she'd ever met, that I had a great plan, that I just had to stick with it, that I had to be patient. I'd done all my charts and calculated my ratios, and Mesa still looked good, really good. It was like Zoellner had said, the market just hadn't seen it yet.

The sun was shining as I walked up Trinity Place. The guard at the "Members Only" door called me by name; when Joey Dee handed me my blue smock, it already had my "Martin Schwartz & Co., 945" badge attached to it; I remembered to change into my crepe-soled shoes and to check in with my clerk to pick up my daily printout from Bear Stearns. I got my cup of tea, with a lemon to save my voice, and headed for the floor. I walked around with a new spring in my step, thanks to my crepe soles. I checked the Trans Lux and the Dow Jones news wire. The bell rang. Mesa opened at 60½. All right. All right. Don't panic. This has to be the bottom. Audrey's right, I just have to be patient.

I waved hello to my friend Hayes Noel. Hayes was a southern boy, a tall blond from Nashville, who spoke with a drawl and had a bit of a cracker sense of humor. Hayes had gone to Sewanee, "The College of the South," and had been on the floor since 1970. It was Hayes who'd gotten me onto the floor with visitor passes before I bought my seat and had shown me how things worked.

I nodded to Jerry Muldoon, another old-timer. Jerry used to run outside the Exchange and sell crates of vegetables off of trucks back in '73 and '74 when the market was slow and he needed to make a few extra bucks. Over to his left, next to Donnie Gee, the specialist who made the book on Texaco options, were Allen Applebaum and Eddie Stern. They were the Exchange's sharp dressers. Allen was a wiry, whippet-looking guy who always wore a starched shirt, and Eddie, whose father had a seat on the New York Stock Exchange, always wore a suit rather than a blue smock.

Tick. 60⅜.

Oh, man. "Chickie. Chickie. The Oct 65 calls, what's happening?"

"Newboy. You still here?"

"Yeah, yeah. Just gimme a quote."

"Two and an eighth bid, offered at two anna quarter."

Holy shit, Chickie. "What's the size?"

"Fifty by thirty." That meant that Chickie was willing to buy fifty options at 2⅛ or sell thirty options at 2¼.

What do I do, what do I do? Sell? Do nothing? Buy? Time to call Zoellner.

"Bob, Bob, whaddya think, Bob? I'm down $1,750 and I'm dying. Are you sure you're right?"

"Marty, listen. I've done a lot of work in my day. I've had a lot of winners and a lot of losers; this is a winner. Just hold tight. It's undervalued. It has to come back."

"Thanks, Bob. I know I believe in you, baby. I know you're good." I trotted back to Chickie.

"How're the Oct 65 calls now, Chickie?"

"Same as before. Two and an eighth a quarter. Fifty by thirty."

"Three teenies bid for twenty, Chickie!"

"Sold! Newboy." I'd just bought another twenty options at 2³⁄₁₆. I'd committed another $4,375 and was now "long" fifty call options.

I didn't sleep at all that night. I tossed and turned, thinking and rethinking my position. Mesa had closed at 60. My options were threatening to sink below 2. The phrase "shoot dying quails" kept racing through my mind. How far could I ride this loser down? Was I going to give up everything I'd been working for?

For the past twelve months, I'd locked my door at my office at E. F. Hutton and worked feverishly, trading live rounds. I'd been playing the market with my own money to make more money so that I'd have enough capital when I moved to the Exchange and, more importantly, to prove to myself that I could be successful. Some analysts thought they were hot stuff because their hypotheticals, or "paper trading" models, showed how much money they could have made, but they were just shooting make-believe bullets and couldn't get hurt. You'll never know how good you really are until you've performed under fire. I was like Rose in the candy store, pushing ahead all the time. I'd subscribed to a dozen or more periodicals. I'd studied the floor with Hayes Noel. I'd borrowed $50,000 from my in-laws, Mac and Sally Polokoff. I had it all figured out; this was where I wanted to be.

I got up out of bed, went to my desk, and reviewed my plan. What was I doing wrong? I had spent a year and a half planning this trade. I'd made up a whole list of rules, and I'd already bent two of them badly. My first rule was never to risk more than I could afford to lose, yet I now had half of my working capital riding on one play. That couldn't be helped; I only had enough of a grubstake for two plays and given the information I had, dumping half of it on Mesa was my best bet.

My second rule was to try to book a profit every day, yet here I was, stuck for two days in the red, but that couldn't be helped either. It was the third rule, "shoot dying quails," that was bothering me. When was I going to pull the trigger? When would I have to admit that I was wrong and get out of the position? Even the best traders, even the Zoellners, had their share of losers. The way they hedged their bets was to maintain a diversified portfolio, only I didn't have enough money to build a diversified portfolio. Mesa was it. Finally, as the first rays of morning light crept through our bedroom window, I made my decision. If Mesa opened down again today, I was out.

Wednesday the fifteenth of August, 86 Trinity Place, "Members Only" door, blue smock, crepe soles, Bear Stearns profit and loss statement showing me down $2,300, cup of tea with lemon, out to the floor, check the Trans Lux and the Dow Jones wire. D-d-dr-ring . . .

Mesa opens 60¾, up ⅝. Yeah, baby, I'm with ya all the way. I run over to Chickie Miceli's post. People are jostling for position. The noise level is rising.

Tick. 61.

Louder, more crowded. People are starting to yell. "How's the market?" "What's offered there?"

Tick. 61½.

Zoellner. I love ya, baby. I knew you were good.

"What's the size?" "What's the quantity?" "What's bid for, how many are bid for?" "How many are offered?" "WHAT'S THE SIZE?"

The day wore on. I was too excited to eat lunch. I was loving it.

"Three to a quarter! Fifty at a quarter!" "TAKE 'EM! I'LL TAKE 'EM!" somebody yelled.

"Three and a quarter bid for fifty! Three and a quarter for fifty more!!" "SOLD!" "SOLD!"

Mesa's stock ticked at 63⅜! Tick. The Mesa October 65 calls were up again. "Three and five-eighths, it's seven-eighths, trades!" "Seven-eighths to four!" The noise level rose to a crescendo. "A hundred Mesa Oct 65 calls offered at four!" "Two hundred trading at four!" The options were really moving. The stock was in orbit. All hell was breaking loose. For what had to be the hundredth time I checked my position. Ten Oct 65s at 3. Twenty more at $2\frac{9}{16}$. And twenty more at $2\frac{3}{16}$. Do I sell now? Do I take profits? Do I buy more? Do I call Zoellner? Fuck it. It was time to hear the cash register ring.

I barged to the front. "Chickie! Chickie! Give me a market on Mesa!"

"Oct 65s, four and an eighth a quarter. Ten up." The spit hit my jacket. I cleared my throat to hit the bid. A big pink pudgy fist shot over my shoulder "Sold! SOLD! TEN AT AN EIGHTH!" The smell of cheap bourbon filled my nostrils. Shit, Fat Mike had taken my trade.

"What's it now?" Chickie was on his phone. "What's it now, Chickie?"

"Four to a quarter, twenty up, Newboy."

"SOLD! Twenty at four!" I squealed.

Tick. The stock moved to $64\frac{1}{8}$.

Someone else elbowed in behind me. "Four and a quarter bid for thirty." It was the guy from Merrill.

"SOLD," I screamed as I turned around and spit in his face. My trades were in, I was out. Sweat dripped off my nose as I worked toward the edge of the crowd. The pit clerk came over to confirm. I took out my pen, turned it around, and stamped the tickets with my "945."

Now it was time to count up my profits. Sold 20 at 4, 30 more at $4\frac{1}{4}$. That was $8,000 on the first sale and $12,750 on the second, a total of $20,750; my cost was $3,000 at 3 and $5,125 at $2\frac{9}{16}$, plus $4,375 at 2 and three teenies. Eight grand, baby eight grand. It felt like a million. I'd found the promised land; this was the American Dream. I hadn't gone tapioca; I wouldn't have to go back to being a securities analyst, no more kissing ass. I wasn't going to be sitting in the burial grounds next to the bums and Alexander Hamilton, and most of all, I wasn't going to be hammered by the Depression like my father. I had my freedom. I was running with the winners.

I strutted over to Digital Equipment, Frannie Santangelo's post. Frannie Santangelo, the toughest fuckin' dude in town. Not Chickie Miceli. Frannie's been through the Korean War. Smoking Camels on the side of the floor. He's tough.

"Rookie, whaddya want?"

"Frannie, I wanna play. How're the Oct 85 Digital calls?"

"One and five-eighths, three-quarters. For you, Rookie, I'll give ya ten at three-quarters."

"One and eleven for ten, Frannie."

"No way, Rookie. Gedoudahere, fahgedaboudit if you wanna play like a pussy. No way." This tough bastard wouldn't even give me a s'teenth, a lousy six and a quarter cents per share.

"All right, Frannie, I'll pay one and three-quarters for ten. Digital. Oct 85 calls." I thought to myself, You beat me for a s'teenth, Frannie, that's $62.50. I know you want to show me who's boss, you fuckin' pizza parlor operator. You got me today, but I'm here to stay. I'll get you next time.

Mashed Potatoes

"It's the latest, it's the greatest, come on baby, it's so easy to do. Oh, mashed potatoes, mashed potatoes, you can do it too. Mashed potatoes, mashed potatoes, yeah, yeah, yeah. . . ."

It was 3:59. Hayes Noel and I were up on the balls of our feet, twisting our crepe-soled shoes in opposite directions, dancing around the floor of the American Stock Exchange singing Dee Dee Sharp's 1962 hit. As my young son would later say, "It had been a big busy day." Discarded buy-sell slips covered the floor and we were getting some good sliding action. We were hot. I was up ten grand on paper for the day with only a minute to go. I'd only been trading on the floor for a couple of months, and I was so happy that I was doing so well and that my positions were all marked up in my favor that I didn't realize that I should have converted the ten grand into real money.

The market opened way down the next day, and because I'd been dancing instead of closing out my positions, I was locked in and lost the whole $10,000 in paper profits. From then on, I always fought back the temptation to start dancing before I'd heard the cash register ring. When you feel like doing the mashed potatoes, it's a visceral clue that you've lost your objectivity, you've gotten too emotional, and you're about to go into the shitter.

The other thing that's stupid is that you actually think you're dancing well. And, of course, you're not.

2

The Plan

"Audrey, we missed the turn. We're still on Route 84 West. We're going to freakin' Newburgh. Can't you read the map?"

"Buzzy, don't blame me. You're the one who's driving like a maniac."

"One job, that's all I give you, Audrey, one lousy job, and you screw it up. How could you miss Route 684? It's the main route to the City!"

"Buzzy, you're driving too fast, I can't read the signs. And how was I supposed to know we wanted 684?"

"Because you plan ahead, Audrey. You study the map before we get in the car. Plan ahead, Audrey, you gotta plan ahead!"

"Here, you plan ahead."

I ducked as the map sailed across the front of our leased Chrysler Cordoba. When I get flustered, I tend to lapse into my Marine Corps persona, which means that I expect Audrey to behave like a good captain's wife. That's usually a mistake, and today was no exception. Audrey was in no mood to have me barking orders at her, and I couldn't blame her. It was July 1978, the temperature was hovering near a hundred degrees, we were hot, we were tired, and now, having missed our turn, we were barreling toward Newburgh, New York, a beat-up old dump of a town on the backwaters of the Hudson River fifty miles north of New York City.

We'd just spent Sunday afternoon with our friends Rich and Susan Bertelli. Rich and Susan were former members of our group summerhouse in Westhampton Beach, out on the South Fork. They'd gotten married the previous winter and had bought a beautiful four-bedroom colonial in Danbury, Connecticut. They'd invited us up to show off their new house. When I saw it, I was impressed and jealous. Here were Susan, a freelance computer jockey, and Rich, a battery salesman for

Union Carbide, building up equity, racking up hefty tax deductions, and watching the value of their new home go up while Audrey, the head of the Paper Recycling Division of the American Paper Institute, and I, a high-powered analyst for E. F. Hutton, were paying rent, getting zero tax deductions, and sitting on the sidelines watching the real estate market boom without us. Together, Audrey and I were pulling down more than $100,000 a year, which had to be a lot more than Rich and Susan, but we couldn't afford this house.

"Rich, Susan," I said, "how can you afford such a beautiful home?" The four of us were sitting in their second-floor study guzzling iced tea. The windows were wide open but there wasn't a breath of air. I was sweating profusely. Obviously, one of Rich and Susan's financial secrets was that they pinched a few pennies by not turning on the air-conditioning.

"A plan, Buzzy," Susan said. "You've got to have a plan."

"A plan?" I said. "I get up, I go to work, I come home, I hope I have enough energy left to get laid, and I go to bed. That's my plan."

"And that's the problem. Tell us more," Audrey said.

And they did. Susan and Rich talked and talked, and Audrey and I listened and listened. The more I heard, the more I began to realize that sitting down and seriously developing a plan might not be a bad idea. I needed to do something. Despite all my college degrees and experience, I had yet to achieve success. Developing a plan with specific goals and setting a time frame for achieving them would at least get me thinking about what I should be doing. But I hated the thought of setting goals. I could feel the knot starting to grow in the pit of my stomach.

Goals meant commitments, and commitments meant obligations, and obligations meant mortgages, second mortgages, car payments, car insurance, life insurance, health insurance, homeowners' insurance, and, in my case, air-conditioning bills. What scared me most was the memory of my father stuck in a series of dead-end jobs, sitting in a mortgaged house, looking at a constant stack of bills, worrying about money. Getting trapped in the middle-class jail and ending up like my father was my worst fear. I couldn't let that happen to me. I mopped my brow with my sleeve. God, it was hot at the Bertellis'.

Freedom, I had to have my freedom, but as the afternoon wore on, I began to think that maybe my freedom wasn't so important. What had it done for me lately? I was a thirty-three-year-old securities analyst going nowhere. I had just flown back from Texas from a sales trip, pitching my stocks to institutional buyers. I'd started at a breakfast meeting in Houston, had four more appointments there, then rushed out to the airport to go to San Antonio for a dinner meeting, and finally staggered into my hotel room in Dallas after dodging thunderstorms through the Texas darkness until one o'clock in the morning. Then I'd tried unsuccessfully to get enough sleep to be halfway rested enough to do the same tap dance the next day. It was getting so bad that Audrey was having to push me out the front door of the apartment to go on these sales trips. As we left the Bertellis', I was thinking that Susan and Rich were right, what I needed was a plan, a script for success.

"Here's the money for the toll," Audrey said, shoving two quarters at me. We were sitting in line at the Fishkill toll booth waiting to cross the Hudson River to Newburgh. The pavement was shimmering. The air-conditioning was on full blast, but still I was drenched in clammy sweat. The eighteen-wheeler in front of us belched out a cloud of smoke as it inched ahead. The Corvair behind us beeped. What the hell was I doing here? I didn't want to be in this line. I didn't want to go to Newburgh. I had to turn my life around.

"Hang on, Audrey!" I floored the Cordoba and yanked the wheel hard to the left. We spun across the Fishkill toll plaza straight into the eastbound lanes. Audrey shrieked, tires squealed, horns honked, fists shook, fingers flipped. What did I care? Finally, I was heading in the right direction.

When we got home, I grabbed a pad of paper and a pencil and sat down at the kitchen table. "This is it, Audrey," I said. "Pull up a chair and gimme some goals. It's time for me to become a star."

Audrey was the only person who could give me goals. Audrey was the only person who understood me. Until Audrey, all my experiences with women had been brief and puzzling. I had no concept of a normal healthy relationship with a woman. In 1976, I'd decided that women were just too complicated, that it would be easier for me to go celibate. Then I met Audrey Polokoff. She was beautiful, self-assured, confident, mature. And she liked me. She told me that I was the smartest guy she'd ever met. And she meant it. I couldn't believe it. In the summer of '76, Audrey Polokoff was just what I needed.

By the summer of '77, Audrey was talking marriage. It was the next logical step in our relationship. I knew that Audrey was what I wanted, and what I needed. When I'd met her, I'd been constantly in debt and consistently losing money playing the market. A year later, I was out of debt and $5,000 in the black. But marriage? How could I get married? What would marriage do to my precious freedom?

In August, Audrey began talking about engagement rings. I began developing a spastic colon. In September, she began considering wedding dates. I began eating Gerber's baby food. In October, she issued the ultimatum. "Buzzy, my lease is up next March and I'm moving with or without you, so make up your mind." She was packing to leave for her nephew Jared's bar mitzvah in Syracuse. Her whole family was going to be there and they were expecting Audrey to show up wearing a big rock, compliments of Martin S. Schwartz. Without the rock, I'd failed to make the traveling team. I was left home to deal with my spastic colon.

I went for a sigmoidoscopy with Dr. Raymond Hochman, my proctologist. "Wow! Take a look at this knot," the doc said, swiveling the screen so that he could share this up close and personal view of my large intestine. "There's your problem," he said, tapping the screen with his pen. "That constriction's shrunk the path through your colon to about the size of a dime. We'll have to loosen that baby up, pronto."

As I gingerly pulled up my pants, I asked Dr. Hochman if I could use his phone to call my broker. I'd taken the $5,000 I'd managed to save, thanks to Audrey, and dumped it into Syntex January 78 calls. My broker told me that Syntex was skyrocketing and my $5,000 had jumped to $15,000. "Sell!" I shouted into the phone. It was time to make the cash register ring, time to straighten out my colon, time to buy Audrey her rock, and time for me to grow up. In March, when her lease ran out, Audrey Polokoff became Audrey Schwartz. Now, four months later, she was telling me how I was going to become a star.

"Buzzy. You're thirty-three years old and you've always wanted to work for yourself. So do it. You've got a good education. That'll always stay with you. The worst that can happen is that you'll go bust and you'll have to go back to being a securities analyst. Become a trader, that's your first goal. Go ahead, write it down."

I picked up the pencil. Audrey was right. I'd always known that I wanted to be a trader. Nothing fit my personality better, and there was nothing I enjoyed more. I was good at math, quick with figures, I loved gambling, and I loved the market. **BECOME A TRADER**, I wrote in big bold letters. It looked good.

"There, that's my first goal, Become a Trader. Now, how the hell do I do it?"

"Buzzy. A plan, you have to have a plan. Remember what Rich and Susan said. Now that you've got a goal, you have to have a plan for achieving it."

I sat and thought. "Well, the first thing I have to do is develop a methodology for trading that fits my style."

"Write it down," Audrey said.

Under **BECOME A TRADER** I wrote **1. DEVELOP A METHODOLOGY FOR TRADING THAT FITS MY STYLE**.

"Okay," Audrey said, "how?"

"Where's the latest issue of *Barron's*?"

We spent the next two hours talking about my plan. We clipped coupons for trial subscriptions to market letters and stock charting services. We calculated how much I would need for a grubstake, the core capital base I had to have before I could go out on my own. We decided on at least $100,000. I couldn't see how I could do it on any less. **2. ACCUMULATE A GRUBSTAKE OF $100,000**, I wrote.

"How long will that take?" Audrey said. "Remember, you have to set a time frame for achieving your goals."

"One year."

"Buzzy. One year? How can you make $100,000 in a year? You've been playing the market for nine years and you've never made anything close to that. You have to be realistic."

"Hey. Remember, I'm the smartest guy you ever met. If I'm gonna be a trader, I gotta prove that I can make the money trading. Not investing, not borrowing, not writing market reports. Trading." **WITHIN ONE YEAR**, I added.

We kept talking. I needed a mentor. Every top trader had a mentor, someone older, someone wiser, someone who was willing to show them the ropes. Michael Marcus had Ed Seykota, Paul Tudor Jones had Eli Tullis. Zoellner. It had to be Zoellner. Zoellner was the best tape reader in the business.

3. MAKE ZOELLNER MY MENTOR.

We talked some more. To be a trader, I needed a seat on some exchange. With a seat, my cost of doing business would go down dramatically. Members of an exchange could trade without paying significant commissions. Furthermore, they got "triple M's," market-maker-margins, much more favorable than the public participants. When I bought an option for one hundred shares at $3 a share as an "upstairs trader" I had to put up the whole $300 *in cash*. Members only had to put up half of that, $150. This gave the members leverage, enabling them to make (or lose) money twice as fast. And the exchanges had great health insurance for their members.

4. GET A SEAT ON SOME EXCHANGE.

I yawned. It was getting late. "Let's wrap this up. We've gotta go to work in the morning."

"Buzzy, speaking of work, how are you going to keep your job while you're making $100,000 trading? We can't live on just my salary."

"Don't worry. Hutton doesn't know it, but I'm going on sabbatical. I've been doing this crap for eight and a half years. I know the companies and the industry cold. Hutton'll get their pound of flesh out of me, but what takes most guys a week, I can do in a day."

"If that's part of the plan, write it down."

5. TAKE A SABBATICAL. I threw down the pencil. "Okay, that's it. There's my plan."

The next day I shut my office door, told my secretary to hold all calls, and started working on my methodology. Developing a methodology that fit my personality was the most important part of my plan. Without a methodology for trading, I had no edge. Up to this time, I'd always been a fundamentalist focusing on inflation rates, interest rates, growth rates, P/E ratios, yields, profit margins, market shares, government policies, things that would affect prices over the long haul. Now I was going to transform myself into a technical analyst, a market timer, a trader, someone who was looking for indicators that would signal moves in the market itself. That's the basic difference between an investor and a trader. A trader looks at the market as one living, breathing organism instead of a collection of individual stocks.

As "Adam Smith" said in *The Money Game*, "The market is like a beautiful woman—endlessly fascinating, endlessly complex, always changing, always mystifying." That quote kept running through my mind. Before Audrey, I'd been a loser with women, so it was easy to understand why I'd been a loser in the market. But now that I had Audrey, I was going to figure out what made this other beautiful woman tick.

I began reading everything I could get my hands on about the market: Richard Russell's "Dow Theory Letter," *Barron's*, *Business Week*, S & P Trendline Charts, Mansfield Charting, CMI Charting. One of my favorites was "The Reaper," a commodity letter written by a good old boy named R. E. MacMaster from Sedona, Arizona. This transformation to technical analysis came to me naturally. I was a synthesizer, taking all these different theories and picking and choosing and blending whatever fit my personality, all the time looking for some mathematical harmony that would unlock the market's secrets for me.

Of everything I read, Terry Laundry's *Magic T Theory* made the most sense to me, so I picked up the phone and called Terry and told him how fascinated I was with his work. Terry was an eccentric genius living out on Nantucket Island. He was a fellow marine, a jughead, who'd graduated from MIT and was now using his considerable engineering skills to analyze the market. Terry believed that the market spent the same amount of time going up as it did going down. What it did prior to going up was a kind of prelude, a cash buildup phase, when it was preparing itself, reenergizing, getting ready to go back up.

When you look at the letter T, there's an equal distance on the left side and the right side of the T, hence, the Magic T Theory. From the moment I saw it, I knew the Magic T was the key to my new methodology. It went back to who I was as a person: bilateral symmetry, Darwinism, evolution, the natural order of things. I totally embraced it. I worked fourteen hours a day, seven days a week. On weekends I'd draw trend lines and formulate opinions for the next week. Every night I'd review my charts, recalculate my averages, figure my inflection points, set my entry and exit prices. With the Magic T, there was order in the universe, a high and low tide every twelve hours. The Magic T and I became as one. Data ebbed and flowed in the most primal way and I rose and fell with it instinctively, viscerally, like a mollusk in the sands of high finance. I had my methodology.

There was never any question who'd be my mentor. I started calling Zoellner three and four times a day. When Edwards and Hanly finally went tapioca in 1975 from the aftereffects of the bear market of 1974, Zoellner retreated to Hackensack and set up a small hedge fund. I used to stop by and see him when I was in New Jersey calling on the hospital supply companies. After Audrey and I got married, we'd drive out to Jersey on the weekends and I'd play tennis with Zoellner while Audrey and his wife, Vickie, would visit.

When Zoellner first started his fund, he ran it out of a two-room office in Hackensack. He'd sit in one room, Vickie in the other. A Dow Jones ticker tape machine, an old stand-up model with a glass bubble over the top, continually chattered away in one corner of his office. Above it on the wall staring down on Zoellner's work was a huge Atlantic salmon. These two objects, the tape machine and the salmon, represented the two great loves of Zoellner's life, playing the market and fishing. I'd sit next to him and watch as hour after hour he gently reeled in the tape through his hands, his fingertips permanently stained a light purple with ink.

"Marty, you have to feel the tape," he'd say. "It'll tell you everything you need to know. It can rise on bad news and sink on good news. If you can read the tape, you know when it's healthy, and when it's sick." Then he'd pause, the tape resting lightly in his empurpled fingers, yards of paper piled up around his feet. "Marty, hold still, we're getting a bite. Look here. Polaroid's up another three-eighths. It's coming to the surface. They must be selling a lotta cameras for Christmas, that means they'll have a good fourth quarter. Check your moving averages. It could be time to pick up some January calls."

By early 1979, I could see that my plan was beginning to work. I was slowly mastering the nuances of the Magic T, adding new pieces here, discarding some there, trying a little of this, and a little of that, synthesizing the Magic T with whatever fit my personality and my mathematical bent. Through this process, I derived a methodology that was uniquely my own and, matched with Zoellner's mentoring, it was starting to pay real dividends. My confidence was rising. I was landing some nice fish.

I was primarily trading options, mostly calls because I was bullish on the market, on a dozen or so companies that I'd been trading for the past two years. These were major companies like Syntex, IBM, Honeywell, Teledyne, Polaroid, and Xerox that, as a securities analyst, I knew had sound fundamentals. All of them were heavily traded and very liquid. Liquidity was crucial because I was scalping, jumping in and out of positions in a matter of hours, or even minutes. Plus, the options were much more volatile than the stocks, which meant that for the same amount of money, I had a much greater upside potential. I'd usually have three or four call positions working at any given time and most of my bets were in the $5,000 to $15,000 range, which was compatible with the size of my grubstake. Typically, I was looking to make between $1,000 and $3,000 on each play.

After breaking even in '76 and '77, I was now consistently making money. Before, when I was trading on a rumor or a hunch and the unexpected happened, it was terra incognita, an unknown land, and I was out there all alone. But now, the nightly routine of doing my charts, reviewing and revising my trend lines, calculating my moving averages, figuring my inflection points, setting my entry and exit prices was giving me confidence. I was like a chess player moving men around on the board in his mind, seeing positions five, six, seven moves in advance. I wasn't trading that much differently, but I was trading a lot smarter. The process of doing the work was giving me an inner resource, a place to reach back in my mind for something tucked away in the recesses of the gray matter. It was helping me make better decisions. When you're trading real time, and things start popping, you're challenged to make immediate decisions. You can't stand still, there's no time to think, it's attack or retreat, increase the position or get out. Having a methodology gave me strength, because in my mind's eye I could see that I'd been there before. It gave me the confidence to pull the trigger NOW.

During the first quarter of 1979 my grubstake passed $50,000, half of what I needed. There was no question in my mind that I was going to make another $50,000 during the second quarter of '79. It was time to start working on the next phase of my plan, **GET A SEAT ON SOME EXCHANGE**.

In 1973, the Chicago Board Options Exchange had been founded to trade listed options. Its instant success prompted other exchanges like the Pacific, Philadelphia, and American that were always looking for ways to increase their volume to go after a piece of the business. As part of my plan, I'd considered moving to Chicago, but why move to Chicago when I could get a seat on the American Exchange and stay in the City.

Bob Friedman, a well-known hospital supply analyst at Montgomery Securities, was an acquaintance of mine. We'd both made the *Institutional Investor* magazine's "All America Research Team" in 1976 and we'd see each other at meetings. One day Friedman mentioned to me that he had a stepbrother named Danny Weiskopf who ran a specialist operation on the floor of the Amex. When I told Friedman that I was thinking of getting a seat, he offered to introduce me. Danny Wieskopf's book traded Bally Entertainment, one of the hottest options on the floor, and when I went to see him, he was as busy as a *mohel* at a bris for quadruplets, so he pawned me off onto Hayes Noel.

Hayes worked for Danny, was about my age, and had been on the floor since 1970. Like me, Hayes was deep into technical analysis and, like me, he was hoping to go out on his own. We quickly became friends. A couple of times a week, I'd tell Beverly Schneider, my secretary at Hutton, that I was going out for a long lunch and hustle over to the Exchange. I'd sign in at the visitors' desk, get a badge, and they'd page, "Hayes Noel! Hayes Noel! You have a visitor at the front desk." Hayes'd come down, and I'd slap on the badge and follow him around the floor. During these visits I was a marine reconnoitering a new objective, figuring out what I had to do to take it. I'd trail ten feet behind Hayes, watching him operate, checking out the terrain, memorizing who traded what and where, who was clerking for whom, where the phones were, where the bathrooms were.

"Marty, you should start by leasing a seat," Hayes said to me one day. "That way, you can conserve your capital until you're sure you're going to make it."

"That's bullshit, Hayes," I said. "I already know I'm going to make it. I'm buying a fuckin' seat."

Seats were bought and sold through the Exchange, which took a nice commission (or "transfer fee" as they liked to call it), on a bid-and-asked basis. There was always a seat available for the right price. The price in the summer of '79 was $85,000 bid, $95,000 asked. That meant that I could get a seat for around $90,000, plus a transfer fee of $2,500, but first I had to become registered as a broker-dealer with the National Association of Securities Dealers and pass an evening course given by the Amex on how to trade options. By the end of June, I'd made my $100,000 grubstake; I was ready to go.

I couldn't wait to quit E. F. Hutton. For almost a year, I'd had my job on cruise control, telling Beverly to hold all calls, going into my office, shutting the door, turning on my Bunker Ramo, and trading. I'd been executing three, four, five, a half dozen trades a day.

Having my own Bunker Ramo had been critical. I was the only securities analyst at Hutton to have his own quote machine. The Bunker Ramo was part of the deal that I'd negotiated in June of 1977 when I'd moved to Hutton. On my first couple of jobs, there was only one quote machine for the whole research department, and it was out in the hall. I was always going over to look at the machine, but the powers that be, the bosses, would see me standing out there and wonder what I was doing. I learned early in the game that on Wall Street, the easiest way to receive a pay increase is to change jobs. Wall Street's principle was to pay you as little as they could, but keep you. When somebody wanted you, they were willing to pay you more because that was the only reason you'd leave. By the time I started getting courted by Dan Murphy, head of the Institutional Research Department at Hutton, I realized that as part of my deal I should ask Dan for a quote machine in my office. That way I could watch the market without anybody knowing what I was doing.

I figured the best time to tell Dan Murphy that I was leaving was the first thing on a Monday morning, early in the day, early in the week. I chose Monday, July 9. My natural inclination was to walk in, tell Dan that I was quitting, and walk out. That was how you did things on Wall Street. But Audrey counseled me to take a different tack.

"Buzzy, be honest with Dan, tell him just what you're going to do. Let him know that you're not going to another firm, and that you're going out on your own to become a trader. He'll respect that. Better to leave on a good note in case you have to come back."

So, when I went in to see Dan Murphy, I said, "Dan, I appreciate all that you've done for me at Hutton, but I've decided I want to change my career. I've been a securities analyst for nine and a half years, I just got married last year, I want to have a family, I don't want to travel anymore; this is not the way I want to live my life. This is my chance to go out on my own. I've always wanted to be an entrepreneur, to be my own boss. I'm going to be a trader."

Dan got up and shut his door. I was in a very strategic position because two other analysts had just left to go with other firms. "Okay," Dan said, "but you've gotta do me one favor. Keep this a secret between you and me because I need some time to hire some more analysts. And if I announce you're leaving, it'll look like the ship's sinking."

I told Dan that I would, and I even went on a couple of sales calls for him. We had a trip scheduled to Philadelphia, six calls to six different institutions, one at 9:00, one at 10:30, luncheon at noon, a 2:00, a 3:30, a 4:30, then catch the Metroliner back to New York. I hated it, but Dan said, "Please do it for me, play it through." When it came time to leave, what was remarkable, unheard-of, was that I left on such good terms that Dan let me keep an office at Hutton for the next six months. On Wall Street, usually when you tell your boss you're leaving, they immediately seal your files, check your briefcase, give you a rectal exam, and escort you to the door. But because I was making a vertical leap, going out on my own, I left like a hero.

My plan had worked. I'd developed a methodology that fit my style, I'd made Zoellner my mentor, I'd made $100,000 trading, I'd bought a seat on the Amex, I'd quit Hutton, I'd **BECOME A TRADER**. On Monday morning, August 13, 1979, I stopped outside the entrance to the American Stock Exchange, took a deep breath, pulled out my badge, and walked through the door that said "Members Only." It was time for me to become a star.

The Grubstake

I fancy myself as a renaissance man. I like to go back to different times and figure out what I'd have been if I'd been born then. If I'd been a young man in the nineteenth century, I would have been a forty-niner. I would have pulled together a grubstake and headed west to California looking for gold.

When I went out on my own in 1979, I mined for stocks and bonds and options and futures. I needed $100,000 for my grubstake. Psychologically, I wasn't ready to go out on my own until I knew that I had made six figures. It should have been more, but I was eager to get going, and that was the absolute minimum amount I figured I had to have before I could make my break. If you're going to trade for a living, you have to give yourself a year. Start with enough money to cover your living expenses, plus enough more so you can trade at a level where you've proven you can make money consistently.

If you keep your "day job," you don't need the reserve for expenses, but you still have to have enough capital to give yourself a chance to succeed and trade at a level that's comfortable for you. The simplest way to control your trading activity is to open a separate brokerage account that's used for trading, and trading only. Don't put any more into the account than you're willing to lose. I can't tell you how much; that's a highly individual decision, but whatever it is, stick to it. And if you lose it, be prepared to walk away.

Before you can go out on your own, you have to master your ego and realize that being profitable is more important than being right. **YOU HAVE TO PROVE YOUR ABILITIES AND TEST YOUR METHODS BY ACTUALLY TRADING, AND MAKING REAL MONEY, BEFORE YOU DEPEND ON TRADING FOR YOUR LIVELIHOOD.** That meant that I had to make my grubstake trading. If I could make $100,000 trading, it would show me that I'd developed a methodology that gave me a good chance of succeeding. I didn't feel that it was right to borrow my grubstake. Gamblers Anonymous is full of people who borrowed their grubstakes. True, I borrowed

$50,000 from my in-laws, but that was just backup and I was determined never to use it, and I didn't. For me, that $50,000 was like Dumbo's feather. I needed that security in order to fly, but I knew that if I ever had to use it, it would have meant that I'd failed. And I was determined not to fail, not this time.

Making $100,000 is one thing, saving it is quite another. Audrey and I sacrificed and saved so that when it came time for me to go out on my own, I knew the importance of money management. Making your grubstake takes enormous self-discipline, and if you've earned it and saved it, you're less likely to blow it. Because we make and lose thousands of dollars every day, big-time traders often give the appearance of treating money with an "easy come, easy go" attitude. That's not right. Just because we don't do the mashed potatoes over our wins or whine about our losses doesn't mean that we take them casually.

One of the most interesting points that Jack D. Schwager makes in his book *Market Wizards* is that almost every trader he interviewed talked about how they'd failed before they'd finally become a consistent winner. Your grubstake has to be large enough to give you the time to be successful and large enough so that no one trade can take you out. When I started on the Amex, I lost 10 percent of my working capital in the first few hours, but my grubstake was large enough, and my "puke point" low enough, so that I didn't stop myself out before the market had a chance to turn in my favor. Plus, I was a singles hitter, I wasn't going for the home run. My trading style was to take a lot of small profits rather than go for one big one, so my grubstake didn't have to be as large as that of someone who was swinging for the fences.

Like the forty-niners who headed west to claim their fame and fortune, the traders who have the best chance of striking it rich are the ones who have earned their grubstakes.

3

Paradise Island

I was sweating bullets. I looked up at the wall to check my position. This was it, I had to cover; if I couldn't, I'd lose everything. All my hard work would have been for naught. I'd be tapioca. Everyone was crowded around, yelling. "Come on, Schwartz, it's now or never." "Yeah, come on, Buzzy, make your play. Pull the trigger." "This is it, Schwartz. Don't choke!" "Make the move, you chicken. Chicken!" "Cluck, cluck, cluck!"

I couldn't wait any longer. I toed the line and looked at Yogi's squatty, swarthy Italian face, kissed his oversized, bulbous nose, flipped my wrist, and sent him flying. The crowd hushed as Yogi curved to the right, then to the left, skipped once off the sidewalk, and came to rest leaning against the wall on top of Pee Wee Reese. I pumped my fists in the air. I'd done it, I'd covered. All the cards were mine.

Flipping for baseball cards was my introduction to gambling. I'd get up on a Saturday morning, pull my little red Radio Flyer out of the garage, and go around the neighborhood collecting soda bottles; 2 cents for twelve-ouncers, 5 cents for thirty-twos. By noon, I'd have 40 or 50 cents rattling around in my wagon, and that was big money back in 1953. I'd wheel the bottles down to Artie's corner grocery store next to the Davis Street Elementary School and trade them in for packs of Topps Baseball Cards.

Each pack cost a nickel and contained five baseball cards. I'd rip open a pack, give away the gum. None of the guys ever ate the gum. It tasted like wallpaper paste and was as tough as shoe leather. Only real little kids were dumb enough to eat it. Then I'd blow the fine pink residue off of the cards, shuffle through each of them, figuring out who I already had, praying for a Mantle or a Rizzuto, hoping against hope that I didn't wind up with more losers from the Pittsburgh Pirates or the

Washington Senators (Washington: "first in war, first in peace, and last in the American League"). Finally we'd go outside where we'd flip cards against the wall and see who was the best.

There's a moral here.

To be a winner, you have to be willing to toe the line and pull the trigger.

By the time I was ten, eleven, twelve, I was big enough to get jobs shoveling snow. A Montreal Express would come howling down from Canada, school would be canceled, and I'd grab my shovel and head out. I'd dig all morning, a dollar for a sidewalk, $2.50 for a driveway. It was tough work, and often, just when I thought I was done, a snowplow would come steaming by and fill everything back in. I'd keep shoveling and by noon I'd have six or eight bucks tucked away in my pocket, and that was big money back in 1957. Then I'd head over to Eddie Cohen's basement to play cards. We had a game called "setback," a six-card game, high, low, jack, and game, with an occasional smudge. Sometimes I'd clear as much as $10 or $12 in an afternoon, which sure beat shoveling snow.

By the time I was fifteen, we'd graduated from setback to poker. On Saturday mornings I'd caddy for Pappy, my maternal grandfather. While Pappy wasn't much of a golfer, he was a great tipper. He'd slip me a sawbuck, and that was big money back in 1960. Then I'd head over to Eddie's basement, where I'd meet up with the old gang from Davis Street Elementary and some new guys from Hillhouse High. One of the new guys was Donny K., whose father owned a big soda distributorship in West Haven. I liked playing with Donny, because he always had lots of money. His father drove a Cadillac and belonged to the Woodbridge Country Club, but Donny wasn't too bright. He never quite grasped the concept that you never split a pair to go for an inside straight. I took a lot of pleasure out of beating Donny, because I always had a chip on my shoulder when I went up against somebody who had more money than I did.

My parents didn't seem too concerned with my gambling, probably because I won a lot, but when Pappy found out what

I was doing with his money, he went nuts. He started complaining to my mother, "Hilde, how can you let him play cards and gamble like this? He's got the fever. He's going to ruin."

I had the fever, but I wasn't going to ruin. I was going to Aqueduct. Once I got my driver's license, I'd cruise on down to the Big A with $50 in my pocket and try to come home with a hundred or more. Lots of times, I did. As with cards, I discovered that I had a way with the ponies. And I was all business. I wasn't there to eat, or drink, or socialize. I was there to make money. I'd study the racing forms, research the trainers, chart the jockeys, get to know the track conditions. I'd look at pedigrees and most recent race results, hoping to spot trends. I'd go through the speed ratings in the *Daily Racing Form* for each horse and try to determine which horse was in the best shape to go that particular distance on that particular day. I'd calculate the projected time for each horse and plan my bets accordingly. Finally, I'd scrutinize the tote board, look for imbalances and discrepancies, identify opportunities, wait until the very last minute, and then play the odds.

I loved Aqueduct. It was clean and green, and the horses were beautiful, and nobody cared that my father had a lousy job, or that I was Jewish, or that we didn't have enough money to get into the Woodbridge Country Club. If you wanted to get into the clubhouse at Aqueduct, you just paid a couple of extra bucks.

Moral:

**Preparation pays. It's essential to know more than
the other players in the game.**

At Amherst, one of my favorite pastimes was going to the track. I went alone; even though Lord Jeffrey is usually depicted on horseback, in 1963 not too many sons of Amherst played the ponies. On Fridays after soccer practice, I'd walk down to the station next to the Lord Jeffrey Amherst Bookstore, get on a Peter Pan bus, and head up to the little track in Hinsdale, New Hampshire. As the bus cruised past beautiful New England farms, I'd look out the window at the fall foliage and think to myself how nice it would be to be somebody, to have a farm with bright orange maples, rustic red barns, pristine white fences, and rolling green pastures, with my own stable of horses grazing contentedly. When I came back late at night I'd sit in the back of the bus, fondling my money and feeling like a winner.

> **Dare to dream. It's not where you are, it's where you're going that counts.**

Or, as Pappy Snyder used to sing,

> **"If you don't have a dream, how you gonna make a dream come true?"**

In the summer of 1967, my parents gave me $1,000 for my trip to Europe, just like they'd given my brother when he'd graduated from Syracuse five years earlier. Off I went with Larry Lincoln, my ex-roommate from Amherst, and his brother Steve. I was gone from the middle of June to the end of August, a total of eleven weeks. My parents figured that that would give me plenty of time to soak up some Continental culture before I started Columbia Business School in the fall.

While Larry and Steve toured the museums and cathedrals, I'd be touring the casinos. They were very Old World with ornate baroque buildings, vaulted ceilings, crystal chandeliers, velvet drapes, and everyone dressed in coats and ties. My favorite, by far, was the casino in Divone, France. When we were staying in Geneva, I took the big-ass Mercedes that Larry and Steve's father bought for us to bring back to the U.S. and drove over the Swiss border to Divone.

I remember crossing the border, showing my passport and car registration, and having the guard ask me, "Monsieur, puis je demander qu'est-ce que vous avez que faire en France?"

"Le gambling," I replied.

"Ah, le jeu. Bonne chance, Monsieur."

"Merci, mon gendarme." I did not have a great command of the French language.

I remember seeing the lights and pulling up in front of the

casino in the big-ass Mercedes. I felt like Bond, James Bond in *Casino Royale*. Like Bond, I played complicated progression systems at roulette. I'd wait for a pattern of four or five blacks, or four or five in a row, or four or five reds or odds or evens. I'd stand at the table and chart the results on cards. I didn't care that the roulette wheel was supposed to be completely random, that the odds were the same on every spin. I had to have a system. I'm not comfortable making decisions about money unless I can fit them into some kind of order. And who knew, on some night some wheel might have a bias.

After I'd been in Europe ten days, I'd made more money than I'd spent. That really excited me. My hope was to make enough money from gambling so that when I got home I could repay my parents the $1,000 they'd given me. I thought that would be terrific.

I stayed ahead all the time we were in Europe, but when we got to London, the last leg of our trip, I was so eager to play that I didn't give myself a chance to rest. The one thing you have to do when you're gambling is give yourself plenty of time to rest. It's like running a race, if you're not in shape, you're going to lose, but the first thing I did after we landed at Gatwick was to head for the first club I could find.

It was early evening, around eight or nine o'clock, when I found one, and the place was almost deserted. I didn't know this at the time, but the clubs in London didn't come alive until much later. I wanted to play craps, but I like to bet against the shooter, and no one else was playing. I decided that I'd throw the dice and bet against myself. I have a firm rule that I never let the shooter beat me more than twice in a row; if that happens, I stop betting and wait for the next shooter. But here, the next shooter was me. I must have been unconscious. I made seven straight passes while betting against myself. "By Jove," exclaimed the croupier, "I don't believe I've ever seen anything quite like it."

I was keeping a journal of my trip and when I got back to my room that night, I wrote:

August 18, 1967. This evening, I hope, finalizes a lesson I paid dearly for, but financially it's not a great price *if I stick to what I've learned. Tonight, I lost almost $400 gambling, far too much for an older person, but irrevocably too much for an unemployed person of twenty-two. I'm writing this while I'm still warm, or should I say cold, because there are things that I have learned tonight that should furnish me with a code that I will never break for the remainder of my life:*

1. *Never gamble for large amounts. Earn my money through hard work and not hope for the easy killing for there is no such thing.*
2. *Never gamble for very much money while on vacation. If one must indulge, make it for small stakes and if the self-discipline is lacking, don't bring very much money. In fact, only take as much as you can afford to lose, which is indeed very little.*
3. *Playing for large stakes at the casinos or the horses is absurd. Small wagers for the sport is the only answer.*

The true value of this evening lies in the future, when I prove whether the price I paid tonight was a large one or a small one for something I'd better remember for the rest of my life. It is time to shake myself out of this crazy mood and return to my past beliefs that hard work creates success and enjoyment. In no other way can I find the satisfaction that comes with productive achievement. This lesson must be learned now before it is too late!

To help alleviate my poor character as a person, I propose that I do exceptionally well at business school while trying to work one day a week.

Of course, it was all bullshit. I wasn't willing to give up gambling. The next day I was back at the tables and before I left London, I'd won some of what I'd lost, but not enough to pay back my parents.

Don't beat yourself; if you've got a plan that's working, stick to it.

Ricky G. took me to the next level. In the winter of 1970, when I graduated from business school and started working for Kuhn Loeb, I transferred from the Marine Motor Transport Reserve Unit in New Haven to the Russian Interrogation Team in Brooklyn. Ricky G. was one of the enlisted men in my unit. Ricky G. was a Runyonesque character who was deep into gambling. Since there weren't too many Russians in Brooklyn to interrogate at the time, we spent most of our free time at our reserve meetings playing cards and talking about gambling.

When we were doing our two weeks of active duty at Camp Pendleton, California, we got a weekend pass, and Ricky G. said to me, "Hey, Lieutenant, you wanna go to Vegas?"

I'd never been to Vegas, so naturally I said, "Conyetchna, duroch!"

"Huh?"

"Conyetchna, duroch! Translated: 'Of course, you fool!'"

Naturally, most of my enlisted men drove up with me to L.A. and we caught a flight to Vegas. It was early August, it was real hot, and there were sandstorms blowing all over the desert. We were being tossed around like cats in a dryer and the pilot didn't know if he could land. It took him three tries to get the plane down; I was sure that we were going to crash and die. When we finally walked into the Sands Hotel and I saw the slot machines, the tables, the drinks, the food, the girls, and the games, it was like I'd been born again, a born-again gambler.

We checked in and the bellhop said, "You boys need anything, you just give the bell captain a call. I mean, if you need *anything*, just give us a call." It didn't take more than a couple of calls before Vegas became my very favorite place in the whole world. I'd gamble, come back to my room, call the bell captain, rest up, have something to eat, go back downstairs, and gamble some more. For a young single guy with a good job, Vegas was heaven. It was the best club I'd ever been in, much better than Aqueduct.

From then on, I went back to Vegas every chance I got. I used to follow a group of companies that were headquartered out west and I developed this route. On Wednesday night, I'd fly from New York to Salt Lake City and spend all day Thursday talking with companies in Salt Lake. On Thursday evening, I'd fly to Vegas, check into Caesar's Palace and gamble all night. On Friday morning, I'd fly over to Phoenix and see a couple of companies, and then on Friday afternoon, fly back to Caesar's. I'd gamble all weekend and fly back to New York on the red-eye Sunday night. On Monday morning, I'd be back at my desk writing my reports and tallying up my wins.

For the pure gambler, there's no other place on earth like Vegas.

One day that fall at a reserve meeting in Brooklyn, Ricky G. asked me to look over his football card. He said he was getting ready to call Carmine, his bookie. "Hotski shitski," I said, "I'd love to have a bookie."

Bookies don't deal with just anybody, you have to be vouched for, so Ricky G. set up an interview for me with Carmine. We met at the Aqua Vitae Diner in Yonkers. Carmine was a dark furtive little Sicilian with his collar pulled up and his hat brim pulled down, and he was always looking over his shoulder. I guess I didn't look like a Fed, because right away Carmine started giving me the lingo, like when I wanted to bet $500 that was a "nickel," and when I wanted to bet $1,000 that was a "dime." He gave me a number to call when I wanted to get the line or make a bet, then said, "Marty, you need a code name. Ricky lives in Vermont part of the time, and since you're a friend of Ricky's, we're gonna call you Maple, for Maple Sugar."

Marty Schwartz aka Maple Sugar. I liked it, so Maple became my handle. I'd go out to a pay phone late Sunday mornings, pull my collar up and my hat down, look around furtively, and call Carmine. "This is Maple," I'd murmur into the phone. "What's the line on the Giants. Detroit plus eight and a half? Okay, I like the points, gimme a nickel on the Lions."

Carmine didn't take checks or credit cards so I started looking around the apartment for a good place to hide money. All gamblers have weird hiding places. I finally settled on a federal taxation book that was left over from business school. I figured it was the last place anybody would look for money, and I liked the irony of keeping my gambling money in my federal taxation book.

"Maple" did all right with football, but during basketball season, he got a little out of control. If Maple had been going to a shrink in those days, he would have been told that gambling was a substitute for a meaningful relationship with a woman. The worse Maple's social life got, the more Maple gambled, and in early 1972, he was in a real losing streak.

I'd joined a group ski house up in Sugarbush, Vermont, but I still wasn't getting far with the women, and in early February I was down about $2,000 that week to Carmine, which was a huge amount of money for me. One Friday night, I was driving up to the ski house in my little TR6 when I decided I was going to go for broke. I'd been down in Louisville earlier that week meeting with Wendell Cherry, CEO of Extendacare.

Carmine had this exotic bet called the "double if-then reversal" where you could win all four sides of the bet and make four dimes on a nickel. I'd been charting college basketball the same way I'd charted horses, jockeys, and roulette, and by this late in the season, I had a pretty good idea of who could win on the road, who could win on consecutive nights, and who could only win at home. As I burned up I-91 past Brattleboro, Bellows Falls, and Bartonsville, I picked the four games for my "double if-then reversal." My fourth and final pick was Louisville by three and a half over Memphis. Everyone in Louisville had been talking about the Cardinals, and I had a wonderful feeling about Louisville. I called Carmine and made my bet.

Late Saturday afternoon and Saturday night I drove around the mountain in my TR6, fiddling with the radio, searching for the best reception, trying to get the scores. It was snowing its ass off, my hands were freezing, and I was getting all kinds of static, but after midnight I was pretty sure that I'd won the first three parts of the bet. All I needed was Louisville to win by four, and I'd be out of the hole and into some big money. I thought I'd heard that Louisville was down by eleven, or maybe it was seven, at the half, but whatever it was, it didn't sound good.

I was going crazy. I had to find out if Louisville covered. Midnight, one in the morning, I was still parked outside the ski house, jiggling the radio. I was getting the Mormon Tabernacle Choir from Salt Lake City, hockey scores from Quebec, cattle prices from Fort Worth, and boxing from Vegas. But nothing about Louisville or Memphis. Everybody else was inside partying. It was no wonder I had trouble forming meaningful relationships.

At two, I was running out of gas. I gave up and went to bed. The next morning everybody went skiing but me. I got in the TR6, drove into town, and picked up a *New York Times*. Louisville had stormed back from fifteen points behind and won 75–71.

I'd won the bet. I'd won four grand. I was out of the hole.

When I got back to the city I called Carmine to find out where we should meet for the payoff. Thanks to pro football, the betting week ends on Sunday and you settle up on the following Tuesday. Carmine said he'd meet me Tuesday after work on the corner of 86th and Third, right in front of the movie theater. I was really nervous about getting $4,000 in cash. There were a lot of people walking around the streets of New York who'd cut your throat for $40. I didn't want to think about what they'd do to you for four thousand.

The Godfather had just opened, and the line stretched around the block. I was standing under the marquee when Carmine came down the street with his collar pulled up and his hat pulled down. He pushed his way through the line and pounded forty hundred-dollar bills into my palm. Everybody was staring at us. There I was, standing beside a big poster of Don Corleone, collecting a big wad of cash from a bookie named Carmine. I had an image of myself sleeping with the fishes. I was sure that somebody named Luca Brasi was waiting to mug me, or worse, before I got home. I didn't stop sweating until the four thousand was tucked safely away in my federal taxation book.

Good gamblers keep their bets in balance. You have to have a life beyond brokers and bookies.

Ricky G. had a friend named Billy H. who was a commodities broker for H. Hentz & Co., and Billy was always on the fringes of something. In August of 1971, the three of us were driving up to Saratoga for the Travers and Billy said that he'd run across a trainer who claimed he could fix a race. I doubted it, but it doesn't make any difference whether you're playing the market or the ponies, everyone's dream is to have the results ahead of time. "Billy," I said, "if this guy ever gets one going, let me know."

The next month at our reserve meeting, Ricky G. pulled me aside. "Lieutenant, Billy says the fix is on. There's a horse running in the sixth at Aqueduct on Thursday, My*Tune, and he's a sure thing. You wanna go?"

"That's a big conyetchna, baby."

Monday I went down to the bank, got a thousand, and tucked it away in my federal taxation book. Tuesday, I told Joanne, my secretary, that I had a very important meeting on Thursday afternoon and not to schedule any appointments. Wednesday, I bought a copy of the *Daily Racing Form* and noted gleefully that My*Tune was at 4–1, but on Thursday morning, I got a call from Ricky G. "Forget it, Lieutenant," he said. "We're not going. Our horse has been scratched."

The following Monday was Columbus Day and even though the banks were closed, the market was open, so I was at the office. I was just getting ready to go to lunch when the phone rang. It was Ricky G. "Lieutenant, we're back on. Billy just heard that our horse is running in the fourth. We're headin' out right away."

"Da, da, da!!"

"But we got a problem. The banks are closed and we don't have any money. You got any?"

"Yeah, about a thousand. But it's at home. Gimme an hour."

"Bring it all and any more if you can get. We'll meet you at Billy's office at one o'clock."

The race was on. I called my brother Gerry to see if he had any money. He wanted a piece of the action. "Meet me at Grand Central, the uptown express platform, in half an hour," I said. I grabbed my jacket and said to Joanne, "I've got to go to that meeting that got canceled last Thursday. It's very important. If anyone's looking for me, I'll be back around three or three-thirty."

I ran down to the Wall Street Station and caught the uptown express. I hopped off at 42nd Street, found Gerry, got a hundred bucks from him, and jumped on the local. I got off at 77th, ran up to my apartment on 78th between Lexington and Park, grabbed the thousand out of my federal taxation book, ran back to the subway, and took the local back down to 59th. My watch read 1:05. The H. Hentz & Co. office was at the corner of 59th and Park Avenue. Ricky G. and Billy were pacing on the sidewalk outside.

"You got the money?" Billy said.

I pulled out my wad and we jumped in a cab. I threw the driver a twenty and said, "Aqueduct, and step on it."

We got there just as the third race was ending. I loaned Ricky G. and Billy $300 and put $800 on My*Tune to win. He went off at 7–2 and that race was the sweetest thing I'd ever seen. My*Tune won by two and a half lengths, and all the time we were yelling, screaming, pounding each other on the back, and jumping up and down. I won $2,800. For once I thought I was on the inside, and that made it feel even sweeter.

Ricky G. and Billy stayed for the rest of the card, but I had to get back to the office. I took out a quarter and started heading for the subway. Then I saw the line of limousines parked in front of the track and I said to myself, "Wait a minute, you jerk. You just won $2,800. You've got over $4,100 in your pocket. Why the hell are you getting on the subway?" For fifty bucks, I hired myself a limo and was chauffeured back to Kuhn Loeb.

Nothing can beat knowing what's going to happen before it happens, except when it doesn't.

In 1972 I discovered Paradise Island in Nassau. You'd fly two and a half hours from New York, pay a couple of bucks to cross over Huntington Hartford's toll bridge, and on the other side was a combination of Aqueduct, Divone, and Vegas. There were lots of trees and water, there were lots of Europeans in coats and ties, and there was lots of action. Unlike Vegas, however, Paradise Island was more of a "couples" vacation place, and since I could never get a date who looked good in a bathing suit, I only went a few times.

Then I met Audrey. Audrey looked terrific in a bathing suit. When it came time to pick a place for our honeymoon, I didn't have to think twice. We were going to Paradise Island. We spent March 26, 1978, our wedding night, in New York City, then caught the morning flight to Nassau. I'd booked us into the honeymoon suite at the Loews Hotel, right on the beach. We checked in at noon and while Audrey started to unpack, I grabbed the phone and began calling my broker at Bear Stearns. I was trying to make money even on my honeymoon.

The casinos opened at one o'clock, so at five to one I finished my calls and yelled, "Audrey, time for some fun?"

"I'll be out in a minute, Buzzy," she purred seductively from the bathroom.

I looked at my watch, "Well, hurry up, honey. I'm really feeling hot."

The door opened and there was Audrey dressed in a flimsy negligee with a bottle of champagne in one hand and a tray of chocolate strawberries in the other.

"Hey, whatcha doin'?" I said. "Why aren't you dressed? The tables open at one. We're going to miss the action."

Audrey didn't say a word. She just turned around, walked back into the bathroom, put down the strawberries and champagne, and locked the door. Her visions of a romantic honeymoon on Paradise Island had just crapped out. Here she was, married to some bozo whose idea of fun was trying to screw a casino.

Keep your priorities straight.

I don't play cards, bet the ponies, or go to casinos much anymore. After Audrey and I developed "The Plan" in the summer of '78, I did my gambling on the stock market, then the options market, then the S&P futures market. But I haven't forgotten the lessons I learned at Artie's corner store, Eddie Cohen's basement, Aqueduct, Hinsdale, Europe, Vegas, the Aqua Vitae Diner, and Paradise Island. As more and more new financial instruments are thrown into the game, and trading moves out of the pit onto the computer, more and more traders are learning their lessons at places like Harvard, Wharton, the Sorbonne, and the London School of Economics. That's important, but all the academic degrees in the world aren't enough once the bell rings. I see that with some of the kids who come to see me looking for advice. Unless they've got that feeling in their stomach, they can't toe the line, they can't pull the trigger, they can't be a winner.

Show me a great trader and I'll show you someone who understands gambling.

Viva Las Vegas

Trading futures is a lot like playing the craps tables. So Las Vegas is a great place to work on the mental discipline it takes to become a successful trader. There's no way to win consistently in Vegas, but, if you're really good, you can win some of the time, not lose too much of the time, and have a good time all of the time. But it takes discipline. The casinos want you betting with your gut, not with your head, and they'll do anything to break your concentration. Unlimited booze, uninhibited women, and unrestricted fun, twenty-four, seven, three sixty-five.

My game is craps. It's a lot like floor trading—fast, loud, crowded, with lots of money moving around. Twelve players are leaning over the table watching every roll, urging the dice to come up a winner. "Boxcars, craps, you lose." "Give me fever." "Aces, snake eyes." "Eighter from Decatur." "Nina from Pasadena." "Thirty-three the hard way." "Yo-leven, winner, pay the line." When someone's on a roll, chips are flying, men squeeze in tighter, women lean over farther, everyone breathes harder, and the shouts get louder. It's just like being on the floor with Chickie, Frannie, and Fat Mike.

I'm a "don't pass" player. That means I bet against the shooters. The odds are the same whether you bet with or against the shooters, but most people bet with the shooters, the people rolling the dice. I bet against them, because I don't want to be associated with the guy in the blue double-knit leisure suit with the gold medallion hanging out of his open shirt or the fat bleached blonde who's bursting out of her sequined minidress and spitting on the dice before every roll. I'm hoping they'll crap out before they make their point. That means that everyone at the table, even the stickmen, who survive on tips and want everyone winning and happy, hate me. That doesn't bother me a bit. At the craps table or in the trading pit, the losers always hate the winners.

Playing craps at Vegas has taught me three rules that I find indispensable in trading. The first rule is, **DIVORCE YOUR**

EGO FROM THE GAME. Don't get emotionally involved. While you're playing against the shooter, it's nothing personal. If you let your ego into the game, the temptation is to double up when Doubleknit wins a few bets, to hang tough so you can get even fast with Sequins. I've found this behavior to be self-destructive and a sure way to go tapioca. You have to be unemotional, like the house. The house never takes anything personally.

The second rule is, **MANAGE YOUR MONEY.** The minute I arrive at the casino, I go to the cashier's cage and get a safe-deposit box for my money. I put all but a few hundred dollars in the box. If I lose that, I have to go back to the box to get more. Having to go back to the box does two things: it makes me physically leave the table, which automatically breaks my losing streak, and it gives me time to relax and consider what I want to do next. It's like splashing cold water on my face. The same holds true for trading: keep money in a separate account that your broker can't get to unless you expressly transfer it into your trading account. That way, you can't get swept up in the excitement of the moment and shoot your whole wad.

The third rule is, **CHANGE TABLES AFTER A WINNING STREAK.** The luckier you've been, the surer it is that your luck is going to change. Changing tables is not easy, especially if you're doing well. Human nature tells you that if you're making money at one table, stay there and make some more. But the best thing you can do is to pick up your winnings, go back to the box, and deposit everything except for a few hundred bucks. Periodically leaving the table with your winnings is the only way you can avoid getting ground down by the house's edge. Then, if you still feel lucky, you still have your concentration, and if you still want to play, go find a new table and hope you get hot again.

This kind of mental discipline may not make you a winner in the market, but if you don't have it, you're sure to be a loser.

4

The Great Pyramid

In early 1970, when I graduated from Columbia Business School, I knew that I wanted to be in the stock market. I figured that there were three ways I could get into the game. I could become an investment banker, a trader, or a securities analyst. I knew that I wasn't cut out to be an investment banker. Investment bankers were smooth operators who made fortunes by creating entities, underwriting stock offerings, and keeping big pieces of the action, but I didn't have the experience, the capital, or the polish to become an investment banker. I didn't want to be a trader because in those days, traders were just middlemen. They got orders from their clients and phoned them down to the floor. I decided I wanted to be a securities analyst. That's what appealed to me and best fit my personality.

When I was in the first grade, the teacher asked each of us what we wanted to be when we grew up. I said, "a detective." Here I was, a smart kid from a good Jewish home, but I didn't want to be a doctor or a lawyer, I wanted to be a detective. My parents must have wondered where they'd gone wrong, but I knew even then that I liked to analyze things, and that's what securities analysts did. They analyzed companies, interviewed managements, and wrote reports. They got to travel all over the country, and I liked to travel.

In the spring of 1970, the economy was in a recession. For the Class of '70, jobs on Wall Street were hard to find, but that hadn't stopped me. I was a hustler and I was selling my favorite product, me. At the beginning of the year, when I was finishing up at Columbia, I started cold calling everybody. Like a detective, I investigated leads, got names of research directors, called them up. They'd say, "We're not hiring anybody, let alone some kid who doesn't know anything. Don't you know there's a recession going on?"

"Well, somebody must have given you your first break," I'd say. I always got them with that line. Usually it was enough to keep the conversation going. Then I'd try to get an appointment, because even if the contact didn't pay off right away, it might pay off later on. I ended up with six job offers.

I went with Kuhn Loeb. Kuhn Loeb was owned by the Schiff family and was an old-line, well-respected Jewish firm. Jack Favia was the head of research and Jack offered me $16,000, which was a princely sum back in 1970. Jack assigned me to Abe Bronchtein, an MIT graduate who was the drug analyst for Kuhn Loeb. Abe was my mentor. He followed the pharmaceuticals and he assigned me to the drug chains, the Rite Aids, the Revcos, the Eckerds. That's how I got into health care.

In addition to the drug chains, Abe exposed me to other companies that were in health care. One of my early assignments was to help him look at a company called Four Seasons Nursing Centers. Medicare had just come in a few years before and nursing home stocks were going crazy. They had become the new rage. Four Seasons was run by a promoter named Jack Clark, and Jack Clark had come to New York to pitch Four Seasons stock to Wall Street analysts. Abe and I met him for a power breakfast in his suite at the Regency Hotel on Park Avenue between 61st and 62nd Streets. Jack Clark was a "dude," a real smooth operator. The first thing I noticed when I walked into his suite was Jack Clark's alligator shoes. I'd never in my life seen anything so beautiful as those alligator shoes. It was like the light had come out of the sky.

Now, no rational person on this earth would pay $1,500 to walk down the street in a depreciating asset. But I kept staring at Jack Clark's feet and thinking, Alligator shoes, that's for me. I'm gonna have to get me some of those someday. I don't remember a thing about the interview. All I remember was Jack Clark's alligator shoes. It was just the shoes, baby. No wonder nobody wants to hire anybody under twenty-five fresh out of business school.

A few weeks later, Abe and I flew out to Joliet, Illinois, to do due diligence on Four Seasons. Abe wanted to see one of the nursing homes. Sure enough, it was a brand-new nursing home, but as we found out later on, Four Seasons's earnings weren't coming from the operation of the nursing homes. They were coming from the construction side of the business. Jack Clark was a crook. What he was doing was building nursing homes, inflating the construction profits, and representing those profits as operating earnings from the nursing homes. That way, the stock would trade at a high multiple as a "concept stock." As everyone learned with the S&L crisis fifteen years later, you can make big profits in construction if you inflate the price. On April 27, 1970, trading in Four Seasons stock was halted. Four Seasons was a fraud, and Jack Clark and his beautiful alligator shoes ended up going to prison.

The hot concept that came after nursing homes was hospital management. Unlike Four Seasons and some of the other nursing home companies, hospital management was no Ponzi scheme. These were legitimate businesses run by businessmen who saw the huge opportunities being presented by Medicare and Medicaid.

I saw this embryonic industry that was allied with the health care field and I started following it. The big ball started rolling. Hospital management became my primary area of expertise. I was a young analyst following a young industry, and this was my first exposure to real wheeler-dealers. Before I knew it, I was one of the players in their game. I wrote favorable reports about their companies, I recommended their stocks, I got Kuhn Loeb to sponsor a big institutional luncheon in New York at the City Midday Club where all the boys flew in on their private planes and I was the moderator. I'd sit with them at the head table and introduce them to the institutional clients. "David Jones is a graduate of Yale and Yale Law School and he and Wendell Cherry, the new owner of the Kentucky Colonels, have made Extendacare one of the fastest-growing companies in America," I'd gush. "In just two short years, Dr. Tom Frist and Jack Massey have taken Hospital Corporation of America to the pinnacle of the industry," I'd trumpet. "Bernie Korman and Bob Goldsamt were the first to see the potential in consolidating hospital management, and thanks to their leadership, American Medicorp has been a pioneer in this explosive field," I'd boast.

It was a real dog and pony show and I was a central part of the act. The stocks were soaring. The more I ingratiated myself with management, the greater the chance that I could attract some big investment banking fees for my firm, and, ultimately, for myself. Investment banking was where the real big money was; to get a shot at it, I needed to be friendly and positive to these potential clients anytime I could. Big ball, please roll my way!

In the spring of 1972, I'd been at Kuhn Loeb two years. My salary was up to $30,000 and I was jetting all over the country, big-shotting it up with my friends from Amherst, analyzing the drug chains, and promoting hospital management companies. Then one day at a luncheon for Columbia B-School alumni, I bumped into a classmate. He'd taken a job at The Great Pyramid.

In those days there were a lot of boutique firms, small brokerage firms that were noted for their hot securities analysts. The Great Pyramid was one of them. It had a glow, an aura, a karma, a charisma. My friend told me that The Great Pyramid was looking for more analysts and that he could get me an interview. Getting an interview with The Great Pyramid was like getting a tryout with the Dallas Cowboys. "Shit, yeah, go ahead," I said.

The Great Pyramid was on the thirty-third floor of one of the new stainless-steel towers adjoining Battery Park, overlooking the harbor right where the Staten Island Ferry came in. I had a great interview. I met with the head of the entire institutional department and the partner in charge of institutional research. They offered me $50,000 to come over to The Great Pyramid. So I did.

The Great Pyramid was quickly becoming one of the most impressive edifices on Wall Street. At the top were King Khufu and King Khafre. Khufu and Khafre were the gods, the Pharaohs who were building this financial wonder, and like the great kings of ancient Egypt, they were loading their chambers full of treasures and precious objects.

The Great Pyramid was in a dazzling new building and also overlooked the Statue of Liberty. There was some irony here, because the Pyramid was full of people whose parents and grandparents had fled the pogroms of Eastern Europe and Russia and had first viewed the Statue of Liberty from the other side. The parents and grandparents settled in Brooklyn and the Bronx, but now their children and grandchildren had forgotten where they were from. They were scrambling up New York's social ladder and acting like their families had come over on the Mayflower. They were joining country clubs, sending their kids to private schools, summering in the Hamptons, patronizing charities, buying boxes at Lincoln Center, sipping wine at the Guggenheim, and munching cheese at the Metropolitan Museum of Art.

Immediately under Khufu and Khafre was the High Priest who was in charge of the Pyramid's entire institutional sales and research effort. It was the High Priest who'd sold me on coming to the Pyramid. On the next level, directly below the Priest, was the Prophet. The Prophet was the head of research and technically he was my boss, but as soon as I got to the Pyramid, I learned that the High Priest and the Prophet weren't going to be mentors to me like Favia and Bronchtein had been at Kuhn Loeb. The Great Pyramid wasn't like Kuhn Loeb.

The Prophet had thirty analysts, including me, under him. His job as director of research was to have meetings with the analysts, keep abreast of what reports they were working on, review their work, brief the High Priest, and ensure that research reports were disseminated to clients, the rest of the investment community, and the public in an equitable manner. The Prophet had reorganized the research group into three sub-groups of ten analysts each and put a senior analyst in charge of each subgroup. Now the Prophet didn't have to go to meetings. He could send Papyrus to meetings instead.

Papyrus was the associate director of research in charge of my subgroup. Papyrus wasn't much older than I was, but already he was a legend on Wall Street. He covered the airline industry, and in those days, airlines were indeed highflyers. But highflyers often went down as fast as they went up, and on occasion a Papyrus recommendation crashed and took a bunch of the Pyramid's retail brokers and their clients down with it.

The big joke around the Pyramid was that Papyrus had lost more luggage than Allegheny.

Hiero Glyphics was also in my subgroup, and there were some jokes about him, too. Hiero had recommended Polaroid at $170. He couldn't see how Polaroid with all of its patents on instant photography could ever stop selling more and more film and making more and more money. He was convinced that Polaroid was going to earn $4, then $8, then $16, then $83. According to Glyphics, there was going to be a Polaroid camera in your brain and up your ass and they were all going to be taking instant pictures forever. When Hiero's projected earnings failed to develop, it produced a bleak picture for the Pyramid's brokers and their clients.

The Sphinx was another member of the group. Sphinx was an accountant who liked to analyze young companies with fast-growing earnings. It was important for research groups to have an accounting sleuth like Sphinx because the figures presented in a company's annual report, especially a young company in a new industry, could be very misleading. The disclaimers issued by the independent accounting firms that certified the financial statements in annual reports always said something like,

> Our examination of these statements was made in accordance with generally accepted accounting principles, and in our opinion, the accompanying balance sheet, statement of income and retained earnings present fairly the financial position of this company.

What these disclaimers really should have said was something like,

> We've gone through the figures that management gave us, but you gotta realize that generally accepted accounting principles leave a hell of a lot of leeway to dick around with earnings. Plus, this company is paying us a boatload of money to certify these numbers, and if we don't, they'll find another independent auditor that will.

That's why every annual report has page upon page of notes in tiny print backing up the financial statements. While these notes are too small and too confusing for most stockholders to digest, they are a veritable smorgasbord for an accountant like the Sphinx. He'd spread the annual report out in front of him, tie on his green eyeshade, and dig in. Once consumed, the notes gave him a real taste for the company. The inventories were stale, left on the shelves too long. The depreciation was overdone. The cost of goods sold was a bit understated. The receivables could use a pinch of discounting. The goodwill had gone bad.

By Labor Day 1972, I'd been at The Great Pyramid for three months. I was still analyzing the hospital management industry, and I was still bullish. Due to Medicare and Medicaid, money was pouring into health care, and thanks to their consolidation of the industry, the hospital management companies were poised to get a large share of it. I was gazing out at the Staten Island Ferry thinking how cool I was to be a hot young stud riding a hot young industry when the Sphinx waddled into my office.

As the Pyramid's accounting sleuth, Sphinx had a hunting license to take a shot at any company or industry where he felt that the accounting presented a good target. When he hit one, he'd go to the analyst who handled that industry and tell him what he'd found. Sphinx parked his portly posterior in a chair and smiled smugly. He had that gleam in his eye that an accountant gets when he's tracked down a debit posing as a credit.

"Marty," Sphinx said, "I've been looking at the hospital management companies and I think the earnings might be fulla shit."

He went on to tell me that the fastest-growing source of revenue for the health management industry was Medicare and Medicaid charges, but that those charges were just estimates of receivables based on customary billing rates. The actual reimbursements from the government were based on audits, and those audits frequently were two or three years behind. The Sphinx thought that the companies were recording their receivables in an overly optimistic manner, thereby inflating their earnings.

"Very interesting," I said, shifting uncomfortably in my

chair. I was the Pyramid's lead analyst for the hospital management industry. Telling me that my boys were playing with their receivables was like telling the head cheerleader that his backfield might be messing around with the local bookies.

"Marty," the Sphinx went on, "the receivables are only part of the story. The real problem is that these companies are selling at thirty to forty times earnings because they're hot stocks with fast-growing earnings, but that ain't right. With all the Medicaid and Medicare money going into health care, the government's gonna tighten up on these existing programs. They're gonna eventually raise the standards, which will increase the costs, and they're gonna lower the payments, which will shoot the profit margins all to hell. These companies shouldn't be selling at high multiples. This is gonna be a utility rate of return business."

It never occurred to me to ask myself what the Sphinx knew about government regulation. Sphinx was older and more respected than I was, and when he talked, it was good to listen. Instead of telling him not to worry, that my boys were wired and could handle any government attempts at regulation, I got concerned. I started asking myself what I was missing. Maybe I'd gotten too close to the industry, maybe I wasn't looking at it objectively. I decided that rather than being a cheerleader for the hospital management companies, I'd better start working on a report that would dig into the problems facing the industry, especially government regulation, and then project what effect these problems might have on future earnings.

I drafted an outline of the report I proposed and sent it to the Prophet. At the end of September, I got this memo back:

INTER-OFFICE MEMO

Date: 9/28/72
To: M. SCHWARTZ
From: THE PROPHET

I like the start of your Hospital Management report and I urge you to devote all efforts to this. It has the potential of being a very, very fine piece of work. Feel free to take the Sphinx's time to help you. I think Sphinx is quite willing and very able to aid you.

TP:mc

cc: T. Sphinx

So I teamed up with the Sphinx and together we started working full-time on the report. On weekends, I'd drive up to his beautiful house in Westchester County and we'd go down to his basement, lay out all the reports, and dig into the numbers. Once we had the numbers digested, we did what analysts do. We started drawing charts and looking for trend lines on everything that might have an adverse effect on the hospital management industry.

We had a chart on hospital expenditure as a percent of GNP (thanks to Medicare and Medicaid, it was soaring). We had a chart on occupancy rates (they had not been increasing at "mature hospitals," those open for three or more years). We had a chart on inpatient days (they had been decreasing nationally due to greater use of outpatient facilities and lower birthrates). We had a chart on hospital prices (during the past year, price increases had been limited to 6 percent annually). We had a chart on new hospital construction, a chart on payroll as a percent of total expenses, a chart on total expenses as a percent of GNP, a chart on reimbursable costs, a chart on nonreimbursable costs, and a chart on total costs. We made assumptions about revenues, contractuals, net revenues, total expenses, and pretax income per patient day and all the while Sphinx kept reciting, "Marty, Marty, these companies shouldn't be selling at high multiples. This is a utility rate of return business."

In our original draft, we discussed trends that might cause the future earnings growth of hospital management companies to decline from the 15 to 20 percent rate recorded by the industry during the past five years. We said that a cost squeeze was developing and that the first effects of this squeeze were manifest in the recent quarterly reports of the two leading companies in the industry, Hospital Corporation of America and American Medical International. These two stocks were selling at the highest multiples, and they stood the best chance of getting hammered if our projections came true. We concluded with a warning, "Although investors have generally accorded hospital management companies premium price/earnings multiples, we caution that any disappointment in future profit expectations could adversely affect their price/earnings multiples."

By the end of October, Sphinx and I were ready to present our preliminary draft to my subgroup. Each subgroup had a weekly meeting where all the analysts would get together and present their ideas. This was basically a waste of time because analysts didn't care about anybody else's companies. They were too worried about their own. The only people who cared what the analysts were doing were the brokers, because research reports, especially from a high-powered firm like the Pyramid, would have a direct and immediate effect on the price of a stock. The brokers weren't allowed at the analysts' meetings. There was a Chinese wall between the brokers and the analysts, which was supposed to ensure the equitable dissemination of research efforts to the clients, the investment community, and the public. Still, the brokers were always hanging around the analysts, sucking them up, trying to squeeze out a tidbit or two that would give them an edge.

I was all fired up about our report. I remembered being at Amherst, watching the weirdos from the Students for a Democratic Society protest the war in Vietnam. I thought they were egghead assholes. Then I remembered being in the marines and realizing that sometimes it took as much guts to protest a war as it did to fight it. I reminded myself that it always took more courage to go against the establishment than it did to go with it, and now, with Sphinx's help, I was going to expose the establishment. Like the Vietnam protesters, I was convinced that I was right.

Predictably, nobody gave a shit. Nobody cared about hospital management; their only concern was whether another stock recommendation would crash. The Great Pyramid wasn't Kuhn Loeb. There was no communal farming. Everybody was working their own fields, and unlike Favia and Bronchtein, the High Priest and the Prophet didn't even show up for most of the meetings.

Every analyst at the meeting got a copy of the draft. Everyone knew that preliminary reports were highly confidential and that the copies were to be destroyed after the discussion. Paul Standish was the only analyst at the meeting who seemed at all interested in our predictions for the hospital management industry. Standish was a drug analyst, and Medicare and Medicaid paid for a lot of drugs. If our assumptions were right, the drug companies could also get squeezed.

I didn't know it, but as it turned out, when Standish left the meeting he didn't destroy his copy. He took it with him and a few days later discussed it on a flight back from California with another drug analyst from Scudder, Stevens & Clark, an old-line Boston-based investment counseling firm.

Telling an analyst from Scudder what was in our report was clearly on the brink, but then on November 7, 1972, Standish went over the edge. He mailed a copy of our draft to the scumball from Scudder. To this day I have no idea what Standish thought he was going to get out of it, but giving a copy of our report to someone from another firm was beyond stupid; it was unethical.

During the week of November 13, word began to spread. The scumball at Scudder passed our draft around to other people at Scudder. Scudder's clients began selling their hospital management company stocks. On November 21, news of the leak appeared in the papers and the price of American Medical International tumbled 5⅞. In a week, Hospital Corporation of America plummeted 22 percent. Rumors of market manipulation were swirling around the Street. The phones began ringing off the hook at the Pyramid. Thanks to our Chinese wall, our clients had been left out in Mongolia, and they weren't very happy. Our retail brokers were even more upset. How could Scudder's clients get a copy of our research report before they did? What the hell had happened? Where were the High Priest and the Prophet? The blocks of the Pyramid began to tremble.

For a kid who'd always wanted to be a detective, I didn't have a clue. When the Prophet called me in and asked me how the report had been leaked, I said I didn't know. That was not the answer he wanted to hear. Besides our brokers and our clients, Uranus J. Appel, the chairman of the board of American Medical International, was going orbital. Uranus was sure that the Pyramid was manipulating his stock and suspected that the leak was part of an orchestrated plan to push the price down. He was demanding that the New York Stock Exchange start an investigation.

On Wednesday, November 22, the General Counsel came into my office. "Marty," he said, "you've been called to testify at the New York Stock Exchange."

Testify? Why should I have to testify? I'd already told the Prophet everything I knew. Why not send the Sphinx? The Sphinx was older and more respected than I and it was his idea to write the report in the first place. I felt the weight of The Great Pyramid coming down on my shoulders. I fought to regain my composure. I hadn't done anything wrong. I was just a small block on one of the lowest levels. Surely the Pharaohs, Khufu and Khafre, would make sure that the High Priest and the Prophet kept me from being crushed.

The General Counsel briefed me on what to expect and assured me that I was a valued member of the team. "Just tell the truth, Marty," he said, "and everything will be fine." Then, as he was getting up to leave, he added, "Oh, and Marty, by the way, if at any time your interests and our interests diverge, we'll advise you that we're not on the same team anymore and that you'll need to get your own counsel."

As soon as the General Counsel left, I grabbed the phone and called my brother Gerry. Gerry was an advertising lawyer for Davis and Gilbert, but he was the only lawyer I could trust. "Gerry, these bastards just handed me a live grenade. What do I do? Do I get my own lawyer or what?"

"No. You didn't do anything wrong and this is just a hearing. It'll look bad if you come in with your own attorney. Just go in there and tell them the truth."

So that's what I did. On Friday, November 24, I marched down to the New York Stock Exchange and for six hours I testified under oath. I'd been through a Marine Corps interrogation training course, but nothing could have prepared me for this ordeal. They had a court stenographer recording everything, and they just kept pushing me, asking me the same questions over and over.

Why did I decide to write a negative report on the industry when before I'd always been positive? Where did I get my information? With whom did I discuss it? Who had access to the report? Did I give copies to anyone outside of my group? Did I, or anybody I knew, sell shares of American Medical International, Hospital Corporation of America, or any other company in the hospital management industry within the last three months? Six months? A year?

I have a great memory and I just kept telling them everything I knew. After six hours, it must have been obvious that I didn't know who leaked the report, and if the leak had been part of an orchestrated effort by the Pyramid or anybody else to manipulate stock prices, I didn't have anything to do with it. I left the Exchange confident that I'd be exonerated, but there was still one problem that had to be resolved. The Great Pyramid had yet to publish the report.

In all likelihood, the report never would have gotten released if the Prophet, or the High Priest, or certainly the Pharaohs, had seen it before it was leaked. Our report was, in effect, a "SELL" recommendation for the hospital management industry, and nobody on Wall Street ever made a "SELL" recommendation. "HOLD" was as low as you went and a "HOLD" recommendation meant run, don't walk, to your broker and dump. If the Prophet had been doing his job, he would have been on top of what Sphinx and I were doing and he would have been at the meeting when we presented the draft. If he had been there, he would've killed the report on the spot. But the Prophet hadn't been at his post, he'd been watching the quote machine, and now it was too late to bury the report.

Under the now watchful eyes of the High Priest and the Prophet, Sphinx and I did a complete rewrite. We omitted all references to American Medical International, we softened our assumptions, we changed a whole mess of "wills" to "mights," "probablys" to "possiblys," and "therefores" to "maybes." Most important, we stressed that we expected the industry to maintain its 15 to 20 percent growth rate in earnings through the rest of 1972 and all of 1973. We made it very clear that this report was not a "SELL" recommendation, but rather an "alert" to clients of potential longer-term problems that might be facing the hospital management industry.

The official report was released on Friday, December 1, 1972, but by that time nobody was buying it. On Monday, November 27, Dan Dorfman's "Heard on the Street" column in the *Wall Street Journal* talked about the leak, and how the original report was much more negative than the one that the Pyramid was publishing. "It was a 'nightmare' for The Great Pyramid, or so, at least, one inside source describes it," Dorfman began. The report got out without authorization, it caused hefty losses for stockholders of the hospital management companies, and due to some short selling, there was suspicion that The Great Pyramid was manipulating the market. Dorfman ended with a quote from one savvy Big Board trader who said, "'I think these are down stocks. What the Pyramid has done is to seriously question the future earnings power of the industry. Who knows if they're right or wrong, but if they're right, the game's over for these stocks.'"

No wonder Uranus J. Appel and other executives in the industry kept pushing the New York Stock Exchange to investigate. On December 1, 1972, Uranus, who had seen a copy of the original draft, was quoted as saying that it was "amateurish" and "shows very little understanding of what the health care field is all about." He added angrily that the stock's sharp decline had caused a major acquisition to be canceled.

The Exchange, through its Stock Watch program, began looking at the trading in the stocks of hospital management companies during the week of November 13. The leak was traced back to the scumball at Scudder and, ultimately, to Standish. Standish, after first denying that he'd leaked the report, admitted on December 12, 1972, that he'd taken our preliminary draft and given it to the scumball. On December 14, George Johnson, CEO of Scudder, acknowledged that one of his analysts had obtained a copy of the draft and that some Scudder clients might have sold stock holdings before the steep price declines that followed wide circulation of the leaked report. At last I was vindicated, or so I thought.

On January 26, 1973, a group of stockholders from California who'd owned American Medical International stock sued The Great Pyramid and me personally, contending that

> [O]ne of its general partners and its security analyst devised a "short-sale" scheme whereby they disseminated false information under the guise of its being "insider information" which reflected unfavorably on the financial condition of American Medical International, Inc., a company in which the plaintiffs held stock. As a result, the market became depressed, causing plaintiffs to sell at a depressed price, allowing the defendants to purchase to cover their short position. This was a concerted plan, a conspiracy to create a short market in AMI stock.

They asked for damages of $74,200 and punitive damages of $742,000 for a total of $816,200. The General Counsel said not to worry, that the suit had no merit, but still, it wouldn't go away. Uranus wouldn't let it go away. By the end of January, AMI's stock had fallen to 24½, a 50 percent drop.

At a meeting of the New York Society of Security Analysts on February 2, 1973, Uranus blasted the Pyramid, the report, and me. He extolled American Medical's 20 percent increase in earnings for the most recent quarter and told the analysts that his company had "never been in a stronger position on which to build for future growth." He assailed the unauthorized release of the report, saying it was an "underground publication" that contained at least seven basic misstatements of fact in addition to "half truths, misconceptions and sins of omission." He stressed that "this inaccurate presentation was served up by two young men after only a two-hour interview in my office."

Executives of the hospital management companies, my former buddies, wanted nothing to do with me. I was an analyst with nothing to analyze. Even worse, by that time, the whole market had gone to hell. The small stocks had started falling in the second half of 1972. In the fall of '72, the only stocks still going up were the "nifty fifty," institutional favorites like Polaroid, Kodak, and Avon. Fifty stocks were carrying the whole show, all selling at fifty to sixty times earnings. In January of 1973, the Dow topped out at 1,017 and we went into one of the worst bear markets this country has ever seen. On March 15, the suits were dismissed for lack of venue, but hardly anybody noticed. Since the whole market had gone into the crapper, the hospital management industry was just another sad face in the crowd.

In July 1973, the Prophet called me in. He told me that due to the downturn in the market, the Pyramid was cutting back on its overhead. "Marty, I'm sorry, but we're gonna hafta letcha go."

I was stunned. I thought that we were a team, and for six months I'd been carrying the ball for these guys. Now they'd dumped me. But I should have seen it coming; once again, the big boys were looking out for Number One. After Standish got caught and admitted that he was the one who'd leaked my report, people on the Street like Dan Dorfman started wondering publicly who was watching the shop at Pyramid. The High Priest and the Prophet weren't about to take the hit. I was the guy who'd written the report, so I was the block that would be crushed. They couldn't crush me as long as the suit was hanging over their heads, because they knew that I knew things that could really rock The Great Pyramid. It was much safer for them just to keep on paying me for a few months until the suit was dismissed and then can my ass.

I was only twenty-eight and still naive in the ways of Wall Street. I'd been to business school, but nobody had ever taught me about *business*. My father was a small-time merchant. My mother was a high school guidance counselor. My degree in economics from polite, gentlemanly Amherst was irrelevant, and the marines were Semper Fidelis, Always Faithful. At Kuhn Loeb, I was part of a team, and Favia and Bronchtein watched out for me. I just wasn't prepared for the Pyramid. At the Pyramid, you didn't wear a bulletproof vest in the front, you wore it in the back.

I had forty-odd thousand saved up, so I wasn't in a rush to find another job. I decided to take the summer off and stay out at my group house in the Hamptons. I ran into some guys on the beach who were playing commodities. They convinced me to take a trip to Chicago to the Mercantile Exchange, where they were trading cattle and pork bellies. The next thing I knew, I was $5,000 into a computer geek named Paul Goldstein who was running a time-sharing computer commodity trading system. Goldstein didn't have his own computer and couldn't afford to buy computer time except at three in the morning. I was also $20,000 into a Russian wheat futures deal I got from my old gambling buddy Ricky G., who had a commodities broker, Billy H., who had a brother-in-law who supposedly had a direct line to a guy in Washington who knew a guy at the Department of Agriculture who'd been to Moscow. Talk about long shots.

By October, I was down $25,000 and things were getting tight. I figured I'd have to go back to being a securities analyst, so I started calling all of my contacts on the Street. "Oh, yeah, Schwartz. Yeah, your résumé is great and everything, but weren't you in the middle of that Pyramid thing? Geez, I'm sorry, with the market down like it is, you know, I don't think we're hiring."

Nobody had the time to find out the facts. They didn't give a shit. Everybody wanted something that was homogenized and pure. So I was a sacrificial lamb, a tar baby, and nobody wanted to get stuck with me. Meanwhile, the rent on my apartment kept coming due. I swallowed my pride, went down to the unemployment office on Broadway and 89th, and got in line. As the line inched forward, I felt my future inching away. Why had I ever listened to the Sphinx?

As it turned out, the great accounting sleuth didn't know his ass from his assets. The hospital management stocks got creamed along with everything else in the severe bear market of 1973–74. But the companies continued to grow over the next two decades as health care expenditures skyrocketed from 6 percent of Gross National Product to 16 percent. With this bullish backdrop, the stocks appreciated several times over, even though they now sell at lower price-earnings multiples. So the report was part right and part wrong.

As for me, while the experience screwed up my career for a few years, it toughened me up and prepared me to become a better trader down the line. And I came to meet Zoellner because of it, which was a very good thing.

In hindsight, I should've kept on being a team player, throwing lunches for the hospital management industry. The Prophet had to have known that. What the hell was he thinking when he told me to team up with the Sphinx and write a negative report?

Standing in the unemployment line, it was clear to me that what the Prophet should have said when he read my proposal was:

INTER-OFFICE MEMO

Date: 9/28/72
To: M. SCHWARTZ
From: THE PROPHET

Schwartz, you idiot. I hate the start of your Hospital Management report and I urge you to shitcan it immediately. It has the potential of permanently wrecking both our careers. Nobody wants a negative report. Trust officers want reports that cover their asses. They put them in their files and then when the stock goes down, they pull them out and say, "Well, this guy who's smarter and better paid than I am wrote this report and that's why we bought the stock." And stay away from the Sphinx. Sphinx is quite willing and very able to destroy you. Start looking out for Number One.

TP:mc

cc: T. Sphinx

Inside Skinny

I'd love to say that I'm above dealing in rumors because playing a rumor negates my very first premise for doing well in the market, hard work. Work makes you strong and when you play a rumor, you have no strength. You are what you eat, and garbage makes you weak. Usually when you get a rumor, you're late and you have no information. If the stock goes south, you have nothing to fall back on. You're intellectually weak, and when you're weak, you're the most vulnerable. Still, like everyone who plays the market, I'm a sucker for a rumor.

The worst tips always seem to come when you're in a losing streak. One of the things that I always used to talk about was that I had a very small coterie of people who I'd deal with, but when you get in a cold streak, you start listening to everybody. You're almost listening to the shoeshine guy. It's like being at the track and you haven't had a winner all day, so you lean over to some guy who's on welfare next to you and ask him, "Who do you like in the eighth?" And he says, "Well, the six horse, Jerry Bailey's on him, it's a layup lock." And Jerry Bailey doesn't pop the neck, and the six horse finishes fourth.

What happens with all these rumor stocks is that they get jostled, they get pushed up and down, it's like bobbing for apples. When the stock heads south is when you're at your weakest point, and that's when you're most apt to panic because you don't have any intellectual bias for being there. You're not weak because you're winning, you're weak because you're losing. Like the old cliché says, the chain breaks at its weakest link. At this point, your darkest fears take over and you say, "I'm an asshole, why am I doing this again, I've done this before, why is this happening to me?" You panic, you puke, you throw up the stock.

If you're going to play a rumor, you want to get it from somebody who's got a good batting average. My main source is Inside Skinny. Inside Skinny is an excellent stock analyst who likes to keep his ear close to the "Street." He's always going to lunch with CEOs, chumming around with guys who sit on corporate boards, giving a little here, getting a little there, scraping for another hit.

So Inside Skinny calls with a tip, and why is he giving you this tip? Some people just like to help other people, it's a feeling of power, of magnanimity, like making a charitable donation of information, but there's two sides to the story. What you've got to understand is that Inside Skinny hasn't just made one call. He's already got his position, so he's making twenty calls. Skinny wants to be a good friend to everybody, but he also wants to help his position along. So the stock ticks up an eighth and you and everybody else jump in. Then Inside Skinny's function changes. He becomes a guidance counselor, he holds everybody's hand while they wait for their college acceptances to come in.

"Skinny, Skinny. What's happening? What's going on here?"

"Everything's still fine," says Skinny.

"How'd the meeting go in Zurich?"

"Oh, everything was fine. Yeah, I know it's taking a little longer, 'cause these things always take a little longer, they gotta do the due diligence, everything's on track to come through, don't worry, stop being so nervous, you're always so nervous."

As soon as you get stroked, you go out and buy some more stock. And nineteen other people do, too, so then the stock starts to look good on the tape. Everyone's relieved because someone else knows something, and the stock's acting better. Then the stock goes down five points and you puke.

You call Skinny and ask him what the hell happened. He doesn't want to hear your problems. "I got killed, too," he says. "And I had more than you did," but in the meantime Skinny's feeding his stock out into the third wave of buying.

That's it, you vow for the umpteenth time that you'll never play another rumor, but then a few months later, right in the middle of a losing streak, the phone rings. It's Inside Skinny. "Hey," he says in a hushed voice, "have I got a good one for you."

5

Auric Schwartz

"Care for some more popcorn, Ellen?" I crooned, accidentally brushing the back of my hand against the front of her sweater, again. It was Christmas vacation, 1964, and we were seated in the back row of the Roger Sherman Theater on College Street in New Haven. I was a sophomore at Amherst and so far my social life had been a complete bust. Part of the idea of going to a good school like Amherst was to trade up into a better social stratum, and from James Hillhouse High, I had plenty of strata to go, but back then, I wasn't much of a trader.

My research was strong. I'd pore over the freshman picture books from Smith and Mount Holyoke and pick out terrific-looking sophisticated girls who'd prepped at places like Emma Willard, Ethel Walker, and Miss Porter's and give them a call. It was my execution that was killing me. "Hi, Susie, Susie Payne from Greenwich? Marty Schwartz from New Haven. How ya doing today?" Click. "Hey, Liz Hunter, great. Listen, this is Martin Schwartz from Amherst. I was wonderin' if ya'd like to play some cards this weekend. Bridge? Yeah, sure, how much a point?" Click. "Hello, Kimberly Williams? Buzzy Schwartz here. I'm calling from Amherst 'cause I see you're from Middleburg, Virginia, and that's horse country, right? Yeah, so I figured ya might like to take the bus up to Hinsdale to play the trotters?" Click.

Now I was back in my own stratum. Ellen Fine was my date. Ellen had been in my class at James Hillhouse High and was a sophomore at Vassar.

The lights dimmed and the smooth, debonair image of James Bond filled the screen, his cool, lithe figure framed inside the barrel of a gun. Bond was about to match wits with another master criminal on behalf of Her Majesty's Secret Service. It was no secret that 007 would also be called upon to

69

service a bevy of beauties. That's why I'd chosen *Goldfinger* for my date with Ellen. I was counting on Bond to break the ice. As he made his moves, I'd make mine.

I didn't have to wait long. The movie had hardly started before 007 was wrapped up with beautiful, blond Jill Masterson. When Bond cuddled up to Jill on the balcony of the Fontainebleu Hotel in Miami, I cuddled up to Ellen in the back row of the Roger Sherman Theater in New Haven. When Bond put his arm around Jill, I put my arm around Ellen. When Bond went to first base, I went to first base. All the while, Jill and Ellen were whispering sweet nothings in our ears. Thanks to 007, things were going great, so I decided I was going to try and steal second. Slowly, smoothly, like 007, I made my move, the classic over the shoulder to the boulder holder. "Hey, Buzzy, slow down," Ellen purred. "Who do you think you are, James Bond?"

She broke from the clinch. Unlike a Bond martini, I was stirred but not shaken. I was sure that Ellen was just pacing herself. I had to be cool, like 007. When I looked up at the screen, Bond was playing golf with Auric Goldfinger. They were at some beautiful English country club. Right away, I liked Goldfinger. He reminded me of when I used to caddie for Pappy Snyder. Bond and Goldfinger were on the sixteenth green and Goldfinger was lining up an easy two-foot putt. "What's your game, Mr. Bond?" he said, addressing his ball. "You didn't come here to play golf."

Plop. Bond dropped a gold bar on the green right next to the cup. Goldfinger's body twitched; he missed his putt. I sat up in my seat. I'd never seen anything as beautiful as that gold bar gleaming on that green grass. I lost interest in Ellen and second base. I became absorbed in Auric Goldfinger's plan to nuke Fort Knox. It was brilliant. Why try to steal the gold from Fort Knox when you could just irradiate it? If the largest deposit in the world suddenly became worthless, Goldfinger's own huge holdings would soar in value. Of course, Bond foiled Goldfinger's plan, but even in defeat, Auric Goldfinger became my new hero.

I'd always been fascinated with gold. In many respects, this fascination was as much cultural as it was mercantile. From the days of the pharaohs, Jews have loved gold because gold has always been a way for people on the run to carry their wealth. When Moses came down from the mountain with the Ten Commandments, his followers had made their graven images from gold. Then came the Spanish Inquisition, the pogroms of Eastern Europe, Hitler and the Holocaust. Jews have always been on the run. When my grandfather Sam Schwartz escaped the pogroms of Eastern Europe and fled to America at the turn of the century, he knew where to keep his savings. As a tailor in New Haven, Grampa Schwartz was pressed for money, but what little wealth he had, he kept in gold. With that history, the desire for gold was in my genes.

Gold is unaffected by air, heat, moisture, and most solvents. Historically, it has been highly valued not only because of its beauty and resistance to corrosion, but because it's easier to work than all other metals, and easier to obtain in pure form. It was hoarded because of its rarity. For these reasons, gold's been used as currency since the days of the pharaohs.

Over time, one country after another valued its currencies in terms of gold (the "gold standard") and when the great increase in commerce in the late nineteenth century created the need for a formal system of settling international trade accounts, gold became the basis for international monetary transactions. With some exceptions, the gold standard lasted until the Great Depression, but between 1931 and 1934, virtually all countries found it necessary to abandon the gold standard. The reason was that most countries figured their exports would be stimulated if they devalued their currency. However, any advantage they got was soon lost as other countries also deserted the gold standard.

FDR was forced to follow suit after he took office. In April 1933, he ordered Americans to turn in their gold coins. Most people did, but there was a lot of hoarding. Grampa Sam wasn't about to turn in his $20 gold pieces. Instead, he squirreled them away. America was falling to pieces and who knew when the Schwartzes might be on the run again.

Grampa Sam held those coins until 1957 when he turned senile. One day, without telling a soul, he walked down to the

Westville Savings Bank at the bottom of Fountain Street and cashed in his Double Eagles for their face value, $20 apiece.

What was left of Grampa's mind must have reacted to FDR's order twenty-four years late. By this time the market value of the Double Eagles had soared to around $100. Fortunately, Gramma Rose had squirreled away a few coins of her own, and when I turned thirteen, she gave me one, a 1925D Saint-Gaudens Double Eagle.

Designed by Augustus Saint-Gaudens in 1907, one side bore the image of a majestic eagle flying over the sun, suspended in its rays. Above the eagle were the words

United States of America
Twenty Dollars

Below the eagle, perched on the rim of the sun like a corona, were the words

In God We Trust

On the obverse was a woman with long, wavy hair, clad in a sheer gown, holding the torch of Liberty in her right hand and the olive branch of Peace in her left. Her left leg was raised upon a rock, pulling her sheer gown tight. She was beautiful. I was sure that I could make out the nipple of her right breast. Just above the rock was the date "1925" and above that, nestled between two sunbeams, the mint mark "D." Low in the background, by her right foot, amid the rays of an unseen sun, was a tiny U.S. Capitol. Above it all was the word LIBERTY, and little stars ran around the circumference. I loved that coin. I fondled it hour after hour until, finally, I turned numismatic.

In 1958, I bought a used copy of the "Red Book," *A Guide Book of United States * Coins * 10th Edition * 1952*, by R. S. Yeoman. The Red Book was the numismatist's bible. A new edition came out every year and listed the approximate price you could expect to pay for any U.S. coin, depending on condition and scarcity. I'd go down to the bank with my Red Book and a ten-dollar bill and get either a roll of quarters or two rolls of dimes. Then I'd go over to the counter, break the rolls open, spread the coins out, and start looking for "Winged Liberty Head" dimes or "Standing Liberty" quarters.

I'd keep going back to the teller, recycling the coins and getting more rolls. Once again, I was the detective. When I finally found a coin I wanted, I'd check the date, where it was minted, and then look it up in my Red Book. I'd see how many of that particular coin was minted and what it was worth, and then I'd shop it around to different dealers, or if I had a whole series, advertise it in *Coin World* or *Numismatic News* and sell it directly to a collector.

I made some good money trading silver coins, but all the time my real love was gold. Finding a Winged Liberty Head dime or a Standing Liberty quarter was neat, but it couldn't compete with fondling my Saint-Gaudens Double Eagle. I'd come home from the bank with my dimes and quarters and lay them out on my pillow and dream that they were all Double Eagles. I wanted gold, but I couldn't afford it, and technically it was still illegal for individuals to hold gold coins other than for numismatic purposes.

It wasn't until December 31, 1974, that Americans were allowed to purchase gold as an investment. And I was always going tapioca playing the market, so I wasn't able to buy much gold. It wasn't until I married Audrey and started trading on the American Stock Exchange that I began buying gold coins on a regular basis. By that time, the price of gold had risen to more than $500 an ounce, but whenever I had any extra money, I'd buy a few Krugerrands and Canadian Maple Leafs. After I had a dozen or so, I'd take them out and lay them out on my pillow, and flip them up into the air like Scrooge McDuck. It was a good thing to do if you're not in a mental hospital, because I remember thinking to myself, You know, these ain't worth $500 apiece, and somebody's making a real killing on them.

But the price of gold kept going up as the fear of inflation drove more and more people into hard assets. Financial bestsellers were coming out one after the other, predicting the end of the world. Doug Casey wrote *Crisis Investing*, Jerome F. Smith *The Coming Currency Collapse*, Harry Browne *How to*

Profit from the Coming Devaluation, and Howard J. Ruff *How to Prosper from the Coming Bad Years*, each disseminating his own brand of fear-mongering and predicting the end of the financial system as we knew it.

I became so fascinated with gold that late in 1979, after I made my first hundred thousand on the Amex, I considered selling my seat and buying one on the New York Commodity Exchange (COMEX). I wanted to become Auric Schwartz, the gold trader. I discussed the idea with Audrey, and we agreed that it wouldn't be such a good idea. "Buzzy, you're doing real well on the Amex," Audrey said. "If you want to trade gold, trade the gold stocks."

Easier said than done. There weren't that many public companies producing gold, and only a few were traded on the Amex. ASA was a closed-end investment company investing in over-the-counter South African gold mining stocks that was traded on the New York Exchange, but Louis "Chickie" Miceli's group, the ones that made the market for Mesa Petroleum options, made the market for ASA options on the Amex. ASA was traded right next to Mesa and Peter the Mustache, who worked for Chickie, handled the ASA options.

As usual, I did my homework before I started playing ASA options. One of my rules was never to get into something until I'd fully researched it and made sure that it fit my methodology. In analyzing ASA, I discovered an interesting correlation between the Canadian and American gold stocks and the price of gold itself. The stock prices tended to rise and fall before the price of gold, which made them a leading indicator for gold prices. ASA, which invested in South African gold producers, would rise and fall more in line with the metal itself, so I knew that when the Canadian and American gold stocks went up, ASA would undoubtedly follow.

I started playing ASA options in December 1979. Gold was skyrocketing and the action around Chickie's horseshoe was fast and furious. Gold was the hot new commodity and blue smocks would be gathered a dozen deep, pushing, shoving, screaming, and yelling. "Fifty offered at three and a half," Peter the Mustache would yell. "TAKE 'EM!" "TAKE 'EM!" would come the chorus. Fights would break out over who made the trade. "Take it outside." "Take it outside." "None of that in here." And we'd keep trading.

Basically, I was playing the long side, buying call options on ASA's stock, betting that ASA stock would go up along with the Canadian and American gold stocks.

There I'd be in my blue smock, with my ticket book in one pocket, red for sell, black for buy, and my ASA chart in the other pocket, packed in with the crowd huddled near Chickie's Mesa options. I had my lozenges, because you gotta have 'em, I always had a sore throat from yelling. I'd be looking at ASA's high, low, and close of the previous day, and the gold prices, and the stock prices of the Canadian and American mining companies, and I'd wait for the price of ASA to take out the previous day's high, and then I'd jump on the options with both feet. I'd holler at Peter the Mustache, "Take 'em, take 'em. I'm buying!" The strike prices were at $5 intervals and on a hot day the stock price would be ripping right through them. The Mustache had a board with ASA puts (options to sell ASA stock) on one side, and ASA calls on the other side, and there'd be people draped over my shoulders, and I'd be trading away, scrawling on my buy-sell pad, with Fat Mike breathing bourbon down my neck.

"Peter! How many offered at four and a quarter? Thirty? I'll take 'em!" Thirty ASA February 50 call options at 4¼, giving me the right (but not the obligation) to buy one hundred shares of ASA stock anytime before the third Friday in February 1980, at a price of $50 per share, $12,750 total. The price I'd paid in exchange for that right was $425 per option. And it'd be sweaty, and hot, and rubber would be burning off the crepe-soled shoes, and the stock would still be going up, and I'd catch something out of the corner of my eye, gold prices moving, the other gold stocks moving, and I'd say to myself, Holy shit. I gotta buy some more ASA.

I had two clerks, Susan and Jimmy. I paid them a couple of hundred dollars a month and for that they'd collect my tickets and input my trades onto the cards that I sent over to Bear Stearns, my clearinghouse. "Susan! Jimmy!" I'd be screaming from the pack. "Where the hell are you? Get me my count. Let me know my position. Where am I? How many of the forty-fives did I sell? How many of the fifties did I buy?" I'd be foaming at the mouth. ASA stock was so volatile, trading ASA options was like being on one continual hot streak at Vegas.

Thanks mainly to ASA options, I made $600,000 in 1980 and $1.2 million in 1981. Then in 1982, the Reagan administration began to get inflation under control and the price of gold began to fall. I stopped playing the ASA options as much because when the gold stocks slowed down, my advantage was gone. I was quick with numbers, I was disciplined, I had the charts and the methodology, and the market was moving so fast that very few people could keep up with it. When gold cooled down, any old junkyard dog in a blue smock could understand it. We moved on to trade Merrill Lynch at the start of the new bull market in 1982.

I've still got my Kruggerands and Maple Leafs squirreled away in a safe-deposit box. They've been a horrible investment. I bought most of them in the late seventies and early eighties when gold was near its all-time high. My average cost is around $500 an ounce and now, almost twenty years later, the price is close to touching $300 an ounce. I've come to the conclusion that unless Auric Goldfinger resurfaces and nukes Fort Knox, I'm never going to make any money by owning gold, but still, I love it. To me, gold represents security. Who knows when the Schwartzes might have to run again? Gold is in my genes.

Going for the Gold I

In August of 1982, I was living my fantasy. It was Friday afternoon, we were out at our new beach house, and I was tucked under a towel out by the pool watching my Quotron. I had Debbie Horn on my direct line to New York and was trading up a storm, making money. Then my other phone rang. It was Inside Skinny. He was as excited as I'd ever heard him.

"Motty, the wheels are about to come off the wagon," he whispered hoarsely into the phone. "Volcker's just called back all the bank presidents from their vacations. Mexico's going under. They've got too much debt in the Banana Republic. There's gonna be a run on the banks. It's a green smoke alert!"

Rumors about Mexico going bankrupt had been floating around all summer. The one thing every trader fears more than death itself is another crash like the one in '29. They say it can never happen again, because of all the safeguards that have been set up over the years, like margin limits, automatic trading stops, bank reserve requirements, federal deposit insurance, and a whole host of other checks and balances, but in our heart of hearts, no trader believes it.

The way the big banks had been throwing money at Latin America, who knew what was going on, but if Skinny thought he knew, I'd be crazy to ignore it. He was no barber or cabdriver; he was connected to captains of industry all over the country. He had a good track record. Listening to Skinny had made me a lot of money. Skinny's business was to know things before they happened. He traded stocks, he traded bonds, but more important, he traded information. If you were big enough and lucky enough to get on his list, and if you were able to give information back, seven times out of ten, you'd be in the money.

I looked at my watch. It was 2:30. I had to get my gold out of the bank before it closed for the weekend. If Inside Skinny was right, it might not be opening on Monday.

I'd been building up a stash of gold ever since I'd started trading on my own three years earlier. Whenever I felt flush in the market, I'd take some money out and buy some

Krugerrands or Maple Leafs, then I'd stash them away in different places like W. C. Fields. It may sound nuts, but I had gold stuffed in several safe-deposit boxes. I figured that they were like an insurance policy, something I could lay my hands on if I ever got in trouble. That's what rich people do. They spread their wealth around. They hide some here and some there so they're always able to get their hands on something if everything goes into the crapper. I'd thrown a dozen or so rolls of Krugerrands into my briefcase when we'd left New York City and put them in a safe-deposit box in Westhampton. Now, I only had a half hour to get them out before the bank closed at three.

"Audrey! Audrey!" I screamed. "You've got to go down to the bank and get the gold while I check all of my positions and put in stop losses. Mexico's going under. There's gonna be a run on the banks."

"Buzzy, what the hell are you talking about? Your brother's just arrived for the weekend, we're going to the beach, and all of a sudden, you're yelling about getting the gold."

"Audrey, don't argue with me. Just go for the gold. Take Gerry with you. He'll be able to help you. You'll be carrying a hundred thousand dollars plus. Get the cash. Get everything. Go!" I kept trading away, shouting orders to Debbie. "Buy, dammit!" "Sell!" "Shit. Hold!" "Get me some more of those futures." "Gold!" "Oil! MORE OIL!!" Ding. Ding. Ding. Stocks, options, futures. I'm under my towel going wild. When I look up, Audrey and Gerry are still standing there openmouthed. "What the fuck! Why the hell are you just standing there? You heard me. Get over to the bank and get that gold. We've got to save our ass. I don't know whether this thing is going to turn or burn." They looked at me like I was totally gonzo. "This is Captain Schwartz," I screamed. "Just do what you're told, Private!"

"Buzzy, this time you've really lost it. You're over the edge."

"WE'LL SEE WHO'S OVER THE EDGE," I shrieked. "When the banks close, everyone's going to be out in the cold, but we'll have the gold to protect ourselves and buy all the crap we'll need to defend ourselves from the crazies."

Audrey and Gerry headed down to the bank and about an hour later they showed up with the gold. "Buzzy, here's your gold," Audrey said, dropping the briefcase on the floor with a thud. She rubbed her shoulder. "My arm's killing me, but now that I've got it, where do you propose hiding it?"

"Under the bed, where else. I'm sleeping on it. If anybody wants my gold, they're gonna have to go through me to get it."

"Well, they're not going through me," Audrey said. "You can sleep by yourself."

Over the weekend, Volcker had his meeting with the bankers and decided that the Fed would reliquefy Mexico. The crisis was over. On Monday, the banks opened as usual and except for Inside Skinny, me, and a few other people who had their ear to the Street, most Americans never knew how close they'd come to taking us down the tubes.

On Tuesday, bond prices soared as rates plunged in one of the biggest rallies on record. On Tuesday afternoon, I said to Audrey, "Audrey, sweetie, dear. I think the crisis has passed. Would you mind taking the gold back to the vault, please?"

"Ha," Audrey said. "My arm still hurts from lugging it over here. I got it, you can bring it back."

And this is the thanks I get for trying to save my family. But when you're under fire, making decisions in a crisis, you have to react, no matter how absurd you might look to other people. Brokers, investment advisers, money managers, consultants, family members, and the rest of your support troops have to go along or get out of the way.

Rumors are only as good as their source, but once you're convinced that you have information that might be reliable, you have to act on it. My family's security is my top priority, so I envision the worst scenario and prepare accordingly.

6

Made to Trade

*And let them gather all the food of those good
years that come, and lay up corn under the hand
of Pharaoh, and let them keep food in the cities.*

*And that food shall be for store to the land
against the seven years of famine, which shall be
in the land of Egypt; that the land perish not
through the famine.*

—Genesis 41:35–36

Ever since Joseph interpreted Pharaoh's dreams to mean
that there would be seven years of plenty and seven years of
want, futures contracts have been the best way to protect buyers and farmers against the rising and falling prices of commodities. Historically, the game in Chicago has always been
futures. That's because the two main exchanges in Chicago, the
Chicago Board of Trade (the CBOT) and the Chicago Mercantile
Exchange (the Merc) were originally set up to trade farm prod-
ucts.

All exchanges, be they in Chicago, New York, Philadelphia,
Boston, San Francisco, or even Kansas City, are like casinos.
The more action they attract, the more money they make.
Casinos make money because the betting odds are in their
favor; exchanges make money because they charge their members fees. In both cases, the bigger the volume, the bigger the
take. That's why exchanges, just like casinos, are always trying
to suck in new players.

But by the early 1970s, the CBOT and the Merc were suffering from a sustained drought. Their problem was that the new
players coming into the markets after World War II weren't
interested in trading commodity futures. What did they know

about wheat, corn, soybeans, live cattle, lean hogs, and pork bellies? To even the most sophisticated investors, commodities were an obscure riddle. All they could picture was the market going into the tank and a boxcar of pork bellies being dumped on their front stoop. Investors didn't want to be buying and selling commodity futures. If they were going to play the markets, they wanted to buy and sell things that they could tuck neatly away in their safe-deposit boxes. They wanted to play financial instruments like stocks and bonds, and that meant that they were going to bet their chips in New York.

The Merc's and the CBOT's inability to siphon off some of the funds that were flooding into New York meant that Chicago, as a financial center, was on its way to becoming another Dust Bowl. Then, in 1969, Leo Melamed became chairman of the Merc. Melamed was the embodiment of the old cliché "any port in a storm." His family had escaped from Poland and the Holocaust by fleeing across Siberia to Japan, and then, just months before Pearl Harbor, setting sail for America. The family settled in Chicago where Leo's parents, Isaac and Faygl, were offered positions in the Sholom Aleichem schools teaching Yiddish. From this decidedly Jewish background, Melamed found his way to the Merc and eventually made his fortune trading, of all things, pork bellies, but fortunately for the Merc, the CBOT, and the city of Chicago, Melamed was thinking about a lot more than just the price of pork.

Melamed was a visionary who realized that investors viewed the Merc and the CBOT as farmers' markets, and when it came to buying cows and corn, the only quotes most people cared about were those on the menu at Delmonico's. He knew that his casino, the Merc, was going to be left in the dust unless it could come up with some new games to lure the heavy hitters west. But what new games could they offer? After he became chairman in 1969, Melamed began studying the feasibility of offering financial futures. He finally saw the opportunity he'd been waiting for when, on August 15, 1971, "President Richard Nixon stunned the international finance community when he announced that the United States would no longer honor its pledge to exchange gold for foreign-held dollars." (*Escape to the Futures*, © 1996 by Leo Melamed and Bob Tamarkin, published by John Wiley & Sons, Inc.)

This surprise announcement marked the beginning of the end of the gold standard. World currencies, which previously had been tied to the dollar, which in turn had been tied to gold at $35 an ounce, would be allowed to float. Suddenly, money was becoming a commodity, and as Melamed relates in his book, it was time to "forget about pork bellies, forget about agriculture, think money—the ultimate commodity—all kinds of money."

Knowing that others were bound to reach the same conclusion, Melamed leapt into action. In January 1972, the Merc launched the International Monetary Market, a separate exchange designed for the trading of currency futures. Not to be outdone, the CBOT, the Merc's older sister and greatest rival, lured Richard Sandor, a distinguished professor of economics from the University of California at Berkeley, out of his ivory tower and made him the CBOT's chief economist. Like that of Professor Henry Higgins in *My Fair Lady*, Professor Sandor's challenge was to transform the CBOT from a country girl clothed in agricultural commodities to a seductive debutante decked out in financial futures, one who'd certainly outclass the Merc and would rival the grandes dames of New York.

Professor Sandor figured that since the Merc had staked out its claim to currencies, he'd try something tied to interest rates. His first effort was a mortgage-backed futures contract called the Ginnie Mae which the CBOT launched in 1975, but the Ginnie Mae had delivery problems, so in 1977, Professor Sandor remade his brainchild into the thirty-year Treasury bond futures contract. He figured that with all the debt that the government was issuing, the thirty-year T-bond had the potential of turning the CBOT into another Eliza Doolittle.

By the end of the 1970s, the Merc with its currencies and the CBOT with its T-bonds felt that they had come up with the games that could lure some of the big money away from New York, but the transformation from cows and corn to currencies and T-bonds didn't happen overnight. The heavy hitters still weren't coming west to bet their chips. Why go to the weeds to play futures with farmers when they could stay on Wall Street and play stocks and bonds with captains of industry?

As is often the case in trading, what eventually saved the Merc and the CBOT was Melamed's ability to turn what at first appeared to be a big loss for the Chicago exchanges into a big gain. A good part of the CBOT's and the Merc's business came from tax straddles, a technique that the designers of tax shelters had been using during the seventies to secure huge tax savings for their clients. "Wash sale" and "short sale" rules forbade the selling of securities at year end in order to establish tax losses if essentially the same securities were immediately reacquired after the first of the year. But these rules didn't apply to commodity futures. By juggling profits and losses through year-end commodity trades, rock stars, movie stars, big-time athletes, and traders like me were able to use tax straddles to postpone millions of dollars in taxes. Tax straddles had become so popular that major brokerage firms like Merrill Lynch had set up special departments to design them for their customers. In the early 1980s, the Internal Revenue Service decided that enough was enough and that it was time to close this loophole.

Tax straddles generated a lot of big commissions for the CBOT and the Merc, and to the boys in Chicago the legislation that the IRS was proposing read like *Grapes of Wrath.* Something had to be done. The CBOT and the Merc were notorious for fighting among themselves, but when trouble came from the outside, they were family. They'd pull together, favors would be exchanged, disputes would be settled, problems resolved. When the IRS launched its attack on tax straddles, the first thing that Melamed and Les Rosenthal, head of the CBOT, did was run to Dan Rostenkowski, the chairman of the House Ways and Means Committee and the congressman from Chicago. According to Melamed, Rosty's first question was always, "Is this important for Chicago?" and "over the years, Dan Rostenkowski was the Chicago futures markets' tallest and most effective soldier."

Rosty put up a good fight, but eastern liberals, led by Senator Daniel Patrick Moynihan from New York, were too strong. As Melamed notes, when the issue came to a vote on the Senate floor, Moynihan exclaimed that until then, he'd assumed that "a butterfly straddle must refer to a highly pleasurable erotic activity popular during the Ming dynasty." That was it for tax straddles. They were defeated in the Senate, and the best that Rosty could do was to get the Conference Committee, of which he was chairman, to throw the boys in Chicago a bone.

Oh, but what a bone! Buried deep in the bowels of the Economic Recovery Tax Act of 1981 was a little miscellaneous provision that, as of June 23, 1981, "all futures contracts were to be marked to market at year end, and any capital gain or capital loss was to be treated as if 40 percent were short term, and 60 percent long term."

It was absolutely Nirvana. Futures were short-term instruments. You could be in and out of a futures contract in twenty minutes, but now 60 percent of your gain would be taxed at the long-term capital gain rate (20 percent) rather than the ordinary income rate (50 percent). How could that be? This provision defied all logic, but logic was the last thing the boys in Chicago cared about. They'd fallen into a manure pile and, thanks to Rosty, had come out smelling like the sweetest gal on the strip. Vegas might be able to offer free rooms, free drinks, free chips, Frank Sinatra, or scantily clad showgirls, but now Chicago could offer something even better, sweeter odds.

Since I'd started on the floor of the Amex, I'd made $100,000 in four months of '79, $600,000 in '80, and was on a million-dollar pace for '81. I was doing real well playing stocks, bonds, some arbitrage deals that Zoellner steered my way, and, of course, options, lots of options, because options were what gave me the most leverage. I was usually in and out of a position in a matter of hours, or even minutes, so most of my profits were short-term capital gains that were taxed at the ordinary income rate. I was living in New York City and getting smacked at a 57 percent tax rate: 50 percent federal and 14 percent city and state (half of which was deductible on my federal, hence, 57 percent overall). It really hurt giving away 57 percent of every dollar I made to the government, and now, with tax straddles gone, I had to consider trading futures.

Everybody who was playing big time had to consider trading futures. The ability to put 18 extra cents out of every futures dollar you made into your pocket (60 percent long-term gains taxed at 20 percent = 12 percent, and 40 percent ordinary income taxed at 50 percent = 20 percent, for a total federal tax of 32 percent rather than 50 percent) amounted to some serious money for traders.

If I wanted to trade futures out of Chicago, I had to find a clearing firm, and at this time the brokerage houses in New York still weren't big into futures. Spear, Leeds & Kellogg was a big clearing firm that had an office in New York, so on March 2, 1982, I set up an account with them by purchasing $120,000 worth of Treasury bills to serve as my performance bond. Futures contracts have a value of fifteen to twenty times the underlying margin requirements. This meant that with my $120,000 in T-bills I could control $1.8 to $2.4 million in underlying assets. On twenty-to-one leverage, a 5 percent move against me would wipe me out, while a 5 percent move for me would double my margin value to $240,000, which would allow me to control $4.8 million in assets.

The other interesting thing about putting up T-bills as collateral was that I'd be earning interest on the T-bills while I was making money on my positions. It was the greatest game in the world. In stocks, I'd have to pay for the stock, so there was a cost of capital. In futures, there was no cost of capital as long as I was winning.

Spear, Leeds & Kellogg gave me a clerk named Debbie Horn to handle my trades. Debbie worked for David Hershkowitz on the floor of the New York Futures Exchange (the "knife"), where she had direct lines to the floors of the Merc and the CBOT. In March and April, I started experimenting with gold futures, Eurodollar futures, some of the Merc's Swiss francs and deutsche marks, and, of course, the CBOT's thirty-year Treasury bond futures contract. But stocks were still my game. I was making good money on the Amex trading options, and to me, currencies and bonds were like blackjack and roulette. I was looking for the craps table, which meant stocks, but there was no futures market for stocks, so I stuck with my Amex options and kept my futures trades in Chicago very, very, small. Plus, I hadn't forgotten 1973 when I'd lost $5,000 with Paul Goldstein, the computer geek who could only afford to run his commodities trading program in the middle of the night, and another $20,000 when I'd gotten into the Russian wheat deal with Billy H., Ricky G.'s friend, the commodities broker who had a brother-in-law who supposedly had a direct line to a guy in Washington who knew a guy at the Department of Agriculture who'd been to Moscow. . . .

Another reason I couldn't focus on futures was that in November of 1981, my personal life suffered a major setback. Audrey was twenty weeks pregnant with our first child, but when she went in for amniocentesis, the doctors discovered that there was no amniotic fluid and that we would soon lose the baby. We were devastated. My grandfather Pappy Snyder used to like to sing the line from *South Pacific* that went "If you don't have a dream, how you gonna make a dream come true?" but what Pappy never told us was how much it hurt when one of your dreams was taken away.

After Audrey lost the baby, we said the heck with it, life was too short. Why was I making all of this money if we couldn't enjoy it? It was time to spend some. Audrey and I had always taken shares in group beach houses—in fact, that's how we'd met—but now that we were married, we were stuck in a two-bedroom apartment in New York with no place to go. It was like living in a cage. We'd always wanted to have our own beach house, so we decided that it was time to get ourselves one. As of January 1, 1982, we had a net worth of $1.2 million. We took one-third of it, $400,000, and bought a beach house out in Westhampton.

Financially, putting that much working capital into a non-working asset was stupid. It took a big chunk of money that I should have been trading out of play, but I had this image of myself out at the beach for three months during the summer, wheeling my Quotron machine outside, sitting next to the pool trading every day. (I subsequently found out that the glare out by the pool was too tough and I had to wrap a towel around my Quotron machine and climb under it like Matthew Brady.) Plus, given my success over the past three years, I was sure that I could always make more.

When I got knocked down, I never took the eight count. I always got right back up because I was a firm believer that when something went bad, something good would be coming along, and if I was still lying on my back, I'd miss it. I was on my feet on April 21, 1982, two months after we'd bought the beach house, when the Merc launched the Standard and Poor's 500 Stock Index Futures Contract, a new financial instrument that Leo Melamed labeled the "ultimate contract." And it was. The S&P futures contract was based on the stock price of five hundred large-cap companies. Right away, I could see that the S&Ps were going to be my game because they were based on stocks. All the techniques I had developed or synthesized, the Magic T, the ten-day moving averages, the oscillators, the stochastics, were geared toward playing this new instrument. It was like I'd been playing at the dollar blackjack table, and all of a sudden, they opened a craps table with a $10,000 limit.

On the morning of April 29, 1982, I made my first S&P futures trade. I bought twenty June SPMs and lost $370. The next day, I tried again. I bought forty June SPMs at 117.20. An S&P futures contract was priced at five hundred times the value of the index being purchased, in this case June SPMs. So the value of these contracts totaled $2,344,000 (40 × 500 × 117.20), but I didn't have to put up any money because my $120,000 in T-bills was enough to cover the margin requirement. This was leverage, baby, real leverage. After a couple of hours I sold out at 117.70 and made $10,000 (40 × 500 × 117.70 = $2,354,000 less my cost of $2,344,000).

All that spring and summer I kept experimenting with the S&P futures. While I was intrigued by the S&Ps, I was still cautious. All new instruments are unpredictable. When they first trade, everybody's trying them out, the volumes are erratic, and it's tough for the exchanges to maintain orderly markets. What I'd do was divide the trading day into half-hour blocks, just like the Merc did, and each half hour, I'd chart the rate of change. I viewed momentum during the day just like the tides, two high and two low, ebb and flow, back and forth. If the S&P 500 composite index was up $0.50, then up $0.30, then up $0.10 in three consecutive blocks, then I knew that the momentum was shifting. The sine curve was about to turn down, the market was coming to a stoplight, it was time to switch gears. Red light, green light, go short, pull the trigger.

I saw lots of possibilities for the S&Ps. In addition to having phenomenal leverage and having the ability to get quickly invested in the market without having to buy a whole portfolio of stocks, the S&Ps were a fantastic hedge. If I thought that the market was going down and I didn't want to sell my stocks because I didn't want to lose my holding period, I could sell an equivalent amount of futures contracts against them to try and net out some of the risks. And there were all sorts of tax advantages that were just starting to evolve.

But I was still playing small, because in August, Paul Volcker, the chairman of the Federal Reserve Board, had given the market a jump start when he called the big bankers at their vacation retreats in Martha's Vineyard, Jackson Hole, Bar Harbor, Newport, and the south of France and told them to come to Washington. Rumors were floating around that Mexico was about to default, and at the meeting in Washington, the Fed decided to reliquefy Mexico so that the big U.S. banks wouldn't go into the tank. On that news, interest rates started to drop, and bank trust departments, pension funds, mutual funds, and insurance companies that had been parking huge percentages of their assets in money market instruments with yields as high as 18 percent started to come back into the stock market. On August 17 the Dow Jones rose a record 39.81 points, and I was too busy whipping my options to fool with S&P futures.

Plus, I was making money trading currencies and Professor Sandor's thirty-year T-bond futures. Thanks to Rosty's little miscellaneous provision and the fact that the government was issuing more and more debt, Eliza Doolittle was looking better and better to a lot of heavy hitters, and the CBOT's thirty-year T-bond was becoming the world's most actively traded futures contract. This increased volume made the T-bonds a safer bet.

I'd also discovered a new tool, a quote machine called the Telerate, that was really helping me play the T-bonds. While the

CBOT was maintaining an orderly market for the T-bond futures, there was no centralized market for the "physicals," the actual bonds already issued by the Treasury. The physicals were the crops in the silos, and they were being bought and sold by the individual farmers, investors, and institutions trading through brokerage firms. As interest rates went up and down, the price of the outstanding physicals would go down and up, but one firm might offer a bond at 101 while another firm was offering the same bond at 98. It all depended on who had what bonds and how much they wanted to buy or sell. Like farmers buying and selling silage, trades were made by calling around trying to find the best price.

Neil Hirsch, a former bond salesman with Cantor Fitzgerald, had recognized the need for a black box service that would list the prices for all of the "physicals" in one place. Hirsch started a company called Telerate. Hirsch's company called around to the different brokerage firms and got up-to-the-minute quotes on all of the different bonds that the Treasury had issued. These quotes would immediately appear on a black box that bond traders could rent from Telerate. It was a simple idea that made Hirsch a very rich man. He ended up selling Telerate to Dow Jones.

Not long after I started spending more time upstairs from the floor of the Amex, I got a Telerate. Everything in this business is about finding disequilibrium, that's what produces opportunity, and I knew that the Telerate would help me play the bond futures. Plus, I loved gadgets and was always buying anything that was new. Even though I was working from upstairs, the Amex had a rule that members had to physically make an appearance on the floor every day. I used to go down to the floor every morning, but because the Amex traded stocks, not bonds, there was not a single Telerate machine on the whole floor, so I'd always head back upstairs around three o'clock to check the bond quotes on my Telerate. The bond futures market closed at 3:00 P.M., but the physicals traded as late as the brokerage firms wanted to trade them, and thanks to my Telerate, I could get a feel for how bond futures would do the next day by monitoring the cash bond prices in the after-hours trading.

On Friday afternoon, September 10, when I came up from the floor to check my Telerate, I noticed something interesting. "Audrey. Come look at this," I said. "I think that there's a correlation between the cash bond and the S&P 500."

"I'm busy, Buzzy," Audrey said. After it had become obvious that I was going to make it as a trader and we'd decided to start a family, Audrey had quit her job at the American Paper Institute and come to work with me. She'd do my charts and my paperwork and listen to me talk about the market. Before too long, she could tell whether I was serious about a trade or was just trying to talk myself in or out of something.

"No, come take a look. I think I might be on to something."

Audrey was doing paperwork and didn't want to be bothered. We'd just moved back to the City from the beach house that week and she was catching up. Reluctantly, she wheeled her chair over to where she could see the Telerate. "I've been looking at the cash bonds as an indicator for the bond futures," I said, pointing at the quotes, "but, you know, stocks also rise and fall on interest rates." That's because when interest rates go up, companies have to pay more for their capital, which increases the cost of doing business and cuts into their profits. And higher interest rates make it more difficult for consumers to buy on credit, which slows down sales and cuts deeper into profits. Lower profits mean lower stock prices.

"So?"

"So, if the T-bonds go up in the after-hours trading, that means interest rates should be going down the next day, which means the S&Ps should open up." I grabbed a handful of charts. "Let me give you an example. On August thirtieth, the price of the physicals broke down three-quarters of a point in the last hour." I took out the chart with my ten-day moving averages. "Here, look at the S&P index on the thirty-first. It opened down 0.80. But here last week, the bonds ticked up half a point. And look, the S&P opened up 0.65 the next day."

"So?"

"Audrey, this could be a great indicator!" I was getting excited. "The bond futures close at three, but the S&Ps don't stop trading until four-fifteen. If the physicals go up between three and four-fifteen, I can buy futures right at the close. If they go down, I can sell the S&Ps short." I pointed to the quotes on the Telerate. "Look, the bond price has moved up half a point in the last hour. If I'm right, that means that the S&P should be up on Monday."

Audrey checked her watch. "Buzzy, it's four-ten. You've got five minutes. If you want to give it a try, give it a try."

I was already reaching for the phone. "If the bonds are up half a point in the last hour, I might be too late. I gotta check the S&Ps . . . Debbie! Debbie, honey," I said to Debbie Horn, my clerk at Spear, Leeds & Kellogg. "Yeah, Marty here. The December S&Ps! Gimme a quote, I need a quote. Beautiful! They haven't budged. Get me thirty contracts at the market."

All that weekend I pored over my charts, trying to correlate the price of the physicals in after-market trading with the opening price of the S&Ps the next day and to see how that matched up with my other indicators. It wasn't perfect, but most of the time, significant after-hours moves in the cash bond resulted in similar moves in the S&Ps the following day. More important, these moves fit right into the patterns established by my primary indicators: the Magic T, my ten-unit exponential moving average, my oscillators and stochastics.

I couldn't wait for the market to open Monday morning. Audrey and I got in early and I sat glued to the Quotron. I was sure that the market was going to open up, and it did, at 119.40. "Yes!" I picked up the phone and called Debbie. "Sell!"

For the rest of that week, the after-hours trading of the cash bonds was inconclusive, down $\frac{3}{32}$ one day, up $\frac{2}{32}$ the next. It wasn't until Monday, September 20, that my cash bonds indicator made a significant late move, up $\frac{9}{32}$. "Okay, Audrey," I said, "this is it. The S&Ps should open up tomorrow."

"How much?"

"I dunno. I've still gotta work that out. I don't have enough data yet. But believe me, those babies are gonna open up, at least 0.20." I picked up the phone at 4:10. "Debbie! Gimme a quote on the December S&Ps . . . 123.40 . . . Okay, load me up. Buy me a fifty lot at the market."

Debbie called back at 4:11 and said that I was filled at

123.45. What I'd done was to buy fifty contracts at a theoretical cost of $3,086,250 (50 contracts × 500 × the value that the marketplace was predicting for the S&P index in December 1982). But once again, I didn't have to put up any cash, because the T-bills in my performance bond account covered my margin requirement. On Tuesday, they opened up 123.65 and immediately ticked up to 0.75. Bingo, an instant paper profit of $7,500. I checked all my other indicators. Everything was pointing up. "What should I do? Audrey! What should I do? Should I take the profit or buy more?"

"Buzzy, just hang in there. They opened up so now you're playing with the house's money."

The S&Ps ran straight up to 124.40 before they stopped to take a breath, and I bailed out at 124.30 with a nice gain of 0.85 and a profit of $21,250. This was all right. Being ahead at the opening was like waking up with a woody. What a way to start the day. That same afternoon, the physicals jumped another $11/32$ in after-hours trading, so again at 4:10 I went long fifty more contracts, and when the S&Ps opened up 0.70 I was up $18,750. Beautiful!

On Thursday the twenty-third, the physicals hit a downdraft in the after-market and gave back $12/32$. Now it was time to test the other half of the equation. "Debbie! How're the Decs? 123.85. Sell me twenty-five short." I glanced over at Audrey. She was nodding. "No, screw it. Make it fifty, short fifty contracts at the market."

At 10:01 the next morning, ding! the register rang up another $18,750 as the S&Ps opened at 123 even. Yesss! AC/DC, it worked both ways!

For the rest of September, I kept sparring, jabbing, punching, counterpunching, long a fifty lot here, short a fifty lot there, poking, all the time playing off my Telerate. The market overall was going nowhere. The S&Ps opened at 119.40 on September thirteenth and closed on the thirtieth at 119.35. But I was up $160,000 on small daily swings.

In October the market went supernova. On Wednesday, October 6, the Dow Jones rocketed 37.07 points, the second greatest one-day rise in history. Everyone on the Amex was going crazy, making fortunes. You couldn't see the floor for the buy-sell tickets. I was blowing their socks off with my option trades, but when everybody else was dancing the mashed potatoes on their way to the bar, I sprinted for the elevator to get back up to the Telerate. "Audrey! What's happening to the physicals? How're the December S&Ps?" By now Audrey was calling Debbie for the quotes.

"Buzzy, the S&Ps moved up to 126.45. The physicals have been rising." So was I. We watched the cash bonds go up steadily over the next half hour. My indicator was up $^{11}\!/_{32}$ at 3:30. Up $1\frac{2}{32}$ at 3:45. This was going to be awesome. I had to take a pee, but I couldn't leave. Up $1^{19}\!/_{32}$ at 4:00!

"Debbie! Buy a hundred and fifty December S&Ps at the market! No, the hell with it. Buy two hundred. Call me right back! Get me these babies and we're all goin' to Vegas!" I hung up. "Audrey, if this works, we're at a whole new level."

The next morning the S&Ps opened at 128.70. I had two hundred contracts at an average price of 126.53. 200 contracts × 500 × a gain of 2.17 = $217,000. Holy shit. This *was* a whole new level.

All through October, I smacked the S&Ps when they went up and I smacked them when they went down. On October twenty-second, on rumors that the Fed was not going to lower the discount rate before the election, the physicals plummeted in after-hours trading, the S&Ps opened down 1.85, I was short 150 contracts, covered at the opening, and in one minute made $138,750. By the end of the month, I was up $1.4 million. My legs were sore from jumping up and down, my voice was shot from screaming at Debbie on the phone, and Audrey's ribs were tender from being hugged. In February, when we'd crawled out on a limb and dumped $400,000 into the beach house, our net worth was $1.2 million. Now, in one month, I'd more than doubled that, I'd made more in a month than I'd made in my entire lifetime. I can't begin to describe that feeling. Every day, for twenty straight days, we'd get in the Eldorado to drive home from work and we'd be, on average, another $70,000 richer. It would have taken me a whole year to make $70,000 if I were still a securities analyst.

All of a sudden, I was a thirty-seven-year-old multimillionaire with seemingly unlimited earning potential. Why? Because I'd been able to find a new game that fit my personality and then see something that made it all mine. I was one of the first to realize that there was a direct correlation between the cash bonds and the S&P futures. That's because I was one of the few people who played stocks, bonds, and currencies. Most traders were specialists who played one but not the others. They had no way of finding an indicator that was a crossover. I was one of the first S&P traders to recognize the extra benefit of using a Telerate to trade S&Ps. And thanks to my trusty Telerate, I was living every gambler's dream. I knew what was going to happen before it happened.

Luck? You bet it was luck, but it was also intellectual because I worked so hard at it. I'd put in the time and figured out something that nobody else could see, and now I felt better than Joseph. I had the ability to take care of my entire family and provide them with financial security for the rest of their lives.

And the fame thereof was heard in Pharaoh's house, saying, Joseph's brethren are come: and it pleased Pharaoh well, and his servants.

And Pharaoh said unto Joseph, "Say unto thy brethren, This do ye, lade your asses and go, get you unto the land of Canaan.

And take your father and your households, and come unto me, and I will give you the good of the land of Egypt, and ye shall eat the fat of the land forever.

—Genesis 45:16–18

Switch Hitting

I made up my mind, but I made it up both ways.

—Casey Stengel

After a couple of months on the floor, I was trading some Digital Equipment options with Frannie Santangelo and complaining about how I was always having to run around looking for quotes. Down on the floor, I could never get the information I wanted when I wanted it. The specialists who were paying the rent on the quote machines decided what symbols they wanted up on the screens. Chickie had Mesa Petroleum on his screen, and Joey had Texaco on his, and Frannie had Digital Equipment, but nobody had all the information I needed in one place.

"Marty, I've got an office upstairs with a Quotron," Frannie said. "Feel free to use it. Make yourself right at home." Frannie stayed downstairs during the day running his book, but Frannie was a big-time operator and he kept his clerk and a couple of guys, Jerry Muldoon and Leon D'Agostino, upstairs. Jerry and Leon traded some of Frannie's capital and got to keep a piece of the action. When Frannie decided that I was a winner, he figured that it would be good to get me upstairs. He figured that while he was working me for s'teenths on the floor, Jerry and Leon could be working me for ideas and information upstairs.

I was flattered. During lunch, while a lot of the boys went out for a quick pop, I'd grab a sandwich and go up to the office. I'd post my charts and prepare myself mentally for the afternoon. I had all the information I needed right in front of me on the Quotron and a direct line to the floor. When I wanted to make a trade, I'd call Fat Mike and Fat Mike would execute my order.

Jerry Muldoon and Leon D'Agostino saw that I was making all this money and they befriended me. I knew that Frannie'd told them to look over my shoulder, but the rent was free, they weren't bad guys, and that was fine with me. I'd call down to

Fat Mike with a trade and Jerry and Leon would go running for their phones. What did I care? Having them come in behind me just bolstered my own positions.

After Mesa options, I started trading ASA, the South African gold stock. With inflation out of control, the gold stocks were jumping all over the place, which was great for a market timer like me.

One day, I called Fat Mike and told him to buy me fifty ASA May options, and Jerry and Leon were listening. I never asked them what they were doing, and never really knew whether they were following me into a position or not. After Fat Mike called back to say that the trade was set, I decided to go down to the floor to see what was going on. While I was on the floor saying hello to Hayes, Donnie Gee, Frannie, and Fat Mike, I was keeping an eye on the tape, and I didn't like what I saw. "This is wrong," I said to myself. "I've gotta change my position." I liquidated my longs and went the other way. Once I'd switched from long to short, I headed back upstairs. When I got there, Jerry was glued to the Quotron. He had a worried look on his face. "Geez Marty," he said, "the market doesn't look so good."

I glanced at the machine. "I know. That's why I'm short."

"Short! When did you go short? You were long just a little while ago!"

"Yeah, but when I got to the floor I didn't like the looks of things, so I switched my position."

Jerry's chubby pink Celtic face turned red, and then crimson. "You son of a bitch," he bellowed, jumping out of his chair. Jerry played in a softball league and he kept a bat by his desk. He grabbed it and started coming after me. "I'm gonna kill ya." His Irish dander was up.

"Jerry, calm down!"

"How the fuck could you change your position?" He was still coming after me, swinging the bat wildly around his head.

"I just did what I had to do," I said ducking behind a chair. "I'm trying to take care of my family and the last time I looked, we didn't have an Irish branch. You know, the lost tribe got lost in Israel, not Ireland."

That calmed him down, and after he put the bat back, I said,

"Look, Jerry, one of the reasons I've been able to make some money is that I'm a switch hitter. It's like in baseball, if they bring in a righty, I'm batting lefty. If I see the market going lefty, I'm switchin'."

When you're a market timer, you have to be equally good at going short and going long, and when the market changes sides, you can't hold your position and hope it turns around. If you're not a natural like Mickey Mantle, you've got to be a student of the game like Rod Carew. Practice, practice, practice.

This tip is not directed at the amateur or hobby investor, but to the aspiring professional. Most average investors are long stocks, and that's all they should be. They shouldn't be going short, and they don't need to know how to do it. Going short's a game for the pros.

7

Never Short a Republican

It was Election Day 1982, and Audrey and I were sitting at our desks waiting for the market to open. We'd just voted and I was feeling guilty. In my heart, I was a liberal Democrat, and in my heart, I'd always be a liberal Democrat. That's how my parents had raised me, with a picture of Franklin Delano Roosevelt hanging on the wall of our house in New Haven. But now that I was starting to make big money, I was starting to forget my roots. I'd just voted Republican.

Living in New York City meant that I was giving 57 percent of every dollar I made to the government in income taxes. To me, governments had become gluttons who just couldn't seem to get enough of my money, and for what? The streets were full of potholes, the subways were covered with graffiti, somebody was always getting mugged, city workers were always going on strike. I wouldn't have minded paying the taxes if I thought that they were doing some good, but when I saw how my tax money was being wasted and mismanaged, I'd decided to vote with my wallet, not with my heart. God, I was even sounding like a Republican, but that's what happens when you start making big money, and thanks to the S&P 500 futures, I was making big money.

I'd been profitable every month since I started trading the S&Ps except for June, when I'd gone back to my fifteenth reunion at Amherst and I'd come back with a big head. College reunions are a great barometer for how well you're doing. At your tenth, you start to get a feel for who's going to make it big time. Doctors have picked their specialties and are starting to practice, lawyers have chosen their areas of expertise and are bucking for partner, academics have gotten their Ph.D.s and their assistant professorships and are being considered for tenure, businessmen have done their rotations through marketing and production and are angling for their own divisions, financiers have built up clienteles and are beginning to get a piece of the action. By your fifteenth, a few guys are becoming stars. They've discovered a new cure, won a big case, published a seminal work, captured a major vice presidency, or pulled off an incredible deal. By your twentieth, it's going to be clear who's got the momentum to go all the way, and by your twenty-fifth, it'll pretty much be over. You'll either be sitting at the president's house sipping sherry and writing out a big check to the alumni fund, or you'll be huddled in the back of the reunion tent, still drinking beer, still networking, still hoping for a break.

I was becoming a star. I was especially pleased with how far I'd come in the last five years. At my tenth reunion, nobody got the feel that I was going anywhere, let alone big time. I was working for Hutton, had no money, was living in my little rent-controlled studio apartment, and was too scared to ask Audrey to marry me. At my fifteenth, I was working for myself, was a millionaire, was living in a posh East Side apartment, had a beach house in the Hamptons, and was happily married.

At our first class meeting in the fall of 1963, Eugene S. Wilson, dean of admissions, had told us: "Most of you have been in the top ten percent of your high school class, but as you look around this room, basic mathematics will suggest that half of you, a full fifty percent, will be in the bottom half of the Class of '67." From that moment on, I was determined to be in the top ten percent of my class, and at my fifteenth reunion, I felt that I'd finally made it. And I wanted my classmates to know it. I'd strutted around the campus in my alligator shoes with Audrey on one arm and my big Rolex on the other, making it easy for everyone to see that I was going big time. Of course, when I got home, I promptly lost $35,000 in June.

But in July and August, trading out at the beach, I'd regained my equilibrium and made $333,000. Then in September, I discovered the correlation between the cash bonds and the S&P and made $160,000, and in October, thanks to my trusty Telerate, I'd made $1.4 million. That was unbelievable. Nobody I knew could match this performance. In October of 1982, I was the fastest gun on the Amex, bar none.

By this time, Audrey and I had a couple of desks on the ninth floor of 74 Trinity Place in space that Bear Stearns, my clearing firm, was giving me. I was supposed to have my own office, but at the last moment, Bear Stearns had given the office they'd promised to me away to some specialist who they thought was going to generate more business for them. But, what else is new. Once again, I'd gotten crowded out of the club.

Audrey and I were stuck in a little alcove. It was not a great setup. Behind us, there was a bullpen where a bunch of small-time traders with accounts at Bear Stearns sat, smoking cigars. Like all traders, they were always yelling and swearing. "Look, asshole, get me the fuckin' quote." "I don't need any of your shit, just sell it." "Fuckin' A, I just hit a home run." "I just got screwed out of a five lot on the OEX calls. Those bastards never fill my orders quick enough." "Fuck. Doublefuck. Chickie just bungholed me on some Mesa options. He took 'em ahead of me." It was pretty rough. I was allergic to the smoke, and it was hard on Audrey, being one of the few women on the floor, but we couldn't beat the price and we were making a shitload of money.

My desk and Audrey's were set in an L at a ninety-degree angle so we could sit shoulder to shoulder. We were a team, a perfectly balanced team. I understood the market, and Audrey understood me. She understood my psyche. I'd mutter at my Quotron, I'd check my moving averages, I'd talk on the phone to Zoellner, or I'd check in with Debbie for a quote, and Audrey would be doing her work, listening, observing, getting a feel for how I felt. Audrey was the real prophet because she could tell from my scribbles, and my body language, from what I was saying and what I was doing, how serious I was. She knew what I really wanted to do.

I'd be sitting there looking at my screens, checking my moving averages, and say something like, "The market looks good. The S&P's hit an inflection point, it's in the buy range," and Audrey would say, "Buzzy, if you like it, get it." Or we'd be glued to the physicals on the Telerate at 4:10, and Audrey would be murmuring in my ear, "Buzzy, you like it. Go for it. Go for it." And I would, and the S&Ps would open up a point and a half the next morning, and we'd make another shitload of money in one minute. Having Audrey sitting there, reinforcing my feelings, gave me just the edge I needed.

We weren't expecting Election Day to be a very busy trading day. The market closed for presidential elections but stayed open for midterm congressional elections. Still, bank closings and uncertainty about the outcome of the voting had led most of Wall Street to believe that on this day, the market would bide its time. Plus, the Street didn't really know if it wanted a Republican victory. This midterm was the first public referendum on Reaganomics and this election, more than most, was focused on the administration's handling of the economy.

The Republicans had captured both the White House and the Senate in 1980, and the question for this election was whether Reagan, the great communicator, had been able to sell his trickle-down supply-side economic theories to the voters. Democrats had been pointing to the 10.1 percent unemployment rate, highest since the Great Depression, and claiming that the administration, once the election was over, was prepared to cut Social Security benefits. Republicans, on the other hand, had been pleading for more time to make their programs work. According to the *Wall Street Journal*, Republicans were urging the voters to "Stay the course," while Democrats were responding, "Stay the curse." The polls were predicting more of the same, that the Republicans would hold on to the Senate, but that the Democrats would pick up some seats in the House. That scenario made sense to me and I didn't expect anything dramatic to happen in the markets.

Somewhat to my surprise, stocks jumped off to an early gain that morning and built on it for most of the day before settling back to a comfortable 16.38 advance on the Dow. Trading volume climbed to 104,770,000 shares, way up from Monday's 73,530,000, and that was heavy, especially for an Election Day. As predicted, the exit polls indicated that voters were staying the course by letting the Republicans retain control of the Senate and the Democrats control of the House, and apparently, buyers were finding reasons for optimism no matter which party prevailed.

I'd gone long in the morning and then started selling short toward the end of the day because when the market rose suddenly, sometimes I'd go get short toward the end of the day and catch a late sell-off. The Dow was up more than 30 percent since August and had just broken the thousand-point level for the first time since 1973. The S&Ps had opened at 137.70, gone as high as 140.90 and then settled back to close at 138.85 for a respectable gain of 1.40 points on the day. All of my indicators had said that the market was overbought, and they were right. I'd caught the market going up and coming down and we'd had a good day. The quotes on my Telerate for the after-hours trading of the cash bonds were just like the election, inconclusive, so I didn't bother to put on an overnight position.

"Buzzy, I need a new coat," Audrey said as we were packing up to go home. This didn't surprise me. She'd just been talking on the phone with her mother, Sally Polokoff, and like all good mothers, Sally Polokoff was forever thinking of things that Audrey needed. "I'm going to take tomorrow off and go shopping with my mother. She knows a furrier down in the garment district that'll give us a good deal on a mink."

So now Audrey was getting a mink. How Republican. But that was all right. If Audrey wanted a mink, she should have one. She'd earned it, plus, we'd just learned that she was pregnant again and what better way to keep both my babies warm during the cold New York winter than by having them swaddled in mink.

"Sure," I said. "It looks like the market discounted the results of the election today, so there won't be much happening tomorrow. You take tomorrow off. You go with your mother and get yourself a nice warm coat."

The next morning I eased into the big leather seat of my gray Eldorado and drove to work by myself. Both the Republicans and Democrats were claiming victory. It was going to take a while to figure out what really had happened, if anything, to the balance of power. To me, it looked like more of the same, and I wasn't expecting to see any big bulls or big bears come out of the woods.

Stocks started off mixed, but bonds were rallying, and the

S&P futures opened at 139.20, up 0.35 from Tuesday's close. Investors must have been convinced that with the election out of the way, the Federal Reserve would lower interest rates. There had been speculation that the Fed was going to lower them on October 25, and when they hadn't, in deference to the election, the market had plunged 36.33 points, its second largest fall in history.

I kept an eye on the news services. Economists were predicting a cut in the discount rate, so I went long on fifteen S&P contracts, but I was very tentative because all of my indicators still said the market was overbought short term and who knew about the Fed? I leaned back to say something to Audrey and realized that she wasn't there. I was hoping that she'd call in, but there wasn't much chance of that. When Audrey got with her mother, there was never any time to think about me.

At eleven, I began to get real edgy. The market was running up without stopping to look back. I could hear the noise level out in the bullpen beginning to rise. "Holy shit. Somebody's lit a rocket under Northern Telecom." "IBM's moving. It's time to get on the Big Blue train." "Look at Electric. Look at the brokerage firms. Even Ma Bell is ticking up. Look at everything, it's all moving; technology, brokerage, transportation." "The tape's running late." "Give me a quote, you shithead." "Fuck the quote, buy me five thousand AT&T at the market." "Get me some Teledyne calls." "Digital is flying."

I checked my Quotron and saw that the market was surging. What should I do? "It's like yesterday," I said. "It won't last. My indicators say that the market's overbought. It's gotta drop back. Audrey, what should I do?" There was no answer. I'd said it, but Audrey wasn't there to tell me whether or not I meant it.

I got on the phone and started selling December S&P 500 futures. "Debbie. Yeah, honey, things are moving, but it can't last. What's the quote? 139.20? Dump those fifteen contracts I bought this morning and sell fifty more short." The market kept rising. Just after noon I went short another twenty-five contracts at 140.05, and at 1:10 P.M., another twenty-five at 141.40. Then at 2:00 P.M., the market started to back off a little. "Debbie, what's the quote? 140.95. Excellent. I knew it was overbought.

Sell fifty more." By 3:30, things were totally out of control. The market had suddenly got a second wind and was surging.

According to my Telerate, the cash bonds were on the fly. The S&P futures had locked limit up at 143.85. There was a rule that the S&Ps could only move five points either way in a day, and once they reached that point, they locked at that price and couldn't be traded above the limit until the next day unless there were offers at up limit or bids at limit down. I sat there cursing Audrey and her mother. How long did it take to buy a fucking mink coat?

The more I stewed, the more I convinced myself that I was right. I looked at the Telerate again. The bonds were still rising. But so what? The market couldn't keep going up. It was over-bought. At 3:47, twenty-eight minutes before closing, I got on the horn to Debbie. "What's the quote? What's the quote, dammit."

"Marty, the market's still locked limit up at 143.85."

"Sell another fifty."

"Into the locked limit?"

"You heard me. Don't give me any shit, just do what I tell you." I'd lost it. If Audrey had been there, she would have been slapping me on the side of the head telling me to stop because selling contracts at the lock limit was more than stupid, it was just completely, totally, undeniably, and unbelievably self-destructive. Why didn't she call? Didn't she care that I was getting killed? Why wasn't she there to say, "Buzzy, just listen to yourself. What are you doing? Stop selling and cover those positions, NOW!"

What made it even worse was that I had another indicator staring me in the face, one that was totally reliable, yet I completely ignored it. When the boys in the New York Stock Exchange saw that the boys in Chicago were going to eat their lunch with the S&P 500 futures, they'd created their own meal ticket, the New York Futures Exchange. While they never achieved the volume of the S&Ps, the NYFE, the "knife," which was based on the value of the New York Stock Exchange Index, was for all practical purposes the same as the S&Ps. The NYFE's traded at about a 4:7 ratio with the S&P; if it was up four points, the S&P was up seven. Normally I paid no attention to the knife, because it was peanuts compared to the S&Ps, but now with the S&Ps locked limit, it was doing what they would have done if trading hadn't been halted. If Audrey had been there, she would have taken the knife and cut my trading off cold. But she was out buying a coat with Sally Polokoff.

At 3:58, according to my Quotron, the knife was up 4.05 and because it sold at lower volumes and lower prices, it hadn't locked limit. Despite this fact, I sold another fifty S&P futures, just to show them who was King of the Pits. That meant that the S&P was really up about seven points (to 145-plus), yet here I was selling fifty more into the locked limit at 143.85. I was immediately losing $1,000 per contract, or another $50,000. What a schmuck!

I have what I call my sunspot theory, which says that 2 percent of the time, you become uncontrollably irrational. This was one of those times. I had the facts on the screen in front of me, but I refused to believe them. "The knife's a less liquid exchange," I was screaming. "Fuck it, it can't be right." Of course, it was right, and I knew it. But where was Audrey to tell me I knew it? Out buying a coat with her mother, Sally Polokoff. This was really starting to piss me off.

When the market finally closed, I was short 250 S&P contracts. I couldn't believe it. I was in a daze as I packed up my briefcase, put on my coat, and headed for the door. Ray Gura, one of the guys in the bullpen, was still at his desk settling up his trades. "Hey, Marty," Ray said, "how about this market? Up eight percent in just the last three days and 43.41 points today? Largest jump in history, you musta made a killing."

"Yeah, Ray, it was a big day." Ray was a good guy, an old Yankees fan. He was older and more polite than most of the other guys and was always very respectful of Audrey.

"I thought for sure we'd see you dancing on the desks today. Say, Marty, you all right? You don't have any color. You don't look so good."

"Yeah, I'm fine, Ray. I just had a tough day."

"Hey, Marty, what's tough about makin' money? I'll take forty-three points any day."

Not if you're on the wrong side, Ray. The drive home was the longest of my life. I'd never lost so much money. I'd never conceived of losing so much money. I figured that when my account was marked to market, I'd be down around $600,000, but because the S&Ps had been locked limit up for the last half hour and the knife had kept moving up, I'd be even deeper in the hole when the market opened the next morning. How could I have done it? How could I have been so stupid? And here I thought I was a star, a guy that was going big time.

Another day like today and I'd be back where I was at my tenth reunion; broke, squeezed into the TR6, living in a rent-controlled studio apartment, working as a securities analyst, and voting Democratic. So what if the government mismanaged and wasted my tax money. I needed a welfare state. In my business, you were never more than a couple of sunspots away from the unemployment line.

"Audrey, why didn't you call me!" I screamed as I walked into the apartment. "I'm short 250 contracts. We could lose a million dollars."

"Buzzy, relax. You just had a bad day. Tomorrow, we'll go in and straighten it out. What's done is done. There's nothing you can do about it tonight."

"A bad day! What, are you shittin' me?! Audrey, I just blew almost a million dollars in four hours. Why didn't you call?"

"My mother and I were busy looking at skins. Wait till you see the coat I'm getting, you're going to love it."

Great. Audrey was looking at skins while I was getting skinned. That's what always amazed me about Audrey: she never got emotionally involved in my trading. To her, the money was never real. Making it and losing it was just something that I did, and she assumed that when all was said and done, I was going to make a lot more than I lost, even if the loss was a million dollars.

Audrey wasn't helping me. I needed to talk with someone who understood trading, somebody who could tell me how I was going to get myself out of this mess. Zoellner.

"Yeah, Vickie, Marty here. . . . Yeah, how ya doing? Look, I'm sorry to bother you, but is Bob there?. . . Yeah, I've had kind of a rough day. I've gotta talk to him. . . . Yeah, Thanks. . . . Bob, Bob, whaddya think, Bob? I'm short 250 S&Ps and I'm dying. What do I do?"

"Marty, you're not thinking straight. It's like we always say, you can't shift to first gear from reverse without going through neutral. You've gotta change direction, you've gotta stop the losses. Cover your position, get back to neutral. Once you're out, things will look better."

"Bob, but the market's gotta turn, all my indicators say it's overbought. I can't get out now, it's gotta turn."

"Marty, come on, get ahold of yourself. You can't outsmart the market. Your indicators are wrong. The market thinks that now that the election is over, the Fed's going to cut the discount rate. Interest rates are coming down, the institutional investors are going to be switching their funds from the money markets into stocks. Sure, the market might take a dip, but you can't count on it. You've gotta clean out your position. Believe me, take the loss. Remember, your winners are ahead of you, not in back of you."

"Thanks, Bob, I know you're good, I know you're right, but a million bucks, that's a hell of a hit."

"Marty, you've got to take it."

I tossed and turned all night. Why was it that just when things seemed to be going right, something always went wrong. A couple of days ago, I felt like Joseph. Now I felt like Job. And what was wrong with Audrey? Didn't she understand that we were going to lose a million dollars in the morning? How could she be sleeping like a log?

The next morning, we got in the Eldorado and headed for the office. I was dreading having to go in and cover my position. I was hoping that S&Ps would open down, then maybe I'd ride it for awhile. Maybe my indicators weren't wrong. Maybe the market would come to its senses and see that I was right, that it was overbought. In any event, I felt better knowing that Audrey was going to be with me.

The S&Ps opened at 145.00, up 1.15 from the closing, which, of course, had been locked limit up at 143.85. "Shit, that's not as bad as I thought," I said. "When the knife closed up

4.10, I thought the S&Ps would open at least 145.50. This market might be coming my way. Maybe I should double up." The old me might have done that, but from over my shoulder I heard Audrey screaming, "Get smaller, Buzzy, get smaller! We've already discussed this and you're going to do what you have to do, so do it, NOW!!"

I started buying in my shorts while Audrey stayed right on my shoulder telling me to "get smaller, get smaller." Every contract I bought meant that much less I could lose. Within the first forty-five minutes, I was completely out of the position. I'd thought I'd lose a million, but by the time I was out, I was only down $800,000, and Zoellner was right, as soon as I was out, I started to feel better. I started to breathe again. I even got some color in my cheeks, all four of them.

I fought like hell for the next four weeks and almost made it all back. By the end of November, I was only down $57,000 for the month. In December, I made $928,000 and ended the year up over $3 million in futures alone. So I'd made a mistake. Without Audrey there, I'd lost my balance. I'd gone crazy and sold into the up limit. That wasn't important. What was important was that thanks to Audrey and Zoellner, I'd realized my mistake and got beyond it. I still had my touch, I still had the inside track on the S&Ps, my ability to make money, lots of money, was still unlimited.

In December, just before the holidays, Audrey came home with her new coat. It was a beautiful Blackglama mink. She took it out of the box, put it on, and spun around like a model. "So, Buzzy. What do you think?"

I went over and rubbed the back of my hand on the coat. No doubt about it, a Blackglama mink was just what we needed to keep my babies warm. "Very nice," I said. "But then it ought to be nice. It cost us eight hundred thousand dollars."

The Losing Streak

Every trader faces it. Only the winners know how to handle it. The dreaded losing streak rears its head every so often and attacks every great trader. It eats away at your judgment; it saps your confidence. Sometimes, it can take you so low that you think you'll never get out. You're sure that something has gone wrong, that you've lost your touch, that you'll never be a winner again. When you're in the middle of it, you think it's never going to end, but mostly, your judgment and rhythm are off and what you have to do is stop and regain your composure.

The best way to end a losing streak is to cut your losses and divorce your ego from the game. I learned this lesson many years ago at the crap tables in Vegas. The old cliché says "never send good money after bad," and it's true. You have to manage your resources and not lose too much of your stake. Many people when they're losing increase their bets; they double up hoping to win it all back on one roll of the dice. That strategy can be devastating. The best way to stop a losing streak is to STOP! STOP THE LOSSES, STOP THE BLEEDING. Take time off and let your intellect take charge of your emotions; the market will be there when you return.

But believe me, this simple advice is much easier to give than to take. In August 1996, I was in the worst losing streak of my career. What was driving me crazy was that I would see the trades, but I was so scared of losing, I wasn't thinking about winning. This fear of losing was slowing down my reaction time, and while I was seeing everything, I was reacting later and later, which meant that I was taking more risks, not less. What I had to do was to step back and recharge my batteries, but I couldn't stop. A guy called me and wanted to play some golf. I knew that I needed a break so I told him I'd play eighteen, but as I got up to leave, I couldn't go out the door without a piece of the action. I couldn't let the market go up without me. I bought ten lousy contracts and ended up losing twenty-five grand. It ruined my day and further sapped my confidence.

You can never shift from reverse to first gear without first

going through neutral. YOU MUST CHANGE THE DIREC-
TION OF BAD TRADING BY FIRST SHIFTING TO NEUTRAL.
YOU MUST STOP. What happens is that as your fear of losing
rises, your emotions start to short-circuit your intellect and you
no longer have confidence in what you're doing. Stopping lets
your emotions calm down and lets you reestablish your
momentum with your intellect. Remember, time is always your
ally. Use it to relax, clear your head, and regain your energies.

Once you've stopped, digested your losses, gone through a
period of preparation, and feel comfortable with your work
habits and methodology, you're ready to start trading again.
The best way to do that is to trade small and to concentrate on
being profitable. DON'T START BY TRYING TO MAKE A
KILLING.

When I came back, I'd see a trade I liked and I'd do it small
with a very tight stop, so if I was wrong, I'd get right out. All the
time I kept telling myself, make little profits, make little profits,
make little profits. Black ink, black ink, black ink. It's all psychological. I felt sick and I wanted to make myself feel good
again. I wanted to regain my confidence because CONFI-
DENCE IS ESSENTIAL TO A SUCCESSFUL TRADER. I had
three contracts the other day, which is a tiny position for me,
but I ended up making $15,000 on them. Fifteen thousand dol-
lars is real money, and I took that and built it into $40,000 the
next day, and all of a sudden, I'm hot again, and I feel great.

If for some reason this process doesn't work initially, try it
again by stopping longer and coming back trading even smaller.
The most important thing is to protect your trading capital until
you can regain your equilibrium and put all the shadows of the
losing streak behind you. Losing streaks are an unfortunate part
of the game, but if you are a good disciplined trader who can
shift into neutral, the losing will end and black ink will start to
flow again.

8

Champion Trader

In *Liar's Poker*, Michael Lewis said that traders liked to picture themselves as "big swinging dicks," but up until 1983, it was impossible to tell who had the biggest dick. Back in the early eighties, traders were a small, private club, bordering on a cult. To the general public, we didn't exist. Here we were punching it out day by day, trading more money in a couple of hours than most people traded in a lifetime, but nobody knew it. Occasionally a spectacular knockout, like the Hunt brothers or Billie Sol Estes, would get reported in the papers, but for the most part, we toiled away in relative obscurity. There was no way that we could get any public recognition unless we went broke big time, Texas style.

Then in January 1983, I saw an ad in a financial periodical that said:

UNITED STATES
STOCK, OPTION & COMMODITY
TRADING CHAMPIONSHIP

Who are the nation's top brokers, investment advisors, and private traders?

COMPETE AGAINST THE NATION's BEST.

OUTLINE OF NEXT CONTEST: For brokers, investment advisors, and the public. Contestants specify an account, begin trading for contest purposes as of Feb. 1, and submit copies of profit/loss statements if they do well. Leaders are published monthly, and are judged on the basis of percentage increase in market value from Feb. 1. Minimum starting balances are $5,000 for the stock, stock and option, and commodity divisions and $1,000 for the option division. Managed accounts may be entered.

ENTER THE NEXT CONTEST. Call Financial Traders
Association.
(213) 827-2503

Right away I knew that this contest was for me. Thanks to my trusty Telerate, I was sure that nobody was smacking the S&Ps like I was, and this contest would give me a way to prove it. Plus, I liked competition. I needed competition to get my juices flowing. I was ready to show the world that I was the biggest swinging dick.

I called the number. "Financial Traders Association, Norm Zadeh speaking." I'd never heard of Norm Zadeh or the Financial Traders Association. Nobody on the Street had. But did I care? "Norm," I said, "whoever you are, sign me up. I'm the best trader in the country and I'm going to kick everybody else's ass."

As it turned out, except for the fact that he was as bald as a billiard ball, Norm Zadeh was the Don King of trading. Like King, Zadeh was a gifted self-promoter with a colorful background. Rated the "fourth most knowledgeable gambler in the country" by *Gambling Times*, he'd been a professional handicapper, a professional poker player, and a professional sports gambler. His 1974 book *Winning Poker Systems* was considered a classic by many card sharks. Zadeh had Vegas written all over him, but thanks to a short teaching stint at UCLA, he chose to bill himself as a mathematician with ties to academia.

According to an article by John Liscio in the July 10, 1989, *Barron's*, "The idea for a stock-picking contest came to Zadeh in the early eighties, while he was a visiting professor at UCLA. Upset that the financial faculty did little more than sniff at him in elevators, Zadeh set out to show up the pedants by proving that their cherished efficient market theory was all wet. He began teaching a course in practical trading, using real money in an active futures trading account and inviting the class to trade along. After netting a return of 140% on his original investment, and watching the enrollment for his course zoom from 10 students to 85, Zadeh was shown the door." Like a true fight promoter, Zadeh divided his United States Trading and Investing Championships into four divisions: stocks, options, stocks and/or options, and the real heavyweight division, futures. I entered the futures and the stock and/or options divisions.

For me, even before this contest, trading was a lot like a prizefight. I'd divide the day into fifteen rounds running from 9:00 A.M. when bonds started trading to 4:15 P.M. when the S&P futures pit closed. I patterned this approach after the Merc in Chicago, which divided its trading day into half-hour blocks, or "brackets," and released many of its trading statistics at the end of each bracket. Because trading volumes often picked up just before the hour and the half hour when the numbers came out, anyone who traded futures on the Merc for any length of time got used to thinking in terms of these brackets.

I was a boxer-counterpuncher. Timing was my key. I'd spot an opening, hit it, and jump back. In and out, in and out, bob and weave, a point here, a point there. I didn't take wild swings, because I never wanted to do anything that would jeopardize my family's security. I outpointed the market by trying to win every round, and if I could help it, I never put myself into a position where I could be knocked out. It was a safe, unspectacular approach that didn't give me too many big victories. For two hundred days a year, I'd end up with reasonably small losses netted out with similar-sized gains. Lose $5,000 here, make $6,000 there, round after round, twenty, thirty, forty times a day. But I'd win the other fifty trading days by clear-cut unanimous decisions. Smack the bonds for $75,000, hit a stock for $100,000, nail a couple of options for $125,000, pound the S&Ps for $150,000. Over time it made me a big winner, to the tune of $5 million a year.

The fact that the contest was open to all comers and the minimum investment was only $5,000 for futures, options, and stocks and/or options, and $1,000 for options, put me at an immediate disadvantage. My style didn't really fit Zadeh's contest. I was going to start with $500,000 and jab away, trying to build up points by making steady daily profits, but with a low minimum investment, only a four-month trading period, and an invitation to all comers, any amateur could throw in $5,000 and hope to land a lucky punch. Amateurs could take chances that I couldn't afford. While I was trying to make a living and provide security for my family, some dentist from New Jersey who fancied himself a great investor could get a tip from a patient on a couple of live takeovers, throw in $5,000, and triple his money. If he got knocked out, no big deal. If I got knocked out, I was out of business. Sure, I could play a smaller account just for the contest and try for the knockout, but that would change my style and I wasn't going to do that. That's how I'd played the market before I met Audrey and came up with my plan. Going for the knockout had made me a loser for nine years. Now that I'd developed a methodology that fit my personality, I was going to stick with it whether I was trading $5,000 or $500,000.

The entry fees for the contest ranged from $150 for the stock division to $195 for the other three divisions, and there were only seventy-four entrants in the first contest, so it was obvious that Zadeh wasn't making much from the fees. He had to have another angle. When I asked him how he was going to prevent people from "bucketing" trades, he told me that in addition to submitting copies of their profit and loss statements each month, every contestant had to phone in trades each day and leave them on a tape recorder.

Aha. This had to be his angle. What Zadeh probably was trying to do was to find the brightest traders in the country and then piggyback their positions. But did I care? There was no way that anybody, except maybe the boys in the pit on the Merc, could steal from me. Zadeh might have thought about it, but when he saw how fast I was in and out of the S&Ps and how often I traded, he waived the requirement that I call in my trades every day. I just had to send in my monthly statement with my P&L.

For the first contest, I placed third in the futures division and third in the stock and/or options division. That just got me more fired up. Third out of seventy-four contestants wasn't bad, but for me, it wasn't good enough. I felt like I was back at Amherst when Dean Wilson told us that 50 percent of us were going to be in the bottom half of the class. Here I wasn't going up against kids from Andover and Exeter who were better prepared than I was. When it came to trading, I was more prepared than anyone, and I was determined to prove it. I was going to be the undisputed heavyweight champion of the world. I immediately entered the next contest. It ran from August 1 to December 1, 1983. This time, there were 133 entrants. I placed sixth in the futures division with a 69.2 percent return (the winner was some amateur who had a 388.4 percent return, probably on the minimum $5,000 investment). But I won the Most Money Made for the Year Award, and as it turned out, I'd made more money than all the other contestants combined. Always the promoter, Zadeh bought ads in *Barron's*, *Futures* magazine, *Investor's Daily*, *Stocks and Commodities* magazine, and the *Wall Street Letter* to announce the winners and solicit contestants for the next contest. I liked seeing my name in print, but still, I wasn't satisfied. I had to be the "Champion Trader."

Frankie Joe had been crowned the Champion Trader for the first year, 1983. Frankie Joe was a forty-two-year-old former order clerk on the floor of the New York Stock Exchange. He'd come in second in the futures division with a 181.3 percent return and first in the stocks and/or options division with a 70.6 percent return. I didn't know how much he'd invested or how much he'd made, all I knew was that he had the bragging rights and I was going to get him. "Norm," I said when I called Zadeh and told him to sign me up for the next contest starting on Febuary 1, 1984, "you tell Frankie Joe that I'm going to kick his Oriental ass."

Confidence is every part of trading. If you're not convinced that you can win, you should never climb into the ring. But confidence quickly turns to ego, and egos, like tired fighters, need to be massaged, soothed, sponged off, and stroked. Zadeh, the hustler/handicapper/gambler/mathematician, had this figured out. Winning is a great balm for confidence, but only public recognition can stroke an ego.

The U.S. Trading Championship was becoming a hot item

on the Street. For the contest starting February 1, 1984, there were 185 contestants and on February 18, the *New York Times* featured the U.S. Trading Championships on the front page of the business section. The article was called "Investing for Fun, and Profit" and had pictures of Frankie Joe and me, the 1983 Champion Trader and Most Money Made winners, at our trading desks. Frankie was smiling like a happy Chinaman, and I was grimacing like a tortured Jew. But Zadeh was the real star. The article described him as a "mathematician in Marina del Rey, California" and "former college professor" who'd started the trading championships last year as a business that would make money from the fees.

But did I care? There was a whole paragraph about me. "The person who made the most money in 1983 in trades reported to the United States Trading Championship—a whopping $1.4 million—was Martin Schwartz, whose futures account rose 175.3 percent. Mr. Schwartz, a 38-year-old former securities analyst who owns a seat on the American Stock Exchange, said, 'I can tell you how I became a winner—I learned how to lose.'"

There's an old Italian proverb that says "revenge is a dish best served cold." I was tempted to make a few hundred copies of the article and plaster them all over the Great Pyramid. I wanted to be sure that the Pharaohs saw it. I wanted them to read it and weep when they thought about all the money I could have been making them if only they hadn't shot me in the back. But I didn't have to, because on February 19, I got a call from Inside Skinny. Skinny was wired in to the Pyramid and knew everything that was going on there. "Motty. Here's a laugh. The High Priest and the Prophet are wondering how they can get you to manage some money for them."

"Yeah, sure, right. Tell 'em to give me a call when the Red Sea opens." Good old Norm Zadeh. This was the best ego stroke I'd had yet.

The contests were becoming so popular that Zadeh started advertising the standings in the financial publications every month. This generated more interest and publicity, especially since Frankie Joe and I were battling for the championship. We were going toe to toe, slugging it out for almost three months. Each month after the ads came out, Frankie Joe and I would start swinging all the harder. Then in mid-May, Frankie Joe called me. We'd never talked before. "Marty," he said. "I've had it. I'm throwing in the towel. I'm going on vacation."

Thinking that I'd won, I said to Audrey, "Let's celebrate. If Frankie Joe's going on a vacation, we might as well take off too." When we got back, I found out that Frankie Joe had sucker punched me. He'd been trading the whole time and with one day to go, he was 0.1 percent ahead. 0.1 percent? It seemed unbelievable, but it was a promoter's dream. I went bullshit. I called Zadeh. "This is war!" I said. Norm loved it. He immediately called the *Wall Street Journal* and let them know that the slugfest between Frankie Joe and me had gotten personal.

On the last day, I came out of my corner swinging. I hammered the S&Ps nonstop until 4:15. When the bell rang, I'd beaten Frankie Joe by 3.4 percent. Over four months I'd parlayed my initial stake of $482,000 into $1.2 million for a total return of 254.9 percent. Frankie Joe had taken his $5,000, or whatever he was trading, and increased it a mere 251.5 percent. The June 7, 1984, *Journal* ended its article by saying, "Mr. Zadeh plans his next contest for August. Mr. Joe, a 42-year-old professional trader, says he may not compete. 'I have the insides of an 86-year-old,' he says. But Mr. Schwartz will defend his crown. 'I want to beat everybody,' he says."

And I did. I entered the next contest and beat 262 entrants by posting a 443.7 percent return in the futures. Frankie Joe didn't enter that contest and died shortly thereafter of a heart attack. Trading is very stressful, especially when you know that everybody's watching, and Frankie Joe wasn't kidding when he said that he had the insides of an eighty-six-year-old. At one time or another, every trader has had the same feeling.

As time went on, I realized that Zadeh was using the contests to do a lot more than just piggyback trades. Through the U.S. Trading Championships, he'd quickly established himself as the most visible expert on the best traders in the country. Having this reputation allowed Zadeh to do three things. He made fees by matching investors with money managers, he started his own fund and recruited hot young traders to manage the money, and he came out with a newsletter called *Summary of Top Managers*. But did I care? Helped in part by the reputation I'd developed, I started my own fund in 1989.

I relinquished my championship belt when I started managing other people's money. Managing OPM gave me all the stimulation I needed, and then some. Then in 1992, I was going through some reevaluation and soul-searching about life. I called Norm and told him that, like every great fighter, I was going to climb back into the ring, that I wanted to win back my title. Having me come out of retirement was good for the contest and good for me. John Liscio announced my return in *Barron's* with a feature article that ended by saying, "Spending a week or so chatting with Marty and following his trades, you're left with little doubt that the man who has been called the Bobby Fischer of the S&P pits is still the grand master. Lock him in a room with the boss trader of your choice with nothing more than their wits, enough phones, a couple of quote screens and an equal amount of cash, and at the end of the day, far more often than not, Schwartz is going to come out on top."

He was right. I came back and regained my world heavyweight crown in 1992 by winning the new $500,000-plus futures division of the U.S. Investing Championship. Still the consummate promoter, Norm was always creating divisions within divisions, because more winners meant more competition, more contestants, and more money. Then I retired for keeps. Until I decide to come out yet again. After all, Sugar Ray Leonard and George Foreman did okay.

Well, maybe not. Ultimately, Zadeh quietly suspended the contests. According to a December 26, 1996, "Heard on the Street" article in the *Wall Street Journal,* "a series of inquiries by the Securities and Exchange Commission coincided with the contest's suspension, and may have helped cause it." Apparently, what attracted the SEC's interest was that Norm was "referring investors to money managers without detailed knowledge of the investors' financial picture," and his claims that the results of the contests were "verified." Once again, it sounded a lot like Don King. Through the contests, Norm made himself a major player in the world of trading. But given all the different hats he was wearing—contest organizer, investment adviser, money manager, newsletter publisher, and private investor—he left himself too open to scrutiny and criticism. Norm, who was described in the *Wall Street Journal* article as "a professor of applied mathematics with visiting posts at Stanford University and University of California at Los Angeles," admitted that he might have had some problems with verifying the results of the contests, "but Mr. Zadeh insists that his multiple businesses didn't interfere in any way with his objectivity."

But do I care? Financial publications were doing articles on me, I was basking in the public recognition, and in addition to stroking my ego, the contests gave me credibility with my family and friends and within the investment community. Norm Zadeh took me out of my dark, lonely office and thrust me into the limelight.

In July 1989, we were waiting for our bags at La Guardia Airport after returning from a vacation in Aspen. I picked up a copy of *Barron's* and as I was thumbing through it, I saw an article by John Liscio on Norm Zadeh's trading contests. In the center of the page was a big picture of me, sitting in my office. I showed the picture to my kids, who were four and six, just old enough to start to wonder why I didn't put on a coat and tie and go to a real job like the other kids' dads, and I said to them, "Who's that?" And they said, "Daddy! Daddy!"

When they got a little older and the other kids started asking them what Daddy did for a living, they could say, "My daddy's the Champion Trader!" That was all I cared about.

Honor Thy Stop

One of the great tools of trading is the stop, the point at which you divorce yourself from your emotions and ego and admit that you're wrong. Most people have a tough time doing this, and instead of selling out a losing position, they'll hang on hoping that the market will realize the error of its ways and behave as they believe it should. This attitude is usually self-destructive, because as Joe Granville used to say, "the market doesn't know whether you're long or short and it could care less." You're the only one who's emotionally involved in your position. The market's just reacting to supply and demand and if you're cheering it one way, there's always somebody else cheering just as hard that it will go the other way.

Taking a loss is hard to do because it's an admission that you've been wrong. But in the market, being wrong some of the time is part of the game. On each trade, you have to establish your "uncle point," the point where you'll get out of a losing position, and you have to have the mental discipline to pull the trigger at that point.

I was out playing golf the other day with my buddy Double Bogey, and D.B. was bemoaning the fact that he was getting killed in Bay Networks. He just couldn't understand where he'd gone wrong. He'd heard about the stock when it was in the thirties, he'd read all the reports while it climbed through the forties, and he'd bought it when it backed off to $43. When it really backed off to $35, he'd committed the cardinal sin, he doubled up. Then he'd sat and watched it sink into the teens. "What really pisses me off," D.B. said, "was that it rallied a couple of times during the fall, and instead of bailing out, I just hung on."

"What was your plan?" I asked.

"My plan? I was going to hold it until it got back to fifty dollars. What else?"

That's the problem with amateurs, they only have half a plan, the easy half. They know how much of a profit they're willing to take, but they don't have the foggiest idea how much they're willing to lose. They're like deer in the headlights, they just freeze and wait to get run over. Their plan for a position that goes south is, "Please God, let me out of this and I'll never do it again," but that's bullshit, because if by chance the position turns around, they'll soon forget about God. They'll go back to thinking that they're geniuses, and they'll always do it again, which means that they're sure to get caught, and get caught bad. What most people fail to understand is that while you're losing your money, you're also losing your objectivity. It's like being at the craps table in Vegas, and the fat bleached blonde in the sequined dress is rolling the dice, and you're losing, and you're determined that you're not going to let her beat you. What you've forgotten is that she doesn't care about you, she's just rolling the dice. Whenever you have jealousy as an emotion, or greed, or envy, it distorts your judgment. The market's like the bleached blonde in Vegas, it doesn't care about you. That's why you have to put aside your ego and get out. If you have trouble doing that, as most people do, be like Odysseus: tie yourself to the mast with an automatic stop and take your emotions out of play.

Stops come in two forms: an actual order to sell at a certain price that you place with your broker, or a contract you make with yourself that you're going to sell at a certain price, no matter what. Either way, a stop is an investment in self-preservation because if you're wrong, it saves you those extra dollars that you'd lose by hanging on to a losing position. It keeps you from digging the hole deeper and it makes it easier for you to climb back out. A stop automatically takes your brain out of reverse and puts it into neutral. Your money's not back to neutral, but your mind's back to the point where you can regroup and try to think up a fresh idea without the pressure of a losing position hanging over your head.

The more you lose in a trade, the less objective you become. **EXITING A LOSING TRADE QUICKLY CLEARS YOUR HEAD AND RESTORES YOUR OBJECTIVITY.** After a breather, you might put the same trade back on if you can intellectually justify it, but you have to constantly remind yourself that there's a myriad of opportunities in the marketplace. By preserving your capital through the use of a stop, you make it possible to wait patiently for a high-probability trade with a low-risk entry point.

9

Little Brown Bags

"So, Mr. Schwartz, if we were to approve your application, how do you propose to pay for the monthly maintenance?" the president of the Park Avenue Co-op Board said.

Monthly maintenance? What the hell was this man talking about? We'd just committed to plunking down $3 million in cash for a twelve-room apartment on the seventh floor, and now he wanted to know if we could pay the monthly maintenance?

"You're in the commodities business," the man continued. "That's like gambling, and we want to make sure that all of our owners are financially stable. What happens if something goes wrong? We'd hate to have to ask you to leave."

I looked over at Audrey. She was getting that worried look, the one she got just before I went ballistic. I took a deep breath and said, "I've had a seven-figure income for the past five years and, as you can see from our application, our net worth is nine million dollars. I don't anticipate anything going wrong."

"Still, things happen. The markets are very unpredictable." God, I hated negative thinkers, they were such losers. "Well," I said, "if something happens, I guess you'll just have to ask us to leave. You know, you have to do what you have to do."

It was November 1984, and we were sitting in the president's living room along with two other senior members of the co-op board. These three old-timers were the screening committee of the board of directors for prospective new buyers and they had to approve us before we could move into the building. They squinted through their thick glasses, taking our measure, like old tailors seeing if we were a good fit. If accepted, Audrey and I would be the youngest people in the building by far.

I knew our money looked good and I figured that this interview was just another case of having to kiss somebody's ass before they'd let you into the club. I was sure that they were just showing us who was boss, putting us in our place, letting us know that not just anybody could walk into their Park Avenue co-op. I hoped that was the case, because we really wanted this apartment.

"Yes," the president said, "if you couldn't make your monthly payment, then I'm afraid we would have to ask you to leave." The other two members nodded in agreement. "And with that understanding, let us be the first to welcome you to Park Ave."

Audrey was three months pregnant with our second child, which is why we decided that it was time to move, but for us to put $3 million, or one-third of our total net worth, into an apartment was another dumb financial decision. That was money I was taking out of play, money that I could have parlayed into a much bigger grubstake, but we'd made the same decision before. Over the last two years there had been many times when I'd said to myself, gee whiz, why did I dump one-third of my net worth into that beach house? If I'd put that money into mutual funds, it'd be worth well over a million now and that would have made my entire family more secure.

That was the trap that a lot of traders fell into. Most big-time traders didn't taste the fruits of their labors until they'd climbed to the very top of the tree, and in some cases, they never tasted them at all. To them, making money *was* the fruit, because to them, money was power, and power was the only way they could feed their giant egos. I wasn't interested in power. I wanted to taste my fruits all the way up the tree, which meant that I didn't mind spending money, lots of money. I figured, so what? I'd found a money machine in the S&P 500 futures, and I could always make more. If Audrey and I wanted a beach house, we'd buy a beach house. If we wanted a twelve-room apartment on Park Avenue, we'd buy that, too. There came a time when you had to spend the money you'd been making so you could understand why you'd been killing yourself. And, to be honest, I didn't mind letting other people see that I'd made it.

On Thursday morning, April 4, 1985, we were scheduled to close on our new twelve-room apartment. We'd planned to move in that afternoon, but as usual, there was a glitch. I'd scheduled the move for Thursday because the next day was Good Friday and the markets would be closed. I thought that I could get my office set up and be trading by Monday, but at the closing, the people we'd bought the apartment from said their movers hadn't come and could they have an extra day?

I'm a guy who signs a contract and says, "This is what it says and this is what it means," but that doesn't seem to apply to the rest of the world. Our movers were sitting out on Park Avenue with our stuff, but what could we do? I was screwed. We couldn't get in until they got out, and I knew that I'd never get my office set up by Monday. I had to call and reschedule the telephone people who were going to put in my extra phone lines and the computer people who were going to set up my screens. I'd be lucky if I could get to work by the end of next week.

Fortunately I wasn't planning on trading much, anyway. What I eventually learned was, don't trade too heavily the month before and two months after your wife gives birth. While her hormones are changing, yours are just trying to keep up. If you're a good husband, you're not staying home at night working on your charts and figuring out your ratios. For the month before the birth, you're going to Lamaze class working on how to breathe, how to rub your wife's back. For the two months after the birth, the baby takes center stage and your whole routine is thrown out of whack. You're not getting any dinner, you're not getting any sleep, you're not getting any anything. You're up two, three, four times a night. You're trying to figure out if you have the disposable diaper right side up or upside down. You're always tired, you lose your concentration. Our daughter was born on June 7, 1983, and the worst stretch of trading I'd had since "Never Short a Republican" was May, June, and July of 1983 when I lost $150,000.

Now, in addition to the birth of our second child, we'd thrown in the move to Park Avenue, and it had gotten all messed up, so our lives were really turned upside down. We finally moved in late Friday afternoon, the fifth, and Audrey, who was eight months pregnant, hit the beach like a marine. All day Saturday and Sunday she was unpacking cartons, moving furniture, barking orders, trying to get our nest settled before our chickee arrived. As I wandered around the apartment listening to Audrey's plans to move walls, put in a new kitchen, redo the bathrooms, and install new window treatments, I began to get a feel for how much this place was really going to cost me. My nut was going to be huge, and the more Audrey kept talking, the more the old garment man's promise to throw us out if we couldn't make our monthly maintenance fee kept ringing in my ears. I was really going to have to make some big money to keep this place going, but I wasn't worried. Once I was up and running again, I was sure I could whack the S&Ps for all the new kitchens, new bathrooms, new window treatments, and monthly maintenance fees we'd ever need.

I'd come a long way since my first S&P trade just three years earlier and I'd made a lot of money playing the S&Ps, but it hadn't been easy. Trading in Chicago was nothing like trading in New York. There's an old joke that says "I went to a fight the other day and ended up trading futures in Chicago." Chicago was still the wild, wild West. It was where Richard Daley had been sheriff and the tombstones voted. It was where Mike Royko, the legendary columnist for the Chicago *Daily News,* often suggested that the city's official motto, *"Urbs in Horto"* ("City in a Garden"), should be changed to *"Ubi est Mea"* ("Where's Mine?"). The rules of the Merc weren't written by the Marquis of Queensberry, and the pits were no place for a gentleman. Being tough and knowing the right people was a lot more important than being honest and having gone to the right schools.

And the Merc was no place for outsiders. If you weren't part of the family, you paid the price, usually up front. In New York, if you were a principal, you were trading for yourself, and if you were an agent, you were trading for a client and getting a commission. That's how the game was supposed to be played, but not in Chicago, because the Merc allowed something called "dual trading." That meant that a broker could act as both a principal and agent at the same time. Being able to trade for his own account while he was executing orders for his clients presented a huge conflict of interest and strongly encouraged a tactic known as "front running."

A front runner was a broker who'd sneak his own trades in

front of a client's, or use his brother-in-law standing next to him as the bagman, knowing that the client's order would be right behind his, backing him up or protecting a no-loss situation. A simple example is the broker who gets an order to buy ten S&P contracts at 80. Simultaneously, the brother-in-law also bids 80 for ten contracts, knowing that if he buys his first he can always turn around and sell them back to the broker, at worst breaking even or scratching the trade. If he buys the ten contracts and the price ticks up, he's in a riskless trade, while the client receives the famous report of "ND," or "nothing done." After seven ticks on the screen at his price, the veins begin to explode at the top of his forehead.

After this happens all day long to you and thousands of dollars have been bucketed out of your pockets, you change brokers.

The way to tell if you have a semihonest broker is to get a partial fill of your order, meaning you've bought four contracts out of ten when it ticked seven times at your price. At least that indicates that he's trying for you. You'd think that brokers would want to fill your orders because they earn their living from commissions on executed orders, but the bagger's "executed orders" provide thousands of dollars versus tens of dollars for commissions. In New York, front running was the exception; in Chicago, it was an art form.

During the first three years that it traded, the S&P contract didn't move as fast as it does today and I liked to play an "accordion." When I thought the market was near a buy point, I'd place a scale of, say, fifty lots, where I'd try to buy five lots every 10 cents down (or two ticks) on the S&Ps, hoping that by the time it bottomed and turned up, I had bought most of the scale, but not all. After the market turned in my favor, I'd pick a reasonable price objective on the upside and scale the contracts out, hoping for the eventual price move to just exceed my last offer on the up side. I might even reverse the process and scale into a short position, then I'd cover my position, and start the game all over again. If my indicators were correct, I'd be scalping the market all the way up and all the way back down the scale. In a slow-moving market, scale trading was a great way to make money, and if my core position was right, there was very little risk.

I used to have a broker named Tony D., and Tony D. had a brother-in-law named Sonny J. Sonny J. would stand right next to Tony D. and after a while, I began to suspect that when I put my order in to scale up or scale down, Sonny J. would jump in ahead of me. I'd be looking at my screen and I'd see trades of .10, .10, .10, but Tony D. wouldn't call and say that my five lot had been filled until they had traded through my price.

And so it would go, all the way up and down the scale. I began to wonder how come I was always getting filled on the last tick. I wasn't naive, I'd been on the floor of the Amex, but trading on the Amex was like playing bingo at the Knights of Columbus compared to trading in Chicago. There was no specialist like Chickie or Frannie making the market at the Merc, so there was no way of putting your order in line. Trading in the pits was a free-for-all, and when I'd call and complain, I'd always get the same answer: "Sorry, Marty, somebody jumped in front of you, but hey, what are you complaining about? You're making money." Big money, but I was still pissed.

Front running was only one of the hurdles you had to jump if you wanted to make money on the Merc. Trades were made by the "open outcry" system. That's where traders in the pit would shout and use hand signals to make their trades. This method of trading led to a lot of disputes, especially in a fast-moving market. "Lennie, we had a trade!" "No, I wasn't looking at you. I was looking at the guy right behind you." "Bullshit, the guy behind me's your kid brother." Members were always getting fined for fighting, unruly behavior, and other forms of misconduct, but that was just a cost of doing business, and if you weren't there to defend yourself, they really beat you up.

The Merc even had its own *Back to the Future* machine, the "pit committee." The committee was generally made up of big players in the pits who got to police themselves. Unfortunately, this was the equivalent of giving the inmates the keys to the asylum. The more they made, the more their seats were worth. The pit committee had the power to repeal time. They could go back in time and "whistle out" trades. They actually had a whistle that they'd blow to make trades disappear. One day, I thought the market was about to peak so I called my clerk and told him to sell, "ten offered at fifty." I saw .55, .55 flash on my screen, which meant that there had been two trades at .55, but still I couldn't get a confirmation that my ten lot had been sold at .50. Then, just as my indicators had predicted, the market started to fall, .40, .30, .20, .10, .00. What the hell had happened to my ten lot? Getting the last tick is one thing. Getting no tick and no fill and then having the market run away from you is something else.

For ten minutes, which is a lifetime when you're trading, nobody could tell me whether or not my order had been filled, or even if I still had the ten lot. I was yelling and screaming at my clerk on the phone, going crazy because the market was moving and I didn't know what my position was. Finally, my clerk told me that the two trades at .55 had been "whistled out" and that my trade hadn't been filled at .50. I still was long the ten lot, only now my winner was a loser.

I called the Merc's legal department. I told them I was sick of getting screwed and I was going on the record. They said that they'd look into it, but, of course, since I wasn't a member of the club, nothing ever happened.

They have a machine that records the time and price of every trade. When they whistle a trade out, they merely take out the printed record as though it never happened—it was just a mistake. It's been going on forever.

Over the three years I'd been trading, I'd learned that the Merc was a world unto itself, and I'd come to accept the fact that in addition to making money for my own family, I was supporting a lot of different "families" in Chicago. Unless I moved to Chicago and climbed into the pit to fight for myself, there was nothing I could do about it; there was always going to be some slippage. Slippage was the price you paid for doing business in Chicago. As Leo Melamed, chairman emeritus of the Merc, acknowledged in *Escape to the Futures* when he described his first days on the Merc, "I knew how a market was supposed to work, keyed to supply and demand; they knew how to work the markets, keyed to their advantage." *Ubi est mea?*

To trade on the Merc, I had to have a member firm to clear my trades. Finding a good clearinghouse was a constant problem. With futures, all trades were "marked to market." That meant that at the end of each day, the clearing firms submitted all the trades that took place that day to the central clearinghouse at the exchange, and all accounts were settled on a cash basis. If you lost money, your account was debited and if you made money, it was credited. Unlike stocks, it didn't make any difference whether or not you still held the position. Every day everybody settled up in cash, and the next day, they all started with a clean slate. It was this ability to have a cash settlement for the S&P futures contract that made trading the S&Ps possible since it would be impossible to deliver a certificate that was properly weighted to represent each of the five hundred stocks in the index.

Debbie Horn had done a good job for me at Spear, Leeds & Kellogg, but SLK's commissions had cost me a fortune. During the first year I traded futures, I'd established myself as one of the biggest players in the S&P pit. I'd done twenty-five thousand "round turns," in and outs, which was about one-half of 1 percent of all the S&P trades, and that was huge. But in and out was the way I traded; scale bid, scale offer, scalp a little here, scalp a little there, make the cash register ring. SLK was charging me $25 a round turn, which amounted to more than $600,000, or 20 percent of my S&P profits. After the first year, I negotiated a better rate, but eventually SLK couldn't match the lower commission rates that others were offering, so I decided to make a couple of moves.

The fact that I was able to clear $3 million playing the S&Ps after all the "slippage" and commissions showed just how good my methodology was. The S&Ps were my game and Chicago was where I had to play, so in 1983 I sprung for an Index Options Membership (IOM) membership in the Merc. The Merc charged a tribute of $1 for each contract it traded, but if you were a member, you didn't have to pay the dollar. A membership went for $53,000, and for me that was a good deal because at a dollar in and a dollar out, I'd make my $53,000 back in a year. But even with the membership, I still had to find a firm that could clear my trades.

Little clearing firms were always calling me, trying to get my business. Basically, all you needed to set up a clearing firm was a membership on the exchange, some phone lines, and a modest amount of working capital. For that reason, a lot of small-time traders on the Merc had their own clearing firms. That way, they could save commissions on their own trades and make some money on other peoples'. I would have preferred to keep my money with a big, well-capitalized New York firm, but in the mideighties, the big New York firms still had just a small presence in futures. They didn't understand futures. To them, futures were still a game played by farmers out west. But now that I was a farmer, I'd have to start sowing some seeds in Chicago.

In March 1984, I got a call from Debbie Horn, my former clerk with Spear, Leeds & Kellogg. Debbie was from Chicago and had moved back there to work for the Marcucci brothers, a couple of small-time bond traders who'd set up their own clearing firm, Third LaSalle Services, Inc. Third LaSalle Services, Inc. was named after the street that anchors Chicago's financial district, which in turn was named after Sieur de La Salle, the seventeenth-century French explorer who set the standard for trading in Chicago by being the first to skin the natives out of their beaver pelts.

Third LaSalle was a member of both the CBOT and the Merc and Debbie had known the Marcucci brothers since way back when. She said that they were good guys who'd treat me right, so I talked with Jackie Marcucci, the president. He said that if I went with Third LaSalle, they'd make Debbie my personal clerk on the floor and only charge me $7.50 a round turn. That was the best deal that I'd heard coming out of Chicago. I liked Debbie, knew that she was good, and I couldn't beat $7.50 a contract.

Despite the boys in Chicago's clout in Washington, the Commodity Futures Trading Commission (CFTC) knew that Chicago had a stockyard mentality, and after the commission had approved a cash settlement of futures instead of delivery, they were worried that investors might get slaughtered. Most of these mom-and-pop clearing firms were set up on a shoestring and to help guarantee the financial stability of the futures markets, the CFTC required that every investor secure his or her account by posting a performance bond. This performance bond was divided into two parts. One was a cash account that was used to settle the actual trades. This account was unregulated, which meant while the cash in it belonged to the client, the clearing firm could have the use of the money.

One of the best investments clearing firms could make was to lend the cash out in repurchase agreements. A repurchase agreement, or "repos" as they were called, was where an investor lends money by purchasing securities with the understanding that the borrower will buy the securities back at a higher price at the end of the agreement. A lot of banks and savings and loans used repos to meet the reserve requirements imposed by the Fed. The agreements were very short term, usually overnight, but they gave the clearing firms another way to make a buck.

The other part of the performance bond was the regulated account. This account was a security deposit that was held by the clearing firm and could be used if the cash account was not enough to settle at the end of the day and the client failed to meet the margin call. The regulated account was made up of Treasury bills and this part of the performance bond was inviolate. The regulated accounts were the lifeboats of the futures markets. If a market sank, the T-bills would be there to guarantee payment, and according to CFTC rules, the boys in Chicago weren't allowed to fool with the regulated accounts. The only way they could touch a regulated account was if a client failed to meet a margin call.

In addition to low taxes and lots of leverage, the performance bond was another thing that made trading futures so attractive to me. Because I was a constant winner, I never had to put up any money in the cash account, and in my deal with Third LaSalle, I was able to negotiate the minimum amount required by the Merc for the regulated account, which in my case was $1.2 million. What made it even sweeter was that I got to keep the interest that was being thrown off by the T-bills. With stocks, I had to pay for the stock, which meant that there was a cost of capital. With futures, there was no cost of capital as long as I was profitable. It was a win-win deal for me. I was earning interest on my million two in T-bills while I was making money on my positions.

I'd been trading with Third LaSalle for about a year when we moved to Park Avenue, and I was very pleased with our relationship. I couldn't have asked for a better clerk than Debbie. She was responsible, efficient, tough, and squarely in my corner. And as she'd promised, the Marcucci brothers took good care of me. Jackie ran the business and was a smooth operator. He had come to New York after I'd started trading with Third LaSalle and taken Audrey and me out to this great Italian restaurant in Little Italy. At Christmas, he'd sent us a case of wine. It wasn't any of that Lafite-Rothschild juice that the guys from Wall Street liked to send out. This was vintage Italiano, the kind of stuff they drank in Chicago. It was stomped in vats by peasants in the old country and you could taste the sweat from their feet.

While Jackie was great at schmoozing up Third LaSalle's clients, Johnny took care of them in the pit. Johnny was 6'5", 280, and whenever Debbie had trouble filling an order, she'd call Johnny to come down and straighten things out. Big guys did well at filling orders, and Johnny had 280 ways of persuading whoever was on the other side of the trade that they'd made a mistake. With Jackie, Johnny, and Debbie working my account, I'd been getting great service.

By Thursday, April 11, we'd been in our new apartment for almost a week and it was time for me to get back to work. After much calling and rescheduling, my machines were finally set up and my phones working, so I picked up my direct line to the floor of the Merc and called Debbie. "Debbie, honey, how ya doing?. . . Yeah, we're in, but this place is going to cost me a fortune. Audrey's got a list of things we gotta do that's a mile long. I need to make some money."

"Marty," Debbie said, "we can't trade today."

"What?"

"You'd better talk to Jackie. There's been some problem with the firm. It has to do with that Bevill, Bresler stuff."

"Bevill, Bresler? What the hell are you talking about?"

"Bevill, Bresler & Schulman, the government securities firm in New Jersey that just went under. It's on the front page of today's *Journal*. Jackie was doing some business with them."

"What the hell! Debbie, where's my money? I want my money!"

"Marty, calm down. Call Jackie. You gotta talk to Jackie, but he says that everybody's money's okay."

"Okay, my ass. I don't trust anybody in Chicago. I want my money!" I slammed down the direct line, picked up another phone, and punched in the number for Third LaSalle. The receptionist sounded frenzied and nervous, like she was expecting everybody who called to yell at her. She was right. "This is Marty Schwartz. Where the hell's Jackie?"

"I'm sorry, Mr. Schwartz, Mr. Marcucci's not here."

"Then give me Johnny."

"I'm sorry, he's not here either. If you'd care to leave a message, I'll ask them to return your call."

"Leave a message? You bet I'll leave a message. You tell those bastards that I don't know what kind of crap they think they're pulling, but I want my money wired out immediately!"

I threw down the phone. My hands were trembling. What the hell was going on? I grabbed the latest sheets from my desk. I didn't have any money in my cash account at Third LaSalle. I'd cleaned out all of my positions before the move and swept the cash into a money market fund so I could get some interest over the long weekend. That was a lucky break. All Third LaSalle was holding was my million two in T-bills, and these were in the regulated account. Thanks to the CFTC, they couldn't fool with them unless I failed to make a margin call. If Third LaSalle was having a problem, it must have something to do with the unregulated accounts. So, I should be all right, but in Chicago, you were never all right until you had your money in your pocket.

I hopped on the elevator and went down to the lobby to pick up my *Wall Street Journal*. Debbie said something about Bevill, Bresler being in the *Journal*. The president of the co-op was there picking up his papers. "Good morning, Mr. Schwartz," he said. "Everything okay?"

"Yeah, sure, just fine." Damn, I wondered if he knew something. "Why wouldn't everything be going okay?"

"Well, moving is always stressful, and with your wife about to have a baby. I was just wondering. . . . "

"Everything's fine. Couldn't be better. Thanks for asking." I grabbed my *Journal* and jumped back in the elevator. That old garment maker was the last person I wanted to see. I was sure he was just waiting to throw us out.

According to the *Journal*, Bevill, Bresler & Schulman was a registered broker-dealer handling mainly U.S. government and municipal securities headquartered in Livingston, New Jersey. It and its sister company, Asset Management, had been doing repos with small savings and loans across the country. Asset Management had collapsed on Monday, April 8, when it couldn't make good on its agreements. Bevill, Bresler & Schulman and its affiliates had gone into receivership on Wednesday the tenth when the SEC charged the companies and their senior officers with fraud, saying that "they obtained control of customers' securities and used the proceeds to their own benefit."

I didn't know how Third LaSalle was tied up with these clowns, but the Marcucci brothers had their own bond business, and they must have been doing repos through Third LaSalle. But with repos, they'd lend cash and get Treasury bills back as security. The only way that I could get hurt was if they'd somehow done a reverse repo where they'd lent out my T-bills, gotten cash, and then lost the cash. But they couldn't have done that because my T-bills were in a regulated account. Still, this was Chicago, where the tombstones voted and *Ubi est Mea* reigned.

My mind was spinning with possibilities, all of them bad. I kept calling Jackie and finally got through. "Jackie, what the hell's going on? I want those T-bills wired out immediately."

"Marty, Marty, calm down. Everything's fine. Have a glass of that good wine I sent ya."

"Fuck the wine, Jackie, I want my money! Those T-bills are in a regulated account. You bastards can't touch 'em. It's against the law. You get 'em wired to me *now* or I'll come out there and rip your fuckin' head off!" Talk about posturing. Jackie was almost as big as Johnny.

"Marty, we got a slight technical difficulty here, a computer glitch, but Johnny's looking into it. Believe me, everything's gonna be fine."

"Bullshit! I'm telling you . . ."

Click. Jackie hung up. Fuck, they'd lost them. I could feel it. They'd done something with my T-bills and they'd lost them. None of these funds were insured. Shit, I couldn't take a million two hit. Not now. We'd just moved into this big-ass apartment and Audrey was about to have the baby. How was I going to trade? How was I going to make my monthly nut? Once more, I called the legal department at the Merc.

"You registered these guys," I said, jumping up and down. "They're your responsibility. I've overlooked a lot of crap that's been going on out there, but I'm a member. You gotta take care of me. You gotta straighten this out. It's your problem." Yadda, yadda, yadda! They said that they were aware of the situation and were "looking into it."

I called my lawyer. "Kornstein! I wanna sue these bastards! I want my money back! I want damages! I want punitive damages!! I WANT THE WHOLE FUCKIN' WORKS!!! They're wrecking my business! They're destroying my livelihood!" My lawyer advised me to wait until I had some facts.

I called Mike Margolis, my broker at Bear Stearns. I knew that Bear Stearns did business in Chicago, and I knew that Jimmy Cayne, one of the top men at Bear Stearns, was buddy buddy with Leo Melamed. "Mike, you gotta help me out. Those bastards in Chicago are trying to fuck me out of a million two. Get Cayne to make some calls. Ya gotta find out what's going on!" He said he would.

I stayed on the horn, bugging people, trying to find out what was happening, but by the end of the day, I still had no idea if I was ever going to see my million two in T-bills again. I didn't sleep that night, and the next morning I started making more calls.

"Debbie, what's happening? You got any news?"

"Jackie and Johnny aren't talking, but everybody else is. It looks like Third LaSalle's going under, and all of their accounts are being transferred to other firms. It's in today's *Journal*."

"But what about my money?"

"Gee, Marty, I don't know."

I went to the lobby to get my *Journal*. There was the old garment man standing right by my mailbox. He was talking with another member of the board. They were looking at the financial pages and shaking their heads. Damn, they must be reading about Bevill, Bresler & Schulman. They knew that I was in trouble, and they were getting ready to throw my ass out. I ducked behind a Chinese silk screen and waited for them to leave.

When they were gone, I grabbed my *Journal* and ran back upstairs. The piece on Third LaSalle read like a press release from the Chicago Chamber of Commerce. "The Third LaSalle affiliate, Broker's Capital of Chicago, a small government securities dealer, is believed to have had exposure to losses of $1 to $2 million on repurchase agreements with Bevill Bresler. . . . At Third LaSalle's request, its customer accounts were transferred to three other Chicago clearing firms. . . . The exchanges said the transfer of Third LaSalle's accounts assures that no customer funds are in jeopardy. . . . Indications are that customers' funds 'are intact and haven't been compromised,' said a spokesman for the Commodity Futures Trading Commission. . . ."

I called the legal department of the Merc. "The *Journal* says that all of Third LaSalle's accounts have been transferred to other firms and that their customers' funds are intact and haven't been compromised. So who's my new clearing firm and where's my million two?" They said they didn't know, but that the CFTC and the Exchange were "looking into it."

"DON'T FUCK WITH ME!" I screamed into the phone. "That's a regulated account. It's inviolate. You know, you guys aren't the only ones with clout in Washington. If you don't get me my money by the end of the day, I'm calling the CFTC and I'm telling them about all the crap that goes on out there. I'm on record." Yadda, yadda, yadda!

I called Kornstein. I called Margolis. I called Debbie. I called Zoellner. I even called Frannie over at the Amex to see if they knew anybody else for me to call. Finally, just before five, somebody called me. It was a representative from Saul Stone & Co., a clearing firm in Chicago. He sounded very upbeat. He said that they'd taken over my account, that they had my million two in T-bills, and that they were willing to take on Debbie as my clerk. "Marty, we're pleased to have your business and you can start trading first thing tomorrow."

I couldn't believe it. For the first time in two days, I felt the stoppage in the plumbing in my backside loosen up. Somehow, they'd made me whole. I picked up my direct line and called Debbie. "Yeah, Debbie, they found our money. It looks like we're back in business. You're working for Saul Stone."

"Huh?"

"My account's been moved to Saul Stone, and I told them you were part of the deal, that you went with the money. That OK?"

"Yeah, I guess so, Marty, but what happened?"

"Honey, I don't know, and you don't want to know. Somehow everybody was made whole. What's a million two to them? They'll get it from the next guy. They just want to keep the game going."

I never really knew how I was taken care of, but I got my money. I don't know whether that meant somebody else didn't get theirs, but my idea was that the boys at the Merc went down to the Merc Club, sat around the bar, and worked things out. They couldn't afford to have the reputation of the Exchange sullied. If one firm could rat out on a client, then they all could. So, somehow, the money was made good.

I slept like a log that night. When I went down to get my *Journal* the next morning, there was the old garment man standing in the foyer. "Morning, morning," I caroled cheerfully. "How's the dress business today?"

"Good morning, Mr. Schwartz," he said as I walked up. "All moved in?"

"Yeah, yeah, everything's fine. I'm back in business."

As for Jackie and Johnny, they ended up back in business, too. Their clearing firm was gone, but they still traded bond futures on the CBOT. In Chicago, having a little shit on your shoes is all part of the game.

To Thine Own Self Be True

I have a friend named Mark Cook. Mark's a farmer out in Ohio, but he's also a very good trader and he's developed some interesting methodologies that he sells through a fax service. One day I picked up the phone, dialed Mark's number, and just as I'd done with Terry Laundry, said, "Hey, Mark, this is Marty Schwartz, how ya doing?" I love talking to other good traders because I'm very willing to share information. I don't mind giving as much as I get, and now Mark sends me his faxes and we trade market strategies.

On January 23, 1997, I received a Mark Cook Special Fax entitled "What Makes a Successful Trader?" People are always asking me what it takes to become a great trader, so I was interested in seeing what Mark had to say.

First, according to Mark, to be a successful trader you have to *have a complete commitment to trading and do it full-time*. Trading must be addressed as a profession, because if you do not treat it as such, those who do will separate you from your money very quickly. Mark Cook watches the market all day long, from the opening bell to the closing bell, and keeps a diary that sometimes has more than forty entries a day. If he doesn't do this, his profits suffer. "There is no shortcut in trading, the market will quickly find out if you are lazy."

Second, he says, *fit your trading habits to your personality*. If you are an emotional person, admit that you are emotional and structure your trading habits to make your emotions a positive influence, not a negative one. If you are greedy, or if you are fearful, that will affect your decision making, and if you don't recognize your dominant emotion, your decisions will be wrong. Mark tends to be fearful, and whenever he is most fearful, recognizing that emotion helps him decide to go long and buy. "Whenever my fears become overwhelming, my discipline tells me to buy, and discipline must win out, or you are doomed to failure."

Third, says Mark, *planning is the objective part of trading*. Start with the worst-case scenario and work from there. You will never be more objective than before you execute a trade. Once you are in a trade, emotions take over, so your plan must be in place beforehand. Know when you are wrong and admit it. "Get out, retreat, and live to fight another day; these are cowardly approaches, but they will keep you from the trader's obituary." I think that Mark's analysis is as good as anybody's.

Another question that I'm always asked is if trading is something that comes naturally or is it something that can be learned. The answer is, both. By nature, I'm quick with numbers, very competitive, and love to gamble. Then Amherst taught me how to work hard, Columbia taught me business, and the Marine Corps trained me how to react under fire. A great trader is like a great athlete. You have to have natural skills, but you have to train yourself how to use them.

10
Lots 204 and 207

On May 8, 1985, Audrey gave birth to our son, a handsome six-pound-eleven-ounce little mensch. Then in November, Audrey was diagnosed with breast cancer. This setback, like the one we suffered when we'd lost our first baby in December of 1981, reaffirmed my feeling that it was crazy not to taste the fruits as soon as we could pick them.

The following spring and summer, Audrey decided to completely renovate the apartment. She moved walls, put in a new kitchen, redid the bathrooms, had all the windows treated, and repainted everything. Money was pouring out, but that was all right. I was still the Champion Trader, I was still making it faster than she could spend it. In fact, I was getting ready to spend some more.

Once you get far enough up the tree, there's no shortage of expensive hobbies you can undertake. Ted Turner had his ten-meter America's Cup yachts, George Steinbrenner his Yankees, Wayne Newton his Arabian stallions, and Prince Charles his mistress. But I wasn't interested in yachts, sports franchises, stallions, and with Audrey around, the market was my mistress. If I was going to sink a lot of money into a hobby, I wanted it to be art.

As a kid, my mother would take me on the train to New York, and we'd spend the whole day visiting the Museum of Modern Art, the Metropolitan, the Guggenheim, and the Whitney. I would have much preferred to have been playing cards in Eddie Cohen's basement, but the seed was planted. My mother would buy prints of the great paintings by Monet, Manet, Degas, and Cezanne and hang them on the walls of our house in New Haven, so seeing fine art on the walls of my house was something I was used to, even if it wasn't the real thing. Now that I had plenty of money, I wanted the real thing.

Once the apartment was done, Audrey and I went to see Al Fresco and Cliff Palette at the Fresco-Palette Gallery on the Upper East Side. Al had been in my class at Columbia Business School. He and Cliff were cousins who had taken over the gallery from their fathers. Their grandmother was related to the early American Impressionist John H. Twachtman and had married a Du Pont. So it was no mystery how Al and Cliff had the genes and the green necessary to operate a gallery on the Upper East Side.

When I started making decent money back in the early eighties, Audrey and I began spending Saturday afternoons scouting out galleries. Fresco-Palette became a frequent stop and, while we liked their art, back then it was still out of our reach. Now it wasn't.

In October 1986, we paid Fresco-Palette $100,000 for Ernest Lawson's *Winter Reflections* (oil on canvas, 1915), which was pretty pricey for a Lawson, and $400,000 for Robert Vonnoh's *Jardin de paysanne* (*Peasant Garden,* oil on canvasboard, 1890). In one afternoon, I'd dropped half a million bucks on two paintings. For my $500,000, Al threw in a book, *American Impressionism* by William Gerdts (Amherst '49), a professor of art history at the City University of New York Graduate School and University Center.

I liked the Impressionists because, here again, the seed already had been planted. In 1984, Audrey and I had taken our first trip together to Europe, and while we were in Paris, we hired a driver and had him take us out to see Monet's home and gardens in Giverny. It was early May, and like the American painters who flocked to the provincial villages of Pont-Aven, Grez-sur-Loing, Concarneau, and Giverny in the late nineteenth and early twentieth centuries, Audrey and I were drawn to the special light and beauty of the French countryside. However, when we got back to New York and started looking for something to buy, I realized that it would be foolish for us to try to collect the best paintings by the top French Impressionists. How was I going to afford a top-of-the-line Manet, Renoir, Degas, or Monet? If I was going to buy French, I'd have to go second line.

On the other hand, American Impressionists like Theodore Robinson, Frederick Frieseke, Winslow Homer, Mary Cassatt, and Robert Vonnoh, who had studied under the great French masters, were well within my budget, and after visiting more galleries and studying Gerdts I came to the conclusion that painters, like everybody else, had good and bad days. A Mary Cassatt on a good day was, at least to my eye, as beautiful, or even more beautiful, than a Degas on a bad day. Plus, because the Americans lacked the snob appeal of the French, a top-of-the-line American painting sold for about one-third the price of a second-line French one. Like options back in my early days on the American Exchange or S&P 500 futures in the early eighties, the American Impressionists fit my style and personality. They were priced right, they had upside potential, they were an emerging market, and I understood them. If I was going to play with art, the American Impressionists were going to be my game.

As I spent more time at the Fresco-Palette Gallery, I began to see that Al and Cliff had a market philosophy a lot like my own. For their inventory, they'd buy only the best paintings by the best artists at the best prices. That gave them the best liquidity, because there were always wealthy people around who wanted to buy only the best. When I was trading, I'd stick with the biggest blue-chip companies because they were the ones that gave me the most liquidity. If I bought fifty thousand shares of IBM, Xerox, or Du Pont, and an hour later I changed my mind, I could bang them right out at little risk because there was always a market. That's what Fresco-Palette had, a lot of blue chips that it could bang right out. My problem was that the galleries were banging them out at retail and my Jewish heritage told me to buy wholesale.

The advantage of buying art through a dealer was that you knew what you were getting. The dealer had done all the work so you were sure that you were buying the best of the best. The disadvantage was that you were paying top dollar. Dealers had to make a living, and unless you were new to the game and didn't know what you wanted, or you were looking for a particular piece, who could afford dealer prices? I knew what I wanted,

American Impressionists, and I wasn't looking for any particular piece. I was just looking for the best paintings by the best artists at the best prices, and that meant that I'd have to go where the dealers went: I'd have to go to the auctions.

Christie's at 59th and Park and Sotheby's at 72nd and York were the two main auction houses for American art. Audrey and I got their past catalogs and started studying. We compared the quality of the artists, paintings, and prices that each house sold, and it seemed to us that when it came to American Impressionists, over the years Sotheby's had the better selection. Sotheby's held its auctions for American Impressionists twice a year, once in early December and once in late May, and we decided that we'd make our debut at Sotheby's December 4, 1986, auction.

Like a good marine, I wanted to be prepared before I went into battle. This was new terrain and I didn't feel comfortable going up against art's most elite troops all by myself, so three weeks before the auction, I went to see Al and Cliff.

"Look," I said, "Audrey and I want to build an American Impressionist collection, but we can't keep paying retail. We want to go to the Sotheby auction, but to do that, we're gonna need your advice. Here's what I figure: if you could show us the ropes, we could pick up some paintings that you like, and then if somebody came along sometime in the future looking for a particular piece, you'd know where it was, and you know I'm a trader, so we could make a deal. That way, you can put your money into other stuff and down the road still make some nice commissions."

This argument must have made some sense to Al and Cliff. They told me that they'd give us any information they had on any paintings that we liked and that we could sit with them at the auction. They even offered to do our bidding. As I got up to leave, Al reached under his desk and pulled out a brand-new advance copy of the Sotheby catalog for the December 4, 1986, auction. "Here," he said, handing me the catalog. "Start studying."

I felt like the professor had just given me the final exam. I went right home and sat down with Audrey. "We're gonna go to the auction with Fresco and Palette. They want us to go through the catalog and pick out all the paintings we like. Then they'll help us decide which ones we should bid on."

Audrey and I spent the next two weeks poring over the catalog, studying all of the American Impressionists, trying to find the best paintings by the best artists at what we thought would be the best prices. Trying to find a good painting was a lot like looking for a good stock. The December 1986 Sotheby's catalog contained 349 items, including sculptures, and about fifty of those were paintings by American Impressionists. As with stocks, we were able to eliminate most of them right away. With stocks, we didn't like the earnings, we didn't like the product, we didn't like the market share, or we didn't like the management; with paintings, we didn't like the price, we didn't like the composition or the color, we didn't like the provenance, or we didn't like the artist.

In a week we had the field narrowed down to five paintings: lot 176, Childe Hassam's *Road to the Sea* (oil on canvas, 1895, $150,000–200,000); lot 190, Theodore Robinson's *Summer Hillside, Giverny* (oil on canvas, circa 1889, $450,000–550,000); lot 196, William Merritt Chase's *Shinnecock Landscape* (oil on canvas, circa 1895, $150,000–200,000); lot 204, Maurice Brazil Prendergast's *The Garden* (watercolor on paper, undated, $140,000–180,000); lot 207, Frederick Frieseke's *On the River* (oil on canvas, circa 1909–10, $250,000–350,000). It was time to go see Al and Cliff.

The auction was on Thursday, December 4. I dropped by Fresco-Palette after the market closed on Friday, November 28. As expected, Al and Cliff knew everything about every one of the paintings Audrey and I had chosen. "You've got a good eye," Al said, "but you can't go by the catalog. You have to see them firsthand."

All the pieces were on exhibit from Sunday, November 30, until Wednesday, December 3. *The Garden* was the only piece we were interested in that wasn't being shown at Sotheby's. It was part of a Prendergast exhibit that was being shown at the Coe-Kerr Gallery on East 82nd Street. Audrey and I went there on Saturday. It sparkled. It looked much better in real life than it did in the catalog. We definitely wanted to bid on this piece and we started to get excited with the prospect that in a week, this very painting might be hanging on our wall.

All of Sotheby's exhibitions were open to the public, except for the one on Monday night. Monday night viewings were "by appointment only," which meant that Monday was when Sotheby's had their private cocktail party for its big hitters. That was the exhibition I wanted to go to, because that's where I could sniff noses with the top dogs of the New York art world, but Audrey and I weren't on Sotheby's Rolodex at the time, so we weren't invited. We weren't members of the club. We were scheduled to meet Al and Cliff to look at the other four paintings at the final exhibition on Wednesday afternoon, but at the last minute our sitter called in sick and Audrey had to stay home.

I didn't know what to expect as I walked into Sotheby's headquarters on York Avenue. I knew it wasn't going to be like walking into Aqueduct or Caesar's Palace. I pictured people strolling around soberly and speaking in whispers as if they were in a museum. But it wasn't like that at all. Walking into the main viewing room of Sotheby's was like walking into the 1948 Republican convention. Stuffy-looking Ivy League Wasps and Wasp wannabes were going around gladhanding each other, working the room, trying to make everybody think they knew something. "This is unquestionably one of Redfield's finest works." "Here is a fine example of Paxton's binocular vision method of painting." "Yes, notice how unifying the focus and relegating outlying areas to a less distinct representation makes the work so much more credible." "Look at the energy and intensity of *Young Girl with Dog*." "It's remarkable how Robinson transcends the ordinary. Look at the condensed treatment of space, how it's suffused with soft filtered light, and the wispy brushwork." What bullshit. But it was good bullshit, certainly nothing worse than I heard every day on the Street.

Al and Cliff's hands were in perpetual motion. This was their market and they knew everybody in it. They kept introducing me to the crowd, but I wasn't there to socialize. I was there to study the paintings and measure the people, the way I'd studied the horses at Aqueduct and measured the specialists on the Amex. I looked at each of the paintings we'd identified and listened to the people who were talking about them, trying to chart what they were saying, to fit them into some kind of system.

When I got home, Audrey and I sat down and went over our notes one more time. We were preparing for the market the next day, finalizing our strategy, checking our inflection points, and setting our entry and exit price levels. I wanted my Marine Corps general orders clear in my head. I wanted to be ready when the shit hit the fan, because trading is all about having your mind disciplined ahead of time. Specifically, my objective was to establish a maximum bid for each painting, plus one. If my maximum bid was $200,000 and the bid went to $210,000, I'd give it one more shot at $220,000. Auctions play on the bidder's emotions so the idea was not to go crazy, to set a firm quitting point and to stick to it. Just before we went to bed, we took our catalog, which by now was dog-eared and covered with notes, and carefully folded back the corners of the pages for our three paintings: lots 176, 204, and 207.

The auction at Sotheby's is divided into two sessions. The morning session covered lots 1–150 and started at 10:15. The afternoon session covered lots 151–349 and started at 2:00. The lots were arranged chronologically, so the American Impressionists were part of the second session, but I wanted to use the morning session to reconnoiter the terrain. Walking into 1334 York Avenue that Thursday morning and seeing the guard reminded me of walking into 86 Trinity Place seven and a half years before. We hung our coats in the cloakroom, went into the lounge, found the Fresco-Palette boys, and followed discreetly as they walked upstairs to the main auction hall.

We entered a room about the size of a small off-Broadway theater and claimed four seats in the front row. Al put me on Cliff's left because Cliff did the bidding. Al sat on my left, and Audrey sat on Al's left. Directly in front of us was a table where a half dozen tweedy young men and women sat manning a bank of phones. "Those are for the phone bids. People call in from all over the world," Al told me. Above and a little to the left of the young tweedies was a computerized electronic currency conversion board that listed the conversion rates for all the currencies in which a buyer could bid: dollars, pounds, French francs, Swiss francs, yen, and deutsche marks. Directly in front of us on a raised dais was a large spindle with the display box. It was lit by bright floodlights and had curtains on either side. "That's where they show the pieces," said Al. "It's divided into three sections like a big lazy Susan. While one piece is being auctioned, behind the curtains they're taking off the item that just sold and mounting the next one." To the right of the display box was a pulpit. It was vacant now, but obviously that's where the auctioneer stood.

Boxes with tinted glass ran along both sides and the back of the hall above the floor. I assumed that these were occupied by really big hitters. The crowd was milling around and chatting, but everyone immediately settled down when at precisely 10:15, John Marion, the chief auctioneer, ascended the pulpit. The only people who remained standing were Sotheby's spotters, strategically stationed against the walls.

In a rich patrician voice, John Marion explained the terms of sale, checked to make sure his phone crew and spotters were set, and called up lot 1. There was a whir and the spindle turned. Buttersworth's *The Mayflower Defeating the Galatea* (oil on artist's board, undated, $6,000–8,000), a 7-inch × 12-inch painting of two sloops racing in a rough sea, sailed into the lights. "Five, do I hear five?" The audience leaned forward en masse for a closer look, the young tweedies murmured into the phones, the currency conversion board began converting, and the spotters' heads started swiveling. The room was suddenly filled with a nervous energy.

"I have six, do I have seven?" proclaimed the rich patrician baritone. "Seven, do I have eight? Yes, thank you, eight. Now, do I have nine?" The bids kept coming, but I couldn't figure out from where. This was nothing like the American Exchange. Nobody waved their hands or shouted; bidding was done silently and very inconspicuously. "Nine, going once . . . going twice. . . . Sold!" Thwack. John Marion whacked the top of the pulpit with a brass knocker that fit snugly into his right hand.

The spindle whirred, the currency conversion board clicked, and before I could finish writing down the first sale, John Marion was well into the second.

Cliff bid on a couple of pieces in the morning session. According to the "guide for prospective buyers" section in the front of the catalog, bidding was "by paddle," but evidently that didn't pertain to established pros. The Fresco-Palette paddle never left his lap. He'd wink, tap his nose, pull his ear, nod his head, tug his tie, or whatever, and John Marion's keen eye would mark each movement. I was afraid to move at all. A wink, a tap, a nod, a tug, or whatever and Thwack! two or three hundred thousand dollars would change hands. It all began to feel very familiar to me: the phones, the numbers, the board, the bids, the confirmations of the trades, the speed at which money was changing hands. This was just a cleaner, more genteel Amex, and John Marion was just a better-dressed, more refined Frannie Santangelo. John Marion made his trades with a brass knocker while Frannie Santangelo made his with brass balls.

At the end of the morning session we went out for a quick bite, but I was too nervous to eat. Most of the lots in the morning session had sold above the estimated prices in the catalog. "Gee, Cliff, do you think I'm too low?" I asked.

"You never know," Cliff said. "Sometimes you gauge it just right, and other times they run right by you. Let's wait and see how it goes in the afternoon before we start changing our strategy."

We were back in our seats at 1:50 P.M. At precisely 2:00, John Marion climbed into his pulpit. Thwack! Lot 151, John La Farge's *The Aesthete* (pen and ink and watercolor on paper, undated, exhibited 1898, $4,000–6,000) sold for $13,000. More than double the estimate; things didn't look good, prices were high. The board clicked, the spindle whirred, it was a merry-go-round of American art as pieces were being sold at the rate of two a minute. They were moving faster than Mesa options.

Twelve minutes later lot 176, *Road to the Sea*, whirred into view. It was time to get me a Hassam. We had it marked at $200,000, the upside of Sotheby's estimate. "Do I have 150?"

purred the rich patrician baritone. Cliff pulled his ear. "I have 150, do I have 175?" Art turned to scout out the competition. "I have 175, do I have 200?"

"It's the Greek," Al whispered. Cliff nodded his head.

"I have 200, 200, may I have 225?" There was a pause. "May I have 210?"

Cliff looked at me for approval. "Go. Go. Give'm 210," I whispered. Cliff winked.

"I have 210, do I see 220? I have 220."

"The Duchess," Al said.

"Go," I mumbled. Cliff tapped his nose.

"I have 230. Yes, 240, may I have 240, please?"

"It's the Greek again," Al said.

Shit. I couldn't let some Greek beat me. I was about to tell Cliff to go to $240,000 when I felt Audrey's nails digging into my thigh. "Let it go, Buzzy," she said. "It's not that pretty, and there's still two bidders." Sonofabitch. Audrey was right. We watched as the Greek and the Duchess battled it out to $280,000. Damn, these auctions were tough. It was like craps. I hated to lose, but you couldn't let yourself get carried away.

Seven minutes later, lot 190, Theodore Robinson's *Summer Hillside, Giverny*, went for $475,000. Too rich for my blood, but the cover girl was still well within Sotheby's estimate, and that was good. Three minutes later, lot 196, William Merritt Chase's *Shinnecock Landscape*, went for $300,000, a full 50 percent over Sotheby's estimate. That was bad. "Damn," I said under my breath. "Hampton money, don't worry," said Al. "It's a sentimental buyer. They overpaid. Get ready."

My heart was pounding. 201, 202, 203. Thwack! Click. Whir. "Lot 204, Maurice Brazil Prendergast's *The Garden*, watercolor on paper," chanted the rich patrician baritone. "140, may I have 140, 140, may I have 160? Thank you, 160, now 180, please. May I have 180?" Cliff nodded. "180, thank you, now 200, may I have 200? I have 200, 220, please."

"It's that Philadelphia gallery," Al whispered. "Could be for themselves, or for a client. I can't tell."

"I don't give a shit who it's for. This baby's mine. Go, Cliff." John Marion looked at Cliff. Cliff nodded.

"220, may I have 240?" There was a pause. "A fine Prendergast, may I have 230?" John Marion was looking to the back. "Thank you, 230, now, 240, please." He came back to Cliff.

"Still Philadelphia," Al said. "No other bidders."

Cliff looked at me. I looked at Audrey. She nodded. "Go," I said. Cliff tugged his tie.

"240, may I have 250?" The catalog was open on my lap. I buried my head in my hands and looked down at the Prendergast. It sparkled back up at me. Please, Pleeease be mine. "240. Going once . . . going twice. . . . Sold." Thwack! I bolted erect. I mean, this was the biggest rush I'd ever had in my life. I leaned over Al and hugged Audrey, shook Al's hand, turned around to shake Cliff's hand. It was like when Hayes and I used to do the mashed potatoes. The people in the seats behind us were congratulating Audrey and me. Not bad, for $240,000 (plus Sotheby's vigorish of $24,000) we were in the club.

Thwack! Holy shit. I'd forgotten that we were still in the auction. Lot 206 had just sold, and Frieseke's *On the River* was on the block. Audrey gasped. "It's gorgeous." She had missed the previous night's exhibition and had never seen the real painting before. "Get it! Get it!" she ordered.

Well, I was a good marine and now I had my marching orders. "I have 240, may I have 260?" Cliff started twitching and tugging. "270, now 280, may I have 290?" "Get it! Get it!" I said. Cliff was bouncing around, pulling various body parts like he had Tourette's syndrome. "Once . . . twice. . . . Sold!" Thwack! That was it, we owned *On the River.* I could feel people slapping me on the back, congratulating us on another fine buy. This was unbelievable. $290,000 (plus $29,000) and $240,000 (plus $24,000). I hadn't spent this much money so fast since I'd bought the co-op.

Six months later, Fresco and Palette came to see me. "Buzzy," they said, "we have a proposition that might interest you. We have a major collector who wants to buy your Vonnoh. He's willing to pay $700,000, which we think is a very good price for a Vonnoh."

"Me too," I said, since we'd paid $400,000 only nine months

before. A 75 percent profit in nine months made sense to Audrey and me, so we sold *Jardin de paysanne* to the major collector, and it now hangs in the Musée Americain in Giverny, France.

Over the years we've sold a few other paintings through the Fresco-Palette Gallery when the price was right, and on one level, good art has to be considered as an investment, a commodity to be bought and sold just like any other financial instrument. Sotheby's and Christie's know that, and thousands of dealers like the Fresco-Palette boys know it. They're the ones who make the market. But on another level, art goes way beyond just being an investment. I know who's owned a painting before I bought it, unlike a bond, or a security, or a future, and I like to know where it's going if I sell it. The difference is emotional, moral.

My paintings are guests in my home. I wake up with Ernest Lawson, I dine with Frederick Frieseke, I read with Winslow Homer and Childe Hassam, I sit with Maurice Prendergast, William Glackens, and Mary Cassatt. As my mother knew long ago, they teach me things that I could never learn in Eddie Cohen's basement, or on the floor of any exchange, things like civility, humility, and humanity. They teach me that making money is not the most important thing in the world. They make me a better person.

After several years at the co-op on Park Avenue, I was elected to the board of directors for the building and soon after that, I was made president. I had just taken office when I got a call from a man who'd lived in the building for over twenty years. "Mr. Schwartz," he said, "may I come see you?"

We sat down in my living room. "Mr. Schwartz," he said, staring down at the floor, "things have not been going so well for me. I'm sure that over time, I'll be fine, but for now, I'm afraid I can't make my monthly maintenance payments."

At first I didn't know what to say. I couldn't believe that anyone who lived there wouldn't be able to pay their maintenance fee. Legally, I could have him declared in default and eventually forced him to sell out to meet his debt. That's what the board had said it would do to me seven years earlier, but I was a street kid from New Haven, I wasn't a member of the club. When they have the power, they skewer you; when you have the power, you show humanity because you've been skewered and you know how it feels.

"Look," I said, "you've been here, what, twenty-five, thirty years? Take your time, get your affairs in order, and don't worry about your maintenance fee. I'm sure that you'll be able to work out of this and be able to pay it eventually, and we'll carry it for a reasonable period of time."

He was very relieved and as he got up to leave he paused a moment to look around the room. By that time, the art on the walls was worth more than the apartment. "You have a very fine collection," he said.

"Thanks," I said. "We like it, and it's nice to have hanging around, you know, just in case something happens."

Big Shots Make Big Targets

When you're trading, it's important to have your guns on. You can't be wandering around the Street unarmed, and if you don't know the terrain, you're going to get killed. That's why I spent so much time working on my methodology and reconnoitering the floor of the Amex with my friend Hayes Noel before I started trading. Unfortunately, I forgot this rule on one of my trips to the Windy City.

In the spring of 1987, Audrey and I were six months into collecting art and we were having a ball. When Al Fresco and Cliff Palette told us that for a reasonable donation they could get us an invitation to the opening of the Windy City Museum in Chicago, I grabbed my checkbook and pulled out my pen. The founder of the museum and his wife were major collectors of American Impressionists and the opening of their museum was going to be one of the big art events of the year. It was black tie all the way and muckety-mucks from the art world would be flying in from all over. I sent off my check and shined up my alligator shoes. I was going to the ball.

We checked into the Drake Hotel the night before the opening and since I had nothing to do the next day, I decided I'd go over to the Merc and visit with my clerk, Debbie Horn. For the past five years I'd been one of the biggest individual traders in S&P 500 futures, but I'd never been to the S&P futures pit and I figured it would be fun to watch the boys trade. I took a cab over to Wacker Drive, Chicago's equivalent of Park Avenue, and got out at The Chicago Mercantile Exchange Center. I looked up at the twin forty-story towers clad in granite and thought to myself, I own this place!

I strode up to the membership desk. "I'm Marty Schwartz. I'm a member. May I have my badge, please."

I expected the girl at the desk to snap to attention when she heard the name Schwartz, but instead, she gave me a blank stare and said, "How are you spelling Schwartz?" Well, what did she know? She wasn't part of the action. Wait until I got to the floor. Then we'd see some heads snap.

I walked onto the floor sporting my Armani suit, my Bally alligators, my shiny badge. Holy shit, the place was huge! It was as big as a football field and I had no idea where to find Debbie. The market was open and everybody was moving at a frantic pace, running this way and that. It looked like Grand Central Station at rush hour. I needed help so I tackled the first runner who came by. "Hey! I'm Marty Schwartz! Where the hell's the S&P futures pit?"

"Hey! Who cares! It's over there." He waved aimlessly at the crowd and kept moving. I started to make my way across the floor. Raised octagonal platforms with steps descending toward their centers were all around me. These were the pits. People were yelling, waving their arms, frantically giving hand signals, trading by the "outcry system." Palms in to buy, palms out to sell, fingers waggling bid or offer prices. "Six bid for ten!" "Give me a quote on June bellies?" "I need September lean hogs." I was in meats. I kept wandering.

"What's the offer on the forward Swiss franc?" "Thirty deutsche offered at eighty-five." "What the fuck's going on with the peso?" I was out of meats, into currencies.

"Eighty bid for five Junes!" "Ten Septembers offered at ninety-five!" Finally, something sounded familiar. I looked up at the screens.

	Open	High	Low	Last	Chg
June	286.50	289.30	286.50	289.15	+2.65
Sept	288.60	290.90	288.40	290.60	+2.15
Dec	290.50	292.25	290.40	292.20	+1.70

I'd found the S&Ps.

Debbie wasn't hard to spot. There weren't a lot of women on the floor of the Merc. She started to introduce me around and much to my delight, heads began to snap. It was like Billy the Kid had come to town. "Hi." "How ya doin'?" "Nice ta meetcha, hearda lotta boutcha." "This your first time at the pit?" "Wanna do some trading?"

What could I say? I'd been blasting the S&Ps like nobody else for the last five years. I was the quickest draw in the west, and now the boys wanted to see me in action. "Sure, let's go." I moved next to Debbie. According to the rules, I wasn't sanctioned to trade in the pit, so I'd have to place my orders through Debbie and her clearing firm.

The market was really hopping and immediately I realized that I was in trouble. I'd forgotten to strap on my guns. I had no charts, no Quotron, no moving averages, oscillators or stochastics. Here, everybody was getting ready to draw on me, and I was standing out on the street naked. The only feel I had for the market came from the shouts and the hand signals coming from the pit, and I could hardly understand them. From what I could hear and see, the market was going up, but it seemed to be cresting. "Twenty bid for five," some pimply-faced kid across the pit from me hollered. "Come on, Schwartz, you here to look, or you here to trade?"

Fuck you, touchhole, I muttered under my breath. A lousy five lot. "Debbie! Let's whack this punk. Fifty! Fifty offered at twenty!" If he was going long, I was going short.

A chorus rang out across the pit. "Sold! Sold! Twenty bid for fifteen." "Twenty bid for ten!" "Twenty for twenty more!" "Hey Schwartz, give us some more." "Yeah, c'mon, New York. Show us what you got. Twenty bid for twenty more!" "Schwartz, ya wanna try some Septembers? Sixty bid for twenty!" Damn! What the hell was going on here?

The next hour was as painful as an hour can get. Stubbornly I persisted on going short, but I was firing blanks. The market never looked back. When I was down $90,000, I covered and called it quits. As I crawled out of the pit, one old trader yelled to me, "Hey Schwartz! Come back again! You've been taking our money over the phone for years! We like to take yours in person!"

I went back to the Merc in 1989, but I declined to trade. I'd learned my lesson. Don't get in a shootout if you've left your guns at home. The markets are no place to be trying to impress people. The only way to impress anybody is to stay on your toes, be consistent, and trade within your means. Between my donation to the Windy City Museum and my trading, being a big shot in Chicago had cost me $100,000.

11

Going for the Gold II

The most commonly asked question on Wall Street is, "Where were you on October nineteenth?" On Monday, October 19, 1987, I was long and I was wrong. If I had it to do over again, I'd still be long, and I'd still be wrong.

It was the roaring eighties. Ever since Paul Volcker bailed out Mexico in August of 1982, the market had been on the rise. During those five years, the Dow Jones Industrial Average had climbed from 790 to over 2600, a gain of 230 percent. In the first nine months of 1987 alone, the Dow had risen 650 points, or 33 percent. Wall Street was like Pamplona, everyone was running with the bulls. I was up $8 million for the year, and making money was so easy that only a fool would think it was ever going to end.

I was up to my eyeballs in stocks and getting bigger. I was so confident that I took Audrey, Andre the tennis pro from Westhampton, and Gaby, his wife, to Paradise Island for the Columbus Day weekend. The markets stayed open on Columbus Day, but a lot of the Mediterranean types, the Jews and the Italians at the Amex, took the day off. It was the Northern Europeans, the Wasps and the Irish over at the Big Board, who kept the market going on Columbus Day. But in eight years, nothing had changed. I still couldn't take a vacation. While Audrey, Andre, and Gaby sat out under the thatched bar at the Ocean Club drinking piña coladas, I got on the phone and started trading. "Buy me another ten thousand Tenneco. What? You think Tenneco is going to be taken over? Then buy me another twenty thousand. Buy! Sell! Hold! Audrey, what time does the casino open?"

The market had been getting jittery around the Columbus Day weekend. On Thursday the eighth, the Dow Jones Industrials were down 35, and down another 34 on Friday the ninth. Monday the twelfth, down 10; Tuesday the thirteenth, up 36. Then on Wednesday the fourteenth, it really headed south, down a record 95. Thursday, down another 58; and then came Black Friday. The *Wall Street Journal* described Friday's record drop as follows: "As the Dow Jones Industrial Average fell a record 108.65 points, volume swelled to an unprecedented 338.5 million shares. It was the third major decline in as many days. But several technical analysts said that the big volume accompanying Friday's session might mean better things ahead."

That was how most professionals looked at Friday's dramatic drop, as the finale to a major correction. "Big market declines always end in a 'final death rattle,'" claimed Jack Solomon of Bear Stearns. "The market has reached a 'capitulation point,'" opined Dennis Jarrett of Kidder, Peabody. "Friday's session is a classic 'selling climax,'" agreed a number of technical analysts. I, too, thought that the market had bottomed out, and even though one of my rules is that a down Friday is usually followed by a down Monday, I started buying. After all, how much lower could it go? Just before the close on Friday the sixteenth I called Debbie. "Get me forty S&Ps at the market." She did, at 283.50. That wasn't a big position for me, but my gut told me that it was enough in this market. Then over the weekend, two things happened that made me really nervous.

Friday night, as usual, I was ready to collapse. I was too tired to go out, so Audrey made me a nice meal and I lay down on my couch to watch *Wall $treet Week* with Louis Rukeyser. When Rukeyser asked Marty Zweig, a money manager and market forecaster who was a regular on the show, what he thought about the 108-point drop, Marty said, "The market's in danger. I think we can go down another five hundred points from here."

Marty lived in my building, so on Sunday I called him. He came down to the apartment and we talked for an hour or so. Bonds were sinking rapidly, and Marty told me that all of his monetary indicators were terribly negative. He reaffirmed his position that the market could go down another five hundred points. Of course, he was saying that it might happen over the next few months. Neither of us ever imagined that it would happen in the next twenty-four hours.

The other thing that scared me was that over the weekend Treasury Secretary Baker put a chill in the air when he started lambasting the Germans for nudging up short-term interest rates. Baker was trying to reduce the U.S. trade deficit by controlling the price of the dollar, and he felt that this action by Bonn was contrary to an agreement he'd reached with the Germans back in February. This type of tough talk upset the market. When I heard Baker, I knew I was in trouble.

On Monday I was very, very cautious. Between Zweig's comments on *Wall $treet Week* and Baker's jousting with the Germans, I was thinking that the market was in for a rough day. I had "uncle points," mental stop losses, on just about everything, but now the question was whether I was going to be strong enough to honor them. Having a price in your mind of where you're going to sell is one thing. Actually selling, for a thumping loss, is something else. Being able to honor your stops is what separates the top dogs from the mongrels on Wall Street.

At the opening bell, the market jumped out the window. The Dow plunged in a 150-point death spiral in the first fifteen minutes. I sat at my desk in horror as the forty S&Ps, a ton of options, and two tons of stocks crashed through my "uncles." My positions were being overrun. I couldn't pull the trigger. I couldn't react. The marines teach you never to freeze under fire, either go forward or backward, don't just sit there and get the crap kicked out of you. But they were talking about conventional warfare. I was getting nuked.

My eyes were darting from screen to screen. Holy shit. All the lines were pointing straight down. Dow Industrials? Down two hundred in half an hour. S&Ps? Down nineteen at the opening and still plummeting. The "knife"? Blown away. The NASDAQ? Medevac'ed. The Chicago options? KIA. I started muttering to myself. "What the fuck? This is unreal. Where's my support? Rally, baby, you've gotta rally."

Finally, around 10:30, there was a pause, then a little bounce. I started calling around, doing my reconnaissance, trying to get a handle on my position. "What's the volume?" "How many on the sell side? How many on the buy?" "New buyers, or are they just covering shorts?" "Shit, can you believe Merck, down 12 to 172? And Digital, down 20 to 152? These are great prices, people GOTTA buy!" In the next twenty minutes the Dow regrouped and rallied one hundred points off the lows, and I went into action.

I jumped on the horn to Chicago. "Debbie, dump those forty S&Ps. At the market. NOW!" I sold at 267.50, which was a loss of 315 big ones, but it was one of the greatest trades of my life. I pride myself on being a market timer, and I can't think of any trade I timed any better. I sold the forty S&Ps at just 1.50 off the high for the day. From there, the market started to ooze back downhill and I kept selling, throwing it all overboard. By 11:30, I was out of just about everything except a few options that I'd bought on Columbus Day between the piña coladas. I couldn't get out of them. They'd just stopped trading altogether, no bids at all.

The Dow was back down around 150 by noon. I figured that I'd lost about $2 million, which was horrendous, but at least I was out, and I couldn't lose any more. I was gravely wounded, but I'd stopped the bleeding. According to the U.S. Marine Corps, even a retreat can be an offensive move, because you're saving yourself for another day. That's what I was doing, retreating and saving myself for another day.

The question was, had I retreated far enough? I wondered whether the whole system was about to come down. Was it going to be 1929 all over again? From the recesses of my mind came the image of my father, working two jobs, trying to make ends meet but never able to quite put it together. I started to think about other things I could do to protect my family. That was always my very first rule, protect my family. I left the office and went into the apartment. "Audrey," I said, "the whole system's coming down. I'm goin' for the gold."

Audrey started to test my emotions. "Buzzy, do you really think it's that bad?"

"The market's down over 150 points. It's not good."

"Where are you?"

"I'm out of everything except for some options that have stopped trading." I could see that Audrey was remembering 1982 when we were out at the beach and I made her go for the gold. Damn, that gold was heavy. I really didn't want to do that again. "Maybe I've done enough."

I walked into the bedroom where our son was asleep in his crib. I looked at him lying there sucking his thumb, and I thought to myself, what if everything did go down the tubes and we ended up with bupkas? How could I ever face my children knowing that I hadn't done everything in my power to protect them? I had to go for the gold.

I ran to the closet, pulled out an old battered briefcase, and started for the elevator. I was a trader. Above everything else, I trusted my gut, and my gut told me that everything was falling apart. If I was right, Reagan was going to have to declare a bank holiday, like Hoover did in 1929, and I wasn't having my gold tied up in some bank. I was going to clean out our safe-deposit box.

"Buzzy, where are you going?"

"It doesn't feel right. I'm going for the gold."

"Buzzy, if it doesn't feel right, go for it. But be careful."

Our apartment was on the corner of 65th and Park. My bank, the East New York Savings Bank, was on the corner of 64th and Third, down next to our old apartment building. I rushed outside into a beautiful fall day and started off down 65th Street toward Third, the briefcase flopping at my side. David Rockefeller, the chairman of the Chase Manhattan Bank, had a double-wide town house on the south side of 65th, right next to the town house Nixon had before he moved to Saddle River, New Jersey. At about 12:30, I reached Rockefeller's house and saw half a dozen limousines double and tripled parked outside. "Uh oh," I said to myself, "what's happening here? Must be an emergency meeting of the Tri-Lateral Commission."

From there it wasn't hard for me to convince myself that Vice President Bush, Henry Kissinger, George Shultz, Milton Friedman, Margaret Thatcher, Helmut Kohl, and the ghost of Herbert Hoover were all in Rockefeller's town house figuring out how they were going to save their own asses, and then the rest of the world's. I quickened my pace. I had to get to the vault. All these bastards had to do was pick up the phone; one call from 65th Street to the White House and the banks would be shut tighter than Jimmy Hoffa's coffin.

The sweat began to drip from my brow as I scribbled my safe-deposit box number onto the bank's card. I handed it to the security guard and we went into the vault. He unlocked my box with his key and left. I unlocked the box with my key. I yanked out the box and nearly fell to the floor. I'd forgotten how heavy forty pounds was. I started packing the plastic tubes of Krugerrands into my briefcase. There were a bunch of them, at least $250,000 worth. Maybe more; with the world falling apart, the price of gold probably was soaring.

I cleaned out everything: antique jewelry, my 1925D Saint-Gaudens $20 gold piece from Gramma Schwartz, the deed to the apartment, the whole schmear. The briefcase was bulging, but I was leaving nothing behind. If the system was falling, I wanted everything with me. I locked the box, picked up the briefcase, and called the guard. "You got anything in here, you better get it out," I mumbled to myself. "You might not be open tomorrow."

I walked out onto the street. There were people everywhere, on their lunch break enjoying the Indian summer day. I was sure that they all were staring at me. It felt like the time Carmine the bookie smacked forty hundred-dollar bills into my palm in front of the crowd waiting to see *The Godfather*, only now I was carrying almost $300,000, not $4,000. I kept crossing the street from corner to corner, trying to hail a cab, but with a forty-pound handicap, I was too slow; I kept getting beaten to the wire by people who were poorer, quicker, and blissfully ignorant of the imminent crash.

Fuck the cab, I'd walk. I started shuffling down 65th Street, the briefcase pulling me over to one side like Quasimodo. By the time I reached Rockefeller's house, my shirt was plastered to my body and I was gasping for breath. The leaders of the club might be in there screwing everybody else, but they weren't going to screw me. I was the chosen one, I was fulfilling my responsibility, I was taking care of my family.

I stumbled into the apartment and crashed down on the couch. "Buzzy, what're you doing? Look at your face. You're as red as a beet," Audrey said.

"Gold," I gasped, pointing to the briefcase. "I got the gold. Put it in the safe in the bedroom. I've got to go down to Morgan Guaranty and get some cash."

"Buzzy, you're going to kill yourself. Are you sure it's worth it?"

"It's going down, Audrey. Everything. The whole damn system. I saw the limos. The boys in the club, they're all meeting at Rockefeller's." I got up and wobbled into my office. It was 1:30; the market was down 265 points. Capitalism was crumbling before my eyes. I wanted to change my shirt, but I didn't have time. That call to the White House from 65th Street could come at any minute.

"Good afternoon, Mr. Schwartz," the doorman said. "Going out again. I don't blame you. It's a beautiful day."

"A cab," I groaned. "I need a cab. I gotta get my money for the monthly maintenance."

Morgan Guaranty kept some branches uptown so the gray-haired bluebloods wouldn't have to have their chauffeurs drive them all the way downtown. I told the cabbie to take me to the branch at 58th and Madison in the GM building. I wrote a check for $20,000 and went over to one of the desks where a pert young woman in a neatly tailored business suit was sitting trying to look busy. I needed her approval before I could cash the check because in this country, you can't cash a check for more than $9,999.99 without filling out a form. Anything more than that and they want to make sure that you're not a drug dealer. The sign on the young woman's desk identified her as "Kimberly Van Pelt—Ass't Vice President."

"I have an account here and I want to cash this check," I said handing her the check.

She looked at the check. "Just a minute, please, Mr. Schwartz." She tapped on her keyboard and pulled up my record.

"That will put you below the minimum balance. Are you sure you want that much cash?"

"You bet I do! The market's probably down four hundred points by now. You might not be open tomorrow, and I'm not sure the bank's check's gonna clear by the end of the week. I want my money. And if I were you, I'd get some of yours, too."

When I walked back into my apartment building, I had $20,000 in my breast pocket and a sly smile on my face. I felt like John Dillinger and Willie Sutton rolled into one. "Everything okay, Mr. Schwartz?" the doorman said. "You seemed a little upset when you left."

"Everything's fine, William, just fine," I said. "By tomorrow, half the people in this building might not be able to pay their monthly maintenance fee, but not me." I patted my breast pocket. "I'll show those bastards. The banks will be closed, and I won't care, 'cause I'll pay 'em in green."

I tucked the cash away in the safe with the gold. It was 2:30. I checked the market. As I'd predicted to Kimberly Van Pelt, Asst. Vice President, the market was down 409 and still falling. I grabbed a phone and called my brother. "Gerry! You've got half an hour! Get to the bank! Get some cash! The banks might not be open tomorrow."

"Buzzy, I don't have time to go running to the bank. I'm busy. I've got clients."

"Gerry, fuck the clients. You gotta listen to me. The banks are in structural meltdown. They're like Three Mile Island. You gotta get to the bank, NOW!!"

"Buzzy, you sound hysterical. Like in eighty-two when you went nuts out at the beach. I can't go running off to the bank. I've got too much to do."

"Yeah, well, what are ya gonna do if the banks close and you don't have any money?"

"I'll come over and borrow some from you." Click.

After the market closed down 508 points, I called Zoellner. "So, Bob, whaddya think?"

"I don't know, Marty, but you know what I always say, 'When it gets so bad that you want to puke, you probably should double your position.'"

Tuesday morning was like taking a walk on the beach trying to assess the damage after a hurricane. How much was cosmetic and how much was structural? Rumors were flying all over the Street. . . . The NYSE wasn't going to open. . . . The Merc wasn't going to open. . . . Nobody was going to open. . . . And the biggest rumor of all was that Morgan Stanley, the bluest of the blue-chip investment banks, might go belly up. I called Inside Skinny.

"Motty. The Wasps got it backward," rasped Skinny. "They had all these arbitrage positions, short stocks, and long S&P futures, but because of the selling panic, they got fucked. The futures're tradin' at a forty-point discount and the stocks ain't tradin' at all. After goin' mark-to-market last night, they're tapioca. They owe the Merc over a billion. They can't make the margin call."

What Inside Skinny was telling me was that anybody who had a long position in futures was screwed, bankrupt, because they'd all had to go mark-to-market at a forty-point discount from the actual value of the S&P index. This meant they had to come up with huge amounts of cash overnight to meet their margin calls, because in commodities, everyone starts the day with a clean slate.

I called Zoellner. "Greenspan's thrown open the Fed discount window," he told me. "I heard that at the very last minute, the biggest losers borrowed enough margin to cover their positions on the S&Ps. If they hadn't, the Merc wouldn't have been able to open, and we'd've been heading straight into the next Depression." Wow. My gut had been right again. I was glad I'd gone for the gold. Just an hour or so earlier, we'd been within minutes of the whole financial system collapsing.

Just before the Merc was supposed to open, I called Debbie to see how things were going. The Merc was a total madhouse; she'd never seen anything like it. On Monday, the pit committee had been blue in the face from whistling out trades. Traders had been ratting out on orders left and right. Even as we spoke, Leo Melamed was in the S&P pit telling everyone that everything was going to be all right, but nobody believed him. A lot of brokers and traders just hadn't come in; that way, they wouldn't have to face the music. Seats were up for sale at fire-sale prices by members who'd pledged them as collateral against margin calls.

With stocks, a specialist made the market and could "close the book" (suspend trading) if the buy and sell orders got out of whack. And that's what had happened with a lot of stocks on Monday. But there was no specialist for the S&Ps, which were traded on the open bid outcry system. Orders were thrown into the pit and somebody would always offer to buy or sell something at some price or other. That was why the S&Ps had traded at such a huge discount. With all the sell orders, traders were making bids, but they were way below the last prices listed for the actual index. For the majority of stocks on the NYSE, there weren't really any prices at all. A lot of the prices used to compute the S&P index were the last available quotes from the close on Monday.

With the market so out of balance, I decided that I wasn't going to trade. I'd be crazy to get into the S&Ps. The bigger the fluctuations in the market, the bigger the boys in the pit would screw you. I got screwed on my trades regularly, even in the best of markets. On a day like today, they'd chew me to pieces. All Tuesday morning, I kept my eyes on my screens and my hands in my pockets. Stocks were bouncing around in extremely heavy trading. Debbie called at 11:30. Leo Melamed and Jack Sandner, the chairman of the Merc, had just gone into the S&P pit and called a temporary halt to all trading. They were afraid that the NYSE was going to shut down, and if that happened, the Merc would be left alone for everyone to dump on it. But, just after noon, the Dow Jones news wire began reporting that many blue-chip companies were initiating stock buyback programs. This positive news sent the blue chips soaring and the Merc reopened. The Dow ended the day up 102.27, the largest one-day gain ever. I'd missed the whole run, and for once was content to be on the sidelines. I still had a $6 million profit for the year, my nerves were shot, and my gold was in the safe. It was like after you make a big score in Vegas. I needed a break.

On Wednesday, a wide array of stocks followed the blue chips and by 3:00 P.M. the market was up another 175 points, easily surpassing Tuesday's one-day record and regaining over half of Monday's 508-point drop. The market was going crazy. I had to get back in the game.

I looked at my Magic T, my moving averages, my oscillators, my channel bands. They were kaput, useless, mahullah, busted. The market had not experienced these types of fluctuations in my lifetime. There was no order in this universe, no symmetry, no high and low tides; prices were bobbing around like lifeboats in a hurricane. I had to go with my gut, and my gut told me that this dramatic rebound couldn't last. "Debbie," I barked, "we're going back in. But slow and easy. Try selling a contract at the market, and let's see what happens."

What happened was that the market kept going up and I kept selling into it, one or two contracts at a time, with the boys in the pit filling my orders late every time, front-running me all the way, clipping me for 0.10 here, 0.15 there. The S&Ps closed at 258.25, and I ended the day short twelve contracts at an average price of 255, which, for me, was nothing. I'd often have 100, 150 contracts long or short at the end of the day, but not in this market.

At five o'clock, I dialed up the Elliott Wave Hotline to see what Bob Prechter had to say. Prechter was down in Gainesville, Georgia, and published a market advisory newsletter called *The Elliott Wave Theorist*. Prechter had predicted the start of the bull market back in 1982 and had become the market guru of the eighties. There was a whole cult of believers who hung on his every word. In addition to the newsletter, he had a hotline that came out on Mondays, Wednesdays, and Fridays at five. On Wednesday, October 21, 1987, Prechter was negative. According to the hotline, the tide had turned and despite the two-day rally, the market was headed south.

At the opening Thursday morning, I was on the horn with Debbie. Prechter was the guru of gurus. If he said the market was going down, there was a good chance it would. Either way, up or down, this market was so volatile that I had to be on top of it. Ding. There was the bell. The market was open. "Marty!" Debbie screamed into the phone, "Shearson just came with an order for a thousand contracts to sell, at the market!"

"Quote! Quote! Dammit, gimme a quote!"

"Offered at 240!"

"Shit, it closed at 258! What the hell's going on? Lemme

think! I gotta think!" How much was I ahead? A twelve lot short at 255, now offered at 240. Twelve times five hundred times the fifteen-point profit equaled $90,000. "Marty! Offered at 230! Offered at 225!"

"The size! What's the size at 225?" At this price, I stood to make $180,000 if I could cover my twelve lots short. "What's the size?"

"Marty, there's no bids, I dunno! 220! Offered at 215!" Holy shit. What the fuck was happening? The bottom was falling out of the S&Ps. Nobody was making a bid. In over five years of trading S&P futures, I'd never seen this before. "210! 205! Marty, there's a fill at 202!"

"The size? What's the size?"

"I dunno, I missed it! 200! Another fill at 198!"

"COVER!!!" I shrieked. The boys in the pit were starting to buy. "Cover the twelve lot, and input it to the clearinghouse right away. I don't want those bastards ripping up my tickets!" With the market moving like this, it wouldn't be unusual for the boys to conveniently forget about a few of their trades. "GO!" Click.

I turned to my screen. The 202 was just coming up, then the 200. Then a 198, 197, 195. Wait a minute! 197. 200. 204. The market had turned around. But that was all right. I had to be covered at no worse than 200. What a killing!

Ring. "Debbie! Debbie! DO YOU HAVE THE TRADE?"

"Marty! I got five filled at 200, but they won't give me the card on the other seven!"

"Where are they now? 210? They're moving so fast, if they're not gonna give you the card at 200, buy another five at the market! NOW!" Those fucking bastards. They'd buried my order to cover on the other seven. They'd just ripped me off for at least ten points on seven contracts, $35,000 at least, maybe more.

Ring. "Marty, I got five more filled at 210, and the last two at 215. It was the best I could do. They're ratting out on trades left and right."

I was shaking. I didn't know whether to be happy or pissed. I'd made $290,000 on the twelve lot (5 × 500 × 55 points in profit, 5 × 500 × 45 points, and 2 × 500 × 40 points), and the boys at the Merc had taken about $50,000 in "slippage." Two hundred and ninety thousand dollars on a twelve lot! That was unbelievable. What the hell had happened?

It turned out that Shearson's thousand contract sell order at the market had been on behalf of George Soros's Quantum B.V.I. Mutual Fund. Apparently, Soros felt like Prechter and had decided to dump all of his fund's 2,400 S&P futures contracts at the opening bell. According to *Barron's,* when the first order to sell 1,000 contracts at the market hit the pit, "the pit traders picked up the sound of a whale in trouble." They hung back until the offer dropped to around 200, then attacked. The Soros block sold between 195 and 210 and, within minutes, the market had bounced back to 230, leaving a lot of instant millionaires celebrating in the pits. This is one of the most famous trades in the history of the Merc and many of the details subsequently came out in U.S. District Court in Chicago, where Soros sued Shearson for $160 million (subsequently settled out of court). According to Inside Skinny, Soros actually lost $800 million. "Motty. He was long up the ying yang and he panicked." I just remember it as the day I out-traded the great George Soros.

I was still shaking when I went into the apartment. "Audrey," I said, "you're not going to believe this: I just made $290,000 on a twelve lot."

"Buzzy, that's wonderful. How long did you have to hold it?"

"Overnight."

"Good for you. Now, will you get that briefcase out of the safe. I can't get to any of my jewelry."

On Friday, the twenty-third, I took the gold back to the East New York Savings Bank. As I stood all by myself in one of the little private rooms they make available to their customers, putting all of the plastic tubes of Kruggerands back into the safe-deposit box, I thought that twice now, I'd gone for the gold. And both times, the market had came roaring back and I'd made a bundle. Maybe Zoellner was right. Maybe when it gets so bad that you want to puke, you probably should double your position. I haven't had that feeling for ten years, but the next time my gut tells me that the world's going to end, maybe I'll do just that. Maybe I'll double my position, then go for the gold.

Sitting Down by the Lake, Waiting for the Tidal Wave

Bob Prechter is one of the most talented people ever to analyze the market. Bob's very smart, a Mensa, just brilliant. He went to Yale on a full scholarship, and, after graduating in 1971 with a degree in psychology, spent several years of self-education in the field of technical analysis. That led him to a job with Merrill Lynch as a technical market specialist where he became intrigued with the work of Ralph Nelson Elliott (1871–1948).

Elliott, a former accountant and obscure technician who in the twenties and thirties developed the wave principle as a way of analyzing the market, published his life's work (somewhat immodestly entitled *Nature's Law—The Secret of the Universe*) in 1946, just two years before his death. Since then, the wave principle has fascinated a small but loyal coterie of philosophers, mathematicians, psychologists, and theologians as well as investors.

In 1977, Prechter quit Merrill Lynch and moved his family to Gainesville, Georgia, a little town on Lake Lanier about an hour's drive north of Atlanta. From there, he started publishing a market newsletter, *The Elliott Wave Theorist*, and in 1978, he and A. J. Frost, an old accountant and another disciple of Elliott's, wrote a book called *Elliott Wave Principle*, which predicted the big bull market of the eighties with uncanny accuracy. Over time, this book, along with his newsletter, turned Prechter into the market guru of the eighties.

I subscribed to *The Elliott Wave Theorist* because I was always looking for additional information that would help me improve my methodology, and Elliott's wave theory complimented my Magic T. It was based on mathematics and fit my fascination with bilateral symmetry, high tide, low tide, the natural order of things. For a trader like me, it was indeed a Secret of the Universe.

One day in the fall of 1983, I picked up the phone and called Prechter, the same way I'd picked up the phone and called Terry

Laundry back in 1978. Bob had entered one of Norm Zadeh's Champion Trader contests and he knew my name. We started talking about the market, I liked what he had to say, and we worked out a consulting deal where I'd pay him a certain amount every month. I really respected Bob's intellect and it turned out that we'd talk several times a day, just like I talked to Zoellner.

By the crash of '87, Bob had this huge following and was making $20,000 a speech, but then he got tired of being the "Market's Guru." He saw the crash as the end of the bull run and went totally negative. Even though the market recovered and kept going up, nothing could make Bob change his mind. We were at the crest of the tidal wave, the market was about to be dashed upon the rocks, there was nothing to be done.

In 1989, Bob was president of the Market Technicians Association, which is the trade association for all the technical analysts in the country, and he invited me to participate in a panel discussion with Paul Tudor Jones. Bob had been predicting gloom for so long that he was slowly losing his audience, so at the meeting, I took him aside. "Bob," I said to him, "even if the market's going to crash, ride it until it does. Wait until it turns down, then tell 'em it's going down."

He'd hear none of it. He was convinced that we were at the crest of the tidal wave and had gone into a lifeboat mentality. He was sitting high and dry in Gainesville waiting for the flood. I still had tremendous respect for Bob's intellect, but we didn't have much contact after that. I was a trader. I just couldn't sit and wait for the world to come to an end.

In 1995, Bob sent me an autographed copy of his new book, *At the Crest of the Tidal Wave*. Even though the Dow was up more than two thousand points since 1989 when I'd told him that he had to be more positive, Bob was still negative. The book was all gloom and doom, but fascinating. Bob's truly a genius, and a very persuasive writer. After reading *At the Crest of the Tidal Wave*, one of my friends was so scared that he couldn't shit for a week. But so what, the market still kept going up.

As I read through the book, I kept thinking, Bob, look, this is crazy. You may be sure you're right, but the market is never wrong. Sandbag the riverbank when you have to, not before. Wall Street doesn't want to see the emperor naked. He may be old and fat and flabby, but they don't want to know it. They want to see him regal and royal in all his majesty. And as long as they see him that way, that's the way he is, because they keep on buying. Big ball keep on rolling.

Bob's the classic example of somebody who's sure he's right and the market's wrong. His theories are brilliant, he's smart enough to win the Nobel Prize in Economics, and I hope he does someday, but the market doesn't care. Bob himself has now publicly conceded that he's been wrong for so long, he's lost confidence in his ability to pick the top, and until he decides that it's easier and more profitable to go with the flow, he'll remain sitting down by the lake, waiting for the tidal wave.

12

Commodities Corp

The market had just closed and I was working furiously to finish posting my charts and calculating my ratios. I was in a hurry. The doorman would be buzzing me any minute to tell me that the big shiny limousine from Commodities Corporation was here to drive me down to Princeton. I knew I wouldn't get home until late that evening, so I had to finish my work now or my trading would be out of sync for tomorrow.

Normally, I didn't go out during the week. To trade successfully, I needed my rest and at least three hours of nightly preparation. But tonight was an exception. Tonight was Commodities Corporation's Semi-Annual Trader's Dinner, one of the few chances the top dogs in trading had to get together, gather around the hydrant, and sniff each other out. My nose was ready and I was eager to lift my leg. It was going to be my first dinner and I was looking forward to finding out what made these great traders tick. And to prove that I was as good, or better, than any of them.

Mmmmmmp, Mmmmmmp, the intercom buzzed. The stretch limo had arrived. I put on the jacket to my new Armani suit, buffed my new Bally alligator shoes, straightened my new Missoni tie, and checked myself out in the mirror. Excellent. I was ready to woof with the top dogs.

An hour and a half later, we were driving through Princeton, New Jersey. Despite the fact that I'd grown up in New Haven, Connecticut, in the shadow of Yale University, this was only my second visit to Princeton. Princeton reminded me of a classical New England town, like Amherst, where I'd gone to school. I couldn't imagine how any place this nice could be in New Jersey.

The autumn light was just fading into a crisp, clear evening as the limo pulled into the circular driveway in front of

Commodities Corp's bucolic headquarters. The red and gold of meticulously manicured trees reflected in the shiny glass and steel facade of Commodities Corp's ultramodern building. I felt a knot form in my stomach as I entered through the big glass doors. I get nervous going to dinners where I don't know a lot of people. I don't like small talk and I usually let Audrey handle the social niceties for both of us. But Audrey wasn't invited tonight. Commodities Corp's Semi-Annual Trader's Dinner was strictly stag, no spouses, please.

Cocktails were being served in the main reception area. I stopped at the door and scanned the room looking for a familiar face. The first person I recognized was Michael Marcus. He was wandering around clutching his bottle of Evian. Marcus, a 1969 Phi Beta Kappa out of Johns Hopkins with a Ph.D. in psychology from Clark, was the first of the egghead academics that Commodities Corp had recruited as traders. That was back in the early seventies when Commodities Corp was just getting started. Over the next eighteen years, Marcus had parlayed his initial $30,000 grubstake into $80 million. All that pressure had taken its toll. Marcus lived quietly in a compound overlooking a private beach in southern California and carried around his own personal bottle of Evian, probably because the Maharishi Mahesh Yogi had convinced him that every water supply east of the Rockies was contaminated. I'd had dinner with him a few months earlier and wondered if he'd gone over the edge, but with traders, you never know. We're all weird in some way.

Bob Easton, the president of Commodities Corp, glided over to greet me. Easton had previously worked with the American Bar Association and was a Princeton grad with an M.B.A. from Columbia and a J.D. from Georgetown. He was not a trader. He was one of those guys who'd be comfortable in any social situation. He was as smooth and polished as the shiny glass and steel facade of Commodities Corp's ultramodern building. Easton fixed me up with Bruce Kovner, one of the market's brightest stars, and slipped off to welcome some other socially challenged trader and make him feel right at home at Commodities Corp.

Like Marcus, Kovner was another academic who had been

recruited by Commodities Corp. This former political science teacher at Harvard and the University of Pennsylvania had shifted his attention from academia to the financial markets back in the midseventies. Kovner believed that his knowledge of economics and political science would give him an edge in analyzing futures markets. He'd been right. In 1987 alone, Kovner had scored profits in excess of $300 million for himself and fortunate investors like Commodities Corp, yet despite his tremendous success as a trader, he was still a professor at heart. He continually stroked his little salt-and-pepper goatee and shifted his rotund frame awkwardly in his rumpled suit while he expounded on arcane economic/political theories.

As Kovner rambled on about how he'd fallen in love with the yield curve and how his study of the markets coincided with the initial trading in interest rate futures, my mind began to wander back to the previous spring. That was when Harry Denny, a broker with Shearson, first persuaded me to talk with Commodities Corp. Commodities Corp paid brokers like Harry Denny fat fees to scout out hot traders for them. Not that I needed any scouting. Thanks to all the publicity I'd received from winning a string of Norm Zadeh's U.S. Trading Championships and a February 15, 1988, article in *Barron's* that labeled me "the best there is," I had a reputation on the Street.

I'd been thinking about the possibility of managing other people's money for some time. Managing other people's money would be good for me because even though I'd been successful ever since I'd started trading on my own, I felt that I'd left a lot of money on the table. I was usually right at picking the market, but my fear of losing my money and the resulting urge to take profits kept me from letting my best trades run. By playing with somebody else's money, I was pretty sure that I'd be more aggressive and ride my winners longer. That's why Harry Denny's timing was perfect. When he told me that Commodities Corp was interested in having me trade for them and that I should meet with them, I was ready.

Coming out of the Roaring '80s, big managed funds were going gangbusters. Mutual funds were exploding; "defined contribution" retirement plans like 401(k)s and IRAs were bringing millions of new investors into the marketplace. All through the early '80s, inflation had been running rampant, so big money was desperate for big returns. New financial instruments were coming onstream all the time, and heavy hitters were always on the lookout for market pros, Champion Traders like me, who knew how to play them.

Commodities Corp had been the brainchild of Helmut Weymar. In 1969, at the age of thirty, Helmut was an MIT computer jock who'd become the manager of commodity economics at Nabisco. Helmut was one of the first to realize that commodity trading was particularly susceptible to analysis using information generated by computers. Until then, most commodity trading had been done by the old-boy networks that controlled the London Metal Exchange (precious metals), the Chicago Board of Trade (grains), and the Chicago Mercantile Exchange (meats and livestock). Most of these guys traded on instinct, not theory. They'd look at things like weather, politics, and economic conditions and then shoot from the hip. They had no way of analyzing the myriad of forces that affected commodity prices and that's why commodities markets were so volatile and difficult to predict.

Helmut Weymar felt that he could use computer modeling to give his traders an edge. His plan was to recruit the most gifted traders he could find, put them in an environment where they'd have all the latest technological support, give them a grubstake, and turn them loose, but rather than turn to the old-boy network, he sought out the new breed of trader, the ones who were on the cutting edge of technology. His plan worked, and by 1988, Commodities Corp was one of the largest traders of commodities in the world.

On April 26, 1988, I drove down to Princeton with Dan Kornstein, my lawyer, to have lunch with Bob Easton, Elaine Crocker, who was in charge of Commodities Corp's kennel of traders, and a couple of other well-dressed, well-mannered Commodities Corp potentates. I could tell right away that these characters weren't players. They were too smooth to be players. They were salesmen, the ones who lured traders like me into Commodities Corp.

They escorted Dan and me into one of their fancy private dining rooms where we were treated to a gourmet lunch of cold cucumber soup, lobster salad, a raspberry torte, and chocolate truffles, all prepared by Commodities Corp's own in-house chef. Commodities Corp was a long way from the floor of the American Stock Exchange where lunch was a corned beef sandwich served from the pocket of my blue smock.

As Dan and I ate lunch, Easton and his sales force took turns telling us what a great place Commodities Corp was and how well it treated its traders. All I wanted to know was how much money they were going to give me and how much I got to keep, so after my third truffle, I said, "Okay, what's the deal?"

"As one of our new traders," Easton said, "we'll give you two hundred and fifty thousand dollars in margin and you keep thirty percent of your profits."

I laughed out loud. "Two hundred and fifty thousand dollars," I said. "Cut the crap. I'm making five to six million dollars a year now trading my own account. I'll tell you what, I'll give you two hundred and fifty thousand dollars and you can trade it for me."

"Marty, Marty, please," Easton said, straightening his Brooks Brothers tie, "Michael Marcus, Bruce Kovner, even Paul Tudor Jones all started small. That's the way we like to do it."

"Good for them," I said. I stood up, took off my jacket, and draped it over the back of my chair. "I'm going to the john to wash my hands and when I come back, I hope you guys will have thought this over and be able to make me a better proposal."

As I walked out of the room, Dan gave me a look that said, "Marty, what are you doing? You're going to blow this deal," but I was a trader and I knew I was right. These guys needed me more than I needed them, and sure enough, when I came back they upped the ante. Commodities Corp was willing to let me manage $10 million of their capital pursuant to certain margin limitations, and I still got to keep 30 percent of my profits.

Before I left, they wanted me to meet with Helmut Weymar, the chairman and founder of Commodities Corp. Helmut and I hit it off immediately. Helmut was a trader. I showed him my methodology, how I did my charts by hand, how I did moving averages, how I had to massage the numbers and see how they felt. Helmut liked that. "Computers are a great tool," he said, "but you've still got to get your hands dirty with data."

It took Dan a couple of months to work out all the details of my contract, and by mid-June I started trading for Commodities Corp, but right away, it didn't feel right. Having that much money forced me to change my style and my time horizon for holding positions. If I was wrong for myself, I'd get right out and take my loss, but with a position of hundreds of contracts, there was a tendency to wait and give the position more time to work itself out. Unfortunately, if I was wrong, the losses would be hundreds of thousands of dollars, or even millions. Then I'd have to start over and make that money back just to get even. Plus, I didn't like the scrutiny. When I lost my own money, I just sucked it up and moved on. When I lost Commodities Corp's money, I felt like the whole world was watching.

I did some small trades for Commodities Corp, ones that fit my style, but by July, I had pretty much quit trading their account. Then one afternoon, I got a call from Helmut. He was at the Denver Airport. He was on his way to the Aspen Institute to get his brain cells recharged and I must have been the last item on his to-do list. "Hey, Marty," he said, "how come you're not trading for us?"

"I tried working with your money, but it requires a different style, a longer time horizon, and I don't feel comfortable with that. I'm more short-term oriented."

"Hell, trade for us the way you trade for yourself," he'd said. "That's why we hired you." Helmut then gave me a big pep talk about how much they wanted me and how they thought I was the best and how we could make a lot of money by working together.

"Okay," I'd said, "I'll give it another try."

Helmut's speech was all I needed. Over the next two months, I made $700,000 for the Commodities Corp account. That made me one of their rising stars, so by the time of Commodities Corp's Semi-Annual Trader's Dinner, I was feeling like a top dog.

Thwop, thwop, thwop. Kovner stopped in the middle of a

sentence about how "in the prevailing phase of the business cycle, interest rate theory predicted that the nearby contract should trade at a higher price than the next contract," and said, "What's that?"

The whole room moved toward the big glass windows of Commodities Corp's ultramodern building. A helicopter was settling onto the lawn, its lights blinking in the twilight. "It's Jones," someone said with reverence. Paul Tudor Jones had arrived. I had to admit, Paul Tudor Jones was a class act. Not only was he a great trader, he was a real showman, a smooth, good-looking southerner who was always running three steps ahead of the pack. Tudor Jones had started trading cotton back in 1980 and had made millions, but at the time of Commodities Corp's Semi-Annual Trader's Dinner, he was best known for the way he'd doubled his money in the crash of '87. Tudor liked fooling with mathematical models that he called analogs and he had a chart pattern in October of 1987 that showed the market was reenacting 1929. Consequently, he was way short on October 19, and when the market crashed, he sold more into the hole to smash it even further. I was never sold on Tudor Jones's modeling, especially since we didn't have a Depression and the economy turned out to be fine, but Tudor Jones's models made a fortune for him, so they worked for him.

When Tudor Jones entered the reception area, it was like Robert Redford had come into the room. Everybody gathered around. He was every bit as polished as Bob Easton and every bit as smart as Helmut Weymar. Of course, he wasn't staying for dinner. He was choppering down to his three-thousand-acre retreat on the Chesapeake Bay and had just dropped in to pay his regards. Tudor Jones didn't have to sniff anybody. He could buy the whole hydrant.

At precisely 7:30, as Tudor Jones's chopper thumped into the night, Easton invited us into the Commodities Corp dining room. I didn't want to sit next to some dweeb, so I grabbed Louis Bacon. Louis shared an office with Harry Denny over at Shearson, but at the time he wasn't a big hitter. If I'd been smart, I would've hired Louis right then and let him manage some of my money, but Louis was a southern boy, like Paul

Tudor Jones, and I didn't understand these southern guys. Despite Tudor Jones's success, I still thought that because they talked slow, they thought slow. Little did I know that over the next five years, Louis would eclipse me nine times to Sunday. If I had hired him then, he would have made me millions.

Easton was tapping his glass. "Helmut and I would like to welcome you to Commodities Corp's Semi-Annual Trader's Dinner," he announced. "Thanks to all your good work, we've had another fantastic year." Easton went on to tell us what a great team we were, how we were dominating the markets, how we were world leaders in forecasting market trends through the use of computerized technical trading systems. "You are the best and the biggest traders in the world," he concluded. "By my calculations, fifty percent of the pooled commodities money in the country is managed by people in this room." That was impressive. I wondered if any other industry could put 50 percent of the players in one room.

Easton sat down and we were treated to another gourmet meal: eggs stuffed with caviar, oysters in garlic butter, venison steaks, herb potatoes Maxim, butternut squash timbales, and chocolate tarragon. Tuxedo-clad attendants kept our glasses filled with fine French wines. When the chocolate tarragon arrived, Easton got up and clinked his glass. "It's a Commodities Corp tradition at these dinners," he said, "that everyone has a chance to speak and to tell us what they think is happening in their particular markets." With that, he started going around the tables asking people what they thought about different commodities: currencies; grains; cocoa; sugar; pork bellies; cattle; gold, silver, and copper; Eurodollars, T-bills, and T-bonds; and stock index futures. It went on and on. Commodities Corp traded 135 different commodities and it looked like we were going to hear about all of them.

Eventually, they got to oil futures and I thought that this discussion would be pretty interesting because the price of oil had been plummeting. It was trading at $12.50 a barrel, the lowest it had ever been since the formation of OPEC, and nobody seemed to know why. There was speculation that the CIA might be putting pressure on the Saudis to flood the market in order to help our balance of payments, or maybe just to needle the Russians, or the Iranians, or the Iraqis, or all of them; who knew?

To talk about oil, Easton called on some porky cowboy from Texas. To me, the guy looked like Billy Tex Bunghole. He was wearing boots and a spangly silk shirt that was open halfway down the front. A big gold chain hung around his neck and attached to it was a gold medallion that dangled on his furry chest. His porky face was beet red and he was sweating. "Seems lak to me," he drawled, "over the nex six months, the prass of West Texas crewed is headin' down anotha six dollars a barrel. Ah mean to tell you boys, those wells are pumpin' lak a two-dollar hooker on a Sahdy naht. We've got awl comin out our ass. In six months, we ain gonna be able to give it away."

"Thank you, Tex," Bob said. "Now let's hear what's happening in the European market." He called on a dapper little Frenchman. This guy was thin and effete, and wearing a tailored blue serge suit, custom-made shirt, and Hermès tie. "In zee next five years," Pierre Le Flit crooned, "zee supply of oil will far outstrip zee demand in l'Europe."

When Pierre finished, Helmut Weymar caught me by surprise. "We're fortunate to have Marty Schwartz with us tonight," he said. "Marty's a new trader with Commodities Corp, one who's doing very well for us. Marty, what do you think about what you just heard?"

I puffed out my chest a little. I didn't trade crude oil much, but I decided that this would be a good chance for me to shake things up a bit. I was the new dog at the hydrant and it was time to lift my leg. "Helmut," I said, "I appreciate your asking me down here tonight, but I'm something of a heretic. I don't know what the supply and demand of oil's going to be in Europe in the next five years and I don't know what the price of West Texas crude's going to be in six months and, frankly, I don't care. I'm a mark-to-market trader, all I want to know is what the price is going to be tomorrow, and I've got to tell you, when I posted my charts, checked my stochastics, and calculated my ratios just before I left the office today, oil was above my moving averages. As far as I'm concerned, oil's in a positive mode."

The Commodities Corp's Semi-Annual Trader's Dinner wasn't over until after eleven, and by the time I got home, I was too tired to go over my charts. The next day, I was paying for it. I was constantly on the wrong side of the market; I was tired and way out of sync. At midmorning, the phone rang. It was Harry Denny from Shearson. "Marty," he said, "have you seen the price of oil? It's going crazy." I punched oil up on my screens. The Dec 88's were at $13 a barrel and climbing. Tick, $13.10. Tick, $13.15.

"Fuckin' unbelievable," I said. "We talked about oil at the Commodities Corp dinner last night. I said it was going up, but I was just yanking their chains."

I forgot about oil and went back to my own trades. I was down a bundle on S&P futures. The next day, Harry called me again. "Marty," he said, "you watching oil? Sheik Yamani must have ordered OPEC to turn off the spigots or something. It's heading straight up." I punched oil up on my screens again. Tick, $14.30. Tick, $14.35.

When oil hit $15 the following day, it finally dawned on me what was happening. It wasn't Sheik Yamani who'd driven the price up 20 percent in three days. It was Sheik Schwartz, the kid from New Haven, who'd done it. What I should have realized was that if 50 percent of the pooled commodities money in the country was sitting in the same room at the same time, a lot of it was in oil, and most of it was short. When Sheik Schwartz said that his charts showed oil was in a positive mode, it was like yelling "fire" in a crowded room. Now these guys were frantically trying to cover their positions. I felt like kicking myself. What had the smooth-talking Paul Tudor Jones, the politically astute Bruce Kovner, and the Evian-clutching Michael Marcus done with this information? I was sure that it hadn't taken them three days to figure it out. They probably had lifted their legs and gone long and strong on oil, and made millions. That's what a top dog would've done. That's what I should've done. Woof, woof.

How I Read the
Wall Street Journal

Published since 1889 by Dow Jones & Company, the *Wall Street Journal* is the standard-bearer for financial publications. Anyone playing the market has to follow the *Journal* every day.

I'm a scanner, not a reader. As a kid, I used to get up on Sunday morning and beat my brother, Gerry, to the *New York Times* sports section. I'd look at it for twenty minutes and then give it to Gerry, and he'd quiz me on things like scores, batting averages, who were the probable starting pitchers that day, and he could never stump me. If you're going to be a successful trader, that's how you have to read the *Journal*. There's so much information, you have to train your mind to scan it.

I usually go through the *Journal* right after I've reconciled all of my accounts in the morning, just before the bonds start trading at 8:20. The first thing I do is run through to the second column on the front page, "What's News," Evelyn Woods style. I keep a steno pad and a pen next to me and I make a note of anything interesting.

Everything is written down and filed for future reference. In the marines, a good, responsible officer keeps copious records.

Then I glance over at the far right-hand column for the lead story. I was the sports editor of my high school and college newspapers and I instinctively check out all of the lead stories, but I read very few articles. I don't have the time. What I'm trying to get from the front page is a general feel for the markets.

Next I go to section C, "Money & Investing." That's where the data is. I look at "Abreast of the Market," a summary of the prior day's events in the stock market as reported through the eyes of various brokers, analysts, money managers, and other Wall Street professionals. I check to see if any of the seventy or so stocks I'm following are mentioned and, if so, what other people have to say about them. Then I go to "Heard on the Street," which typically profiles an industry, a company, or an individual, and often contains some juicy tidbits. Hopefully this is some of the same stuff I've gotten two or three days earlier from Inside Skinny, my main source for rumors.

After verifying that Skinny still has his ear to the Street, I check the index and flip to the "Listed Options Quotations" to get a feel for the put-call ratios. I want to see what the ratios were on the previous day because that gives me a running indicator. When the put-call ratio runs close to 100 percent for two or three days, that's a buy indicator. When it's below 50 percent, the optimism is too great and I start thinking sell. I write the ratios down on my steno pad. Everything is written.

One other indicator in section C that I like to look at is the "NYSE Highs/Lows." This table lists all of the stocks that hit new twelve-month highs or lows on the previous day. When I was at Edwards and Hanly in 1974, John Brooks, a technician there, taught me a very simple but interesting indicator. The new highs and lows are always listed alphabetically in four columns in the same size print. John told me, "Marty, whenever you can lay a ruler on the new highs or the new lows and they exceed twelve inches, prepare yourself to become a contrarian and go the other way." In 1974, when the lows exceeded twelve inches on several days, it was one of the greatest buying opportunities of the century. In October 1987, just before Black Monday, the new highs exceeded twelve inches several times. What a great time to sell. This is a trick that I've never seen written or heard talked about anywhere and it very seldom happens, but when it does, pull out your ruler.

Once I've checked the "NYSE Highs/Lows," I go to the bond column and scan that to see who is forecasting what for interest rates. Now I'm through with section C and I throw it on the floor to my left. Then I go back to section A and skim through it, looking to see the interpretations of recent economic news and individual corporate events or results, and discard it on the floor to my right.

Sometimes I flip quickly through section B, "Marketplace," where there are some smaller articles on companies I might be interested in. But there is rarely anything in section B to interest a trader.

It takes me less than ten minutes to read the *Journal,* but ten minutes with the *Journal* first thing in the morning gives me my initial feel for what's going on in the markets and a couple of quick and easy indicators that I can throw into my mix. With all the other information I have flowing into me, I can't spend any more time than that reading the *Journal,* but any serious trader wouldn't want to spend any less.

13

Sabrina Partners

Elders Futures Inc., a futures brokerage firm, had started court-
ing me several months before Commodities Corp's Semi-Annual
Trader's Dinner. Elders wanted me to manage a $20 million
fund and was offering me a 6 percent guaranteed management
fee plus a performance fee of 20 percent of the profits. That was
$100,000 a month guaranteed plus whatever I could make on
the performance fees, all risk-free. This deal was a lot sweeter
than Commodities Corp's, so in the last quarter of 1988, I
stopped trading for Commodities Corp and started trading for
Elders. But still, trading for somebody else didn't feel right.

It was the same problem I'd had with Commodities Corp.
Handling larger positions changed my time horizons. I had a
tendency to hold losers longer, hoping that more time would
give them a chance to work themselves out. I talked to Audrey
about it.

"Audrey, I just don't like trading for these people. Having to
check in every two hours cramps my style. It might be a sweet
deal, but I want my freedom."

Nobody was telling me what to do, Audrey would say. I
could make any trade I wanted. I had my freedom. What was
the problem?

"I don't like all these people looking over my shoulder.
Elders has a lot of foreign money that comes in and leaves every
month. When money's pulled out, it's replaced by other Elders
funds, but every time that happens, I feel rejected. I feel like I
haven't done the job."

Audrey would tell me I was crazy to take it personally. It was
one of my own rules, she'd remind me. I had to divorce my ego
from the game.

"But they keep calling me all the time. This is supposed to
be a one-year commitment, but I have to check in practically

every day. I don't like anybody second-guessing me. It's the freedom of knowing that I'm my own boss. That's why I went out
on my own to begin with."

I was still my own boss, Audrey would say. Nobody was stopping me from making trades on my own account, and I didn't
have to report those trades to anybody (except the IRS).

"But I don't feel comfortable with that. I'm conflicted. I'm
always having to decide, Is this trade for me, or for the fund?
Other fund managers can do that. I can't. When I trade for
myself, it's short term. When I trade for the fund, it's longer
term. If I make money for myself short term but then a position
goes bad for the fund, it doesn't feel right."

Well, why do you need a fund? Audrey would say. You're
making millions on your own. Forget the fund.

"But I want to make tens of millions. I want to be the
biggest and the best. And to do that, I need OPM, other people's
money."

Hey, Audrey would say, start your own fund, make your own
rules, put your own money into it, and be your own boss. You
control the lockup period and report once a month, which is all
the regulators say you have to do. No conflicts. No checking in.
No problems.

So, early in 1989, I stopped trading for Elders. I told my
lawyer, John Tavss of Seward & Kissel, who specialized in setting up hedge funds, to start drawing up the papers for my own
fund. By June, John had the papers ready to go, but I still wasn't
sure. I'd think about how I'd never had a losing year since I'd
started trading on the American Exchange back in 1979, how I'd
put together a run of fifty-five consecutive months without a
loss for my own account, how I worked out of an office right in
my home, how I had the one thing I always dreamed of, my
complete freedom. Why did I need to manage other people's
money? Then I'd remember how I'd felt strutting around
Commodities Corp's Semi-Annual Trader's Dinner with the likes
of Michael Marcus and Bruce Kovner and watching Paul Tudor
Jones leave for his retreat on the Eastern Shore in his own private chopper. I liked sniffing around with the top dogs. To do
that, I needed OPM, other people's money.

When the kids got out of school in June, we took a vacation to Aspen. I'd never been to Aspen, but Aspen was where Helmut Weymar and a lot of other big shots went to get their brains recharged, so why not me? The crisp, clear mountain air two thousand miles away from New York City and the markets would give me a chance to reflect. I'd spent nine and a half years as a securities analyst, then nine more trading with success beyond my wildest dreams. Now I had to decide whether to raise the bar another notch.

Every morning I'd step out of the three-bedroom condo right at the base of Snowmass, hop into my Jeep Wrangler, put the canvas top down, breathe in the cool mountain air, and drive like a cowboy into Aspen for the *Wall Street Journal*. I'd pass the airport and see the Cessnas, Lears, and Gulfstreams that belonged to the movie stars, international jet-setters, and big-time executives. I wanted to be one of them. To do that, I needed OPM, other people's money.

The first thing I did when we got back to New York was rent the biggest, fanciest office I could find. It was at the top of a brand-new building at 750 Lexington Avenue and had an unobstructed view of Central Park. It wasn't cheap, but so what? I signed a three-year lease for three thousand square feet at $12,500 a month, $150,000 a year, but so what? That was a pittance compared to what I was going to make. I turned Audrey loose on the furniture. She selected a post-Impressionistic motif with an accent on cubism and overtones of nouveau-baroque that rang the register up to the tune of $75,000, but so what? We had to look good, and I'd always pictured myself sitting in my own fancy offices with my feet propped up on the partner's desk.

My friends Al and Cliff, the owners of the Fresco-Palette Gallery on the Upper East Side, lent me a collection of modern art. Walking into my new offices was going to be like walking into the Guggenheim. I dropped another $30,000 on the latest computers and a new telephone system, but so what? It had to be state of the art. Then I went out and hired my first two employees. I paid them each $20,000 per month. That was a lot, but so what? Working with me would quickly turn them into stars. By the end of the summer, I was feeling and looking like a top dog. Now I needed to dig up some investors with really big bones to pay for it.

Actually, I needed two sets of investors, one for my domestic fund and one for my offshore fund. The big shots had two funds, and I wanted to be big. Two funds meant twice as much money.

Back in the sixties, while I was still in business school, a hedge fund was a limited partnership where the general partner was the fund manager and the limited partners were so-called sophisticated investors who had at least $1 million in net worth. Under U.S. law, there could be no more than ninety-nine limited partners with a typical minimum investment of $500,000, and the funds were invested mostly in U.S. stocks.

By the end of the eighties, that had all changed. Comparing the original hedge funds of the sixties to the hedge funds of the nineties was like comparing John Wooden to Michael Jordan. Managers like George Soros, Julian Robertson, and Michael Steinhardt had raised so many billions that they couldn't find enough good U.S. stocks, so they'd shifted the focus of their funds to larger global markets where they could make bigger plays and get more leverage. They set up offshore funds that weren't regulated by SEC laws and began speculating in currencies and interest rates worldwide. They'd play the dollar against the yen, or the U.S. Treasury against the Bundesbank.

To compete for these really big investors, the ones with the really big bones, I had to set up two funds, Sabrina Partners L.P., a domestic fund, and Sabrina Offshore Fund Ltd. I set the minimum investment for each of the funds at $1 million with the stipulation that the money couldn't be taken out for a year. I thought that that would give me the freedom to trade without worrying about people looking over my shoulder.

Because I was the Champion Trader, I charged a 4 percent fixed management fee, plus the usual 20 percent of profits. Because investors were investing in me, it was important for me to sell my trading style and methodology. In my prospectus, I stressed that, unlike most money managers, I was a triple threat. I traded stocks, options, and futures, and I had a track record of consistently making money in all three. In any one period, I might not make as much as any given trader in any given market, but over time, I'd beat them all. I was the Champion Trader. John Liscio had said so in *Barron's*, and Jack D. Schwager had said so in *Market Wizards*.

Raising money for Sabrina Partners L.P., the domestic fund, was something I could do. I took packs of five-by-eight cards, just as I had done for my honors thesis at Amherst, but this time, instead of theories from John Maynard Keynes and Adam Smith, I marked down the name and number of everybody I knew who had a million dollars. I called them. I wrote them. I met them for drinks. I sent them a prospectus. I sent them clippings about me, the Champion of Wall Street and the Champion Trader. I sent them copies of Liscio's article. I sent them copies of Schwager's book. I called them back. I wrote them again. I supported their favorite charities. I mailed them another prospectus. I sent them more clippings. I implored them to drop by and see me at my new offices, the ones at the top of the brand-new building at 750 Lexington Avenue with the unobstructed view of Central Park. When they showed up, I plopped them into Audrey's post-Impressionistic furniture with an accent on cubism and overtones of nouveau-baroque, and waxed eloquent about Al Fresco's and Cliff Palette's collection of modern art. By October, I'd raised $22 million for Sabrina Partners L.P. (having coughed up $5 million of my own as general partner).

Finding investors for Sabrina Offshore Fund Ltd. was something I couldn't do on my own. I'd been to Europe a few times, but I didn't know any of the international jet-setters. Typically, the way U.S. money managers found international investors was to align themselves with brokers who had international contacts and could make the proper introductions. The problem with that approach was that some brokers were looking for huge fees, but I decided to test the waters anyway. A guy from Dean Witter was the first to call. He claimed that he had some "great" international contacts, but he wanted 25 percent of whatever I made from his contacts. I wasn't about to give him or any other parasite 25 percent of my profits, so I put the word out that the best I was willing to do was to trade contacts for commissions. You send me clients, I'll send you commissions, that was the deal.

Two brokers took it. Paul Saunders and Kevin Brant, with Kidder, Peabody, got in touch. They were in the money-raising business. They had a colleague named Rakesh Bhargava who was Indian and had a lot of big money connections to India and Pakistan. I'd always thought that India and Pakistan were bitter enemies, but apparently when it comes to making money, so what? Kevin and Paul offered to have Rakesh set up some meetings in London during the middle of October. That would be fine, I said, so Kevin and Paul scheduled a meeting in London.

I was looking forward to this trip. I loved London. I remembered being there during the summer of '67 and fantasizing about going to the London School of Economics and getting a master's degree in economics. I remembered taking the tubes through Knightsbridge from a fourth-floor walk-up I was renting out by Old Cromwell Road. I used to walk by the betting parlors, wondering if someday I'd ever make a betting coup. I'd taken the train to Epsom to watch the ponies. I loved it, even though they ran in the wrong direction. I'd taken a double-decker bus to Harrod's and wondered whether I'd be back to do some serious shopping. I'd passed the Ritz, the Connaught, and the Berkeley (which they pronounced "Barkly," probably because of all the top dogs who stayed there). I'd passed Claridge's, the most splendid hotel in all of England, dreaming that someday I'd be staying there, that I'd step out of a Rolls, and a doorman in his bright red doublet with shiny brass buttons, his big black top hat, and his spotless white gloves would bustle over and open the door for me. Claridge's was where I wanted to be this trip, so I called my dear friends Al and Cliff. Because of their connections in the world of international art, they were welcome at Claridge's and all the other finest hotels, and they got me a room.

On Friday morning, October 13, I liquidated all my positions and was just sitting watching the screen waiting for the driver to come and take me to the airport when I saw the market go into free fall. There had been a proposed leveraged buyout of United Airlines for a very high price of $300 per share, but the financing had disappeared and the deal had fallen apart. It was the tail end of the Drexel Burnham junk bond era and everything was unraveling. The market was telling us that it was time to start paying for all those extraordinary excesses of the eighties. I felt right away that the collapse of this deal was a signal, that this was going to be one of those four or five times a decade when a trader has a chance to make some really big money. And here I was, in perfect shape to act on it. All my positions were cleaned out and I was sitting on a pile of cash. I called Paul and Kevin. "Cancel the trip," I said. "I'm not going anywhere in this market."

They understood completely. Personal upheavals like death, marriage, or sickness are unacceptable excuses for a trader to miss a meeting, but canceling to make money is eminently acceptable. They called Rakesh and told him to reschedule the meeting for the following week. Rakesh said, no problem. If anything, canceling the meeting to trade into a favorable market only enhanced my reputation. I was the guy with the Midas Touch, I was the Champion of Wall Street, the Champion Trader.

I watched the market plummet all day and by late afternoon the Dow was down 190 points. All everybody was thinking was, Here we go again. It's going to be another crash of '87. Perfect. I knew exactly what to do. During the crash of '87 investors ran up the price of bond futures figuring that since the bubble had burst in stocks, people were going to move money out of stocks into fixed income securities. The bond futures market closed at 3:00, so at 2:58, I loaded up. The stock market was open until 4:00, and as stocks continued to plunge, bond futures skyrocketed. I quickly dumped my entire position in the secondary bond futures market that stayed open until 4:15. I'd made $70,000. Not a bad day, but I was sure that the best was yet to come. I didn't think this market was like the one in 1987. Interest rates were much lower, the P/E ratios on stocks were much lower. I was thinking of going long.

Right after the markets closed, I got a call from John Liscio. Every now and then, John would call me for my opinion on the market. I told John that I was bullish, that I was going long. On Monday the sixteenth, the following squib appeared in *Barron's:*

> When we first caught up with legendary trader Marty Schwartz after Friday's close, he didn't know what to make of the 190 point stock market rout. "What really started bothering me," he related, "was that everybody had profits. Historically, when the market is up more than 30% within a year, it's very dangerous." But Schwartz, one of the wealthier and more honest traders we know, had the sound of a man who sold out his entire position the day before. "I really don't think it's all that bad," he asserted. "Rates are much lower than they were in '87 and multiples are dramatically lower. Maybe stocks won't even open down 60 or 70 points on Monday like the futures are indicating. My inclination here is to study my chart book and get ready to go long."

Having John Liscio was like having my own publicist, but when you go high profile, you better be right. Fortunately, on this occasion, I was. First thing Monday morning, I jumped into the stocks that I wanted, like Philip Morris, Fannie Mae, and Freddie Mac, ones that had held up well in Friday's fall and were poised to take off when the market turned around.

Based on the crash of '87, I expected the market to open down but when it turned and closed up eighty-eight, I was really off and running. I rode the position through Tuesday noon, then I reversed my field and went short S&P futures. With everyone buying, it was time to sell, and I was right again. I covered my positions on Wednesday. By postponing my trip for a week, I'd made $500,000.

John Liscio called me again just as I was running out the door to the airport. He wanted to know how I was doing. I told him that I'd gone three for three, that I'd hit the bonds, the stocks, and the S&P futures, but I had to quit because I was leaving for Europe to raise money for my new offshore hedge fund. As I settled back in my leather seat and felt the Concorde lift off for London, I started focusing on how I was going to persuade international investors to put their money into my fund.

The breakfast meeting at Claridge's couldn't have gone better. In addition to Rakesh Bhargava, Paul Saunders, Kevin Brant, and me, there was the Sheik, a big real estate developer and international entrepreneur whose father had been the mayor of Hyderabad, or Rawalpindi, or Faisalabad, or some other damn place (which supposedly didn't hurt the Sheik's cash flow); the Rug Man, who to this day remains a mystery to me; Omar Khayyam, the head of the London branch of a major Middle Eastern bank; and Stirling Sixpence, the former chairman of a British holding company well known in the States for engineering hostile takeovers. How they were connected was beyond me, but I did know that all of them would do business with the devil himself if they thought that it would make them more money. That was how international commerce worked.

I liked Sixpence right away. The others were playing with family money, but I got the feeling that he, like me, was a street kid who'd made it on his own. Plus, among his many acquisitions, he'd picked up a professional soccer team. In the summer of '67, I'd seen them play. Back then I was sitting in the cheap seats eating greasy fish and chips. Now, here I was, twenty-two years later, sitting at Claridge's having shirred eggs and smoked salmon with the owner.

When Rakesh Bhargava was through introducing his clients, Paul Saunders introduced me. "If any of you have read *Market Wizards*," Paul said holding up a copy of the book, "then you know about Marty Schwartz, but in case you missed *Market Wizards*, here's an article in this week's *Barron's* you might find interesting."

With that he reached under the table and pulled out a half dozen copies of the October 23 *Barron's*. The headline said "Upward to New Peaks or Watch Out Below." Below it in big bold letters were the names of five great traders whom *Barron's* had interviewed about the volatility in the market. Paul Tudor Jones was at the top. I was at the bottom. Everyone started reading. My picture was on page 15 next to the headline "Two Up and One Down: How Three Super Traders Fared on Friday the 13th." The article went on to describe how I'd made a half million that week and hated to quit, but I had to fly to Europe to raise money for my new offshore hedge fund. It ended with a quote, "I'm going to Europe, but the market gave me a kiss and that's good enough for now."

"Well, here he is," Paul said, "Marty Schwartz."

This was heady stuff. Here I was out trying to raise money by selling my favorite commodity, me, Marty Schwartz, the Champion of Wall Street and Champion Trader, and *Barron's* had just given me their seal of approval. I felt like Donald Trump. When you listen to Donald Trump talk, he always sounds so assured. He's probably full of it, but he's out there selling his best product, himself. Even though only his therapist knows the truth, Donald Trump sounds like he believes in himself more than anything else on the face of the earth.

That's how I felt as I described the financial empire I was going to build. My fund was going to be the biggest and the best, and everyone at the table could feel it. Thanks to the *Barron's* article, I was a celebrity, like Donald Trump. The Sheik, the Rug Man, Khayyam, and Sixpence were people whose only common denominator was making money, and by latching onto me they were getting a piece of somebody who could help them do it.

When the meeting was over, Rakesh Bhargava took me aside, "Marty, do you have any plans for this evening?" he asked. I didn't. Paul Saunders and Kevin Brant were leaving for Europe, but I didn't have to meet them in Geneva until the following week. I was just going to hang around, like when I was a securities analyst back in the seventies. "I have been invited to a party," Rakesh said. "Omar Khayyam's daughter is marrying the Sheik's son, and, as is our custom, the groom's father hosts the parties for the week before the wedding. I have talked to the Sheik and he would be honored if you would join us."

"I'd like that," I said and I really meant it. This party would be my entrée to a whole different world, one based on more money than I'd ever seen before, even in Aspen.

Fine, Rakesh said. "Kamran Khayyam, Omar Khayyam's son and the brother of the bride, will call for you at seven. You will meet some very interesting people. I think you will enjoy it."

Driving up to the Sheik's country home was like driving into a fairy tale. It lay nestled in the rolling fields about twenty miles outside of London. On the way out, I learned that Kamran managed a branch of his father's bank. We pulled into the courtyard behind Stirling Sixpence and his big canary yellow Bentley. It was gorgeous and must have cost a couple of hundred thousand dollars, but all the cars in the Sheik's courtyard were gorgeous and cost hundreds of thousands of dollars. The Sheik was standing by the main entrance greeting his guests. He was a most gracious host. He personally walked me around introducing me to his family and friends. "Marty, this is my brother, a world bridge champion." "Marty, this is the Chief. He controls most of the oil in Nigeria." The Chief's skin was as black as coal, and he had tribal marks all over his face.

The Sheik continued to show me around the house. He told me that the house was more than 350 years old and had been built by King Charles I as a hideaway where he could take his mistresses. For me, this was ironic because the three main streets in New Haven bear the names of three judges who fled to the New World in the seventeenth century after a failed coup during which they sentenced Charles II to die by hanging. These three judges were Dixwell, Whalley, and Goffe, and they'd all probably been in this very house.

He took me to a dining room. There a large mahogany table was ringed by twelve massive silver chairs sculpted in the style of George III. "Here, come try one of these chairs," the Sheik said. I went to pull a chair out, but could hardly move it. "Solid silver. They each weigh eighty pounds."

We moved on to a sitting room. "Marty," the Sheik said, taking the arm of a strikingly beautiful woman. "I would like you to meet Benazir Bhutto, a dear friend of our family." This was not the woman I'd seen on TV, her body covered in drab black tentlike garb, her thin ascetic face devoid of makeup, her straight black hair pulled back under a black scarf. Her sleek figure was clothed in a luxurious gold and silver satin gown. A gold chain hung over one shapely shoulder and attached to it was a quilted black Chanel pocketbook. Chanel beads, Chanel shoes, and Chanel fragrance all adorned Benazir—Coco in her most opulent hour had never worn as many accoutrements as Benazir Bhutto. This woman had money radiating out of every aperture.

"Marty was just on the front page of *Barron's*," said the Sheik proudly. Benazir Bhutto nodded approvingly. I couldn't believe it. Here I was, the kid from New Haven, a celebrity in the house of celebrities.

I walked through the gardens onto the lawn where two big tents had been set up. Cocktails were served in one tent, dinner in the other. There were foods from a hundred different nations: Beluga caviars, pâtés de foie gras, oysters, prawns, roast suckling pigs, spring lambs, countless kabobs and cheeses, opulence, excess, and greed abounding. I couldn't wait to get a taste of it. Jugglers juggled, belly dancers jiggled, sword swallowers gorged, and fire breathers flared. Entertainment beyond entertainment. Food beyond food. I had never seen anything like it.

It was two in the morning when Kamran Khayyam finally dropped me off at Claridge's, but I couldn't sleep. I didn't need to sleep, my dreams had come true. I'd been worried about my offshore fund, but now I was a star, the man with the Midas Touch, the cover boy of *Barron's*, a celebrity in the house of celebrities. I wasn't going to have any trouble funding Sabrina Offshore Fund Ltd. People had been thrusting business cards at me all night. They knew I could make them even richer than they already were.

The rest of the trip was almost as good. Geneva, Zurich, Paris, everywhere I went, there I was, my name on the front page of *Barron's*. When I disembarked from the Concorde at JFK, I couldn't wait to get back to my new fancy office and start sorting and cataloging the bundles of cards that were bulging from every pocket of every suit.

After a couple of weeks, the bank wires started humming in, but there were no names, just numbers. There was nothing to match with my newly cataloged collection of business cards from all my new international jet-setter friends. The wires were from banks in places like Bermuda, the Bahamas, Guernsey, the Isle of Man, and the Cayman Islands. We were getting a half million, a million, two million a day, and we didn't have a clue who was sending any of it. We called the banks in Bermuda, the Bahamas, Guernsey, the Isle of Man, and the Cayman Islands, but nobody would give us any names. They said they didn't know any, all they had were numbers, so that's what Sabrina Offshore Fund Ltd. became, a $20 million fund of numbers with no names. For all I knew, my investors could have been Noriega, Gadhafi, Idi Amin, or, God forbid, somebody worse, if possible. I was told not to worry, I didn't have to know whose money it was. All I had to do was make more and everything would be fine and everyone would be happy.

14

How's My Money Doing?

I lay down on my bed, set the alarm on my night table for 7:00 P.M., closed my eyes, and drifted into a fitful sleep. It was 6:30 on Monday evening, October 29, 1990, and I'd just gotten home from the office at 750 Lexington Avenue. It had been a grueling month and I was trying to catch a nap before I left for a client's dinner at Lutèce, the *most* chic restaurant in all of New York. I'd asked the investors in Sabrina Partners L.P. and Sabrina Offshore Fund Ltd. to let me know during November whether or not they were going to keep their money with me for another year. So all through October, in addition to my regular work, I'd been meeting with clients telling them what a super job I was doing for them. If you're running a fund, you can't afford to lose any of your investors. At this level, they're a small crew, and when somebody jumps ship, others head for the rail.

I was outperforming the stock market with an 18 percent gross return, but during my meetings it was becoming obvious that I was up against three problems. The first was my fees. I'd come out of Jack Schwager's book as a *Market Wizard*, one of the top dogs, and I'd figured that if I was going to go through the hassle of managing other people's money, I wanted to get paid the big bones. I was going to charge the same fees that Paul Tudor Jones, Bruce Kovner, and Louis Bacon were charging. The problem was, Jones, Kovner, and Bacon were running pure futures funds, and I wasn't.

Sabrina Partners L.P. and Sabrina Offshore Fund Ltd. were set up to trade 25 percent in futures and 75 percent in stocks, so they weren't futures funds, they were equity funds. Most equity fund managers charged "1 and 20," a 1 percent annual management fee on the invested capital and 20 percent of the profits. Only the really top dogs, the guys who were running pure futures funds, had the *cojones* to charge "4 and 20," but that's what I was charging. That meant that on a return of 18 percent, I was getting 6.8 percent, more than one-third of the action: 4 percent off the top plus another 2.8 percent of the profits (20 percent of the remaining 14 percent), and a lot of my investors were starting to figure out that that wasn't such a good deal.

My second problem was the market. It had been behaving erratically all year and I'd had trouble identifying any trends. When I started trading for the funds in November 1989, the market was whipsawing above and below my moving averages, so I took what I thought would be a conservative approach and set up several positions in proposed or rumored takeover deals, hoping for a consistent rate of return to underpin my S&P futures trading. I bought some Lin Broadcasting and Georgia Gulf, but with every rumor, the spreads would widen, and concerns about financing would create havoc with my short-term profitability. As a part commodity fund, I was required by the futures regulators to report to my investors every month, and this produced short-term pressures. I thought that these arbitrage positions would provide a favorable rate of return in a nontrending market. I was wrong. They didn't pan out and after only five weeks, I was down 6 percent, or $2.4 million, of the $40 million that I'd raised.

I'd never lost that much money before, and my confidence was slipping away with my money. I started cutting back my positions, protecting my capital, and taking my profits when I could. It worked. By the end of March, the funds were up 7.6 percent while my measuring stick, the New York Composite Index, was down 4.2 percent. Beating the index by 11.8 percentage points in a three-month period was a differential that any reasonable investor would have to consider extraordinary. And many investors did, which led to my third problem.

One of my main concerns when I started trading for the funds was whether I could manage $40 million of other people's money as effectively as I'd been trading $10 million of my own. In two previous experiences, I'd found that handling larger positions had changed my time horizons. I tended to hold my positions longer, which cramped my style of taking profits quickly, but my results for the first quarter of 1990 had convinced me that I could manage large sums of money. So on April 1, I'd raised the bar another notch. I opened the funds up to new capital, and an additional $30 million poured in.

Most managers with $70 million would diversify, look for niche investments, spread the risk, and let their young Turks do all the grunt work while they took a broad overview and planned the grand strategy. But that wasn't my style. I'd always been a control freak and I didn't have any young Turks. I'd gotten rid of the two old Turks I'd hired earlier and was doing all the trading myself. I kept playing my defensive game and posted another 1.5 percent gain in April, but in May and June, the market ran away from me. I completely missed a major rally, and right away, the pressures began to build. All through the rally investors kept calling me, asking, "How's my money doing?"

When you've cut yourself in for more than a third of the action, investors only want to hear one answer, "Fuckin' A Fantastic!" but I couldn't say that. At the beginning of each month, I'd send a letter to my investors telling them how we were doing and the best I could say in June was:

> As the largest investor in the funds, I personally feel far more comfortable trying to be profitable every month as opposed to taking large risks "trying to hit a home run." My investment record has been based on consistent profitability allowing the power of compound growth to work its mastery.

That appeased nobody. They kept calling, faxing, and writing, whining about their returns and comparing me with managers whose results were better, a lot better. The middlemen representing the foreign money were the worst. They'd call two or three times a day while I was trading and say, "Martay, Martay, how's my monay doing?" I couldn't believe these bozos. They were locked in for a year, so what difference did it make how they were doing every day? Didn't they know that I had double-digit profits for ten consecutive years in all kinds of markets, that I was the Champion Trader?

In July, I tried to buttress my June letter by reminding them that they were in for the long haul and attaching a two-page excerpt from Richard Russell's *Dow Theory Letters*. This excerpt showed how the effects of compounding were the best way to accumulate great wealth and for the really smart investor, slow and steady was the name of the game. I ended my July letter by once again staying on the defensive:

> When I set this fund up I knew there would be periods when I would outperform others and then times when I would underperform—that was the reasoning behind requiring a minimum one-year investment period and that is what I believe I should be judged on. As the year draws on, all of you will decide whether or not to continue your investment or increase it as a number of you already have done. All I ask is that you judge the results at the end of the appropriate period and compare them both on an absolute and relative basis to other managers and the opportunities that were available.

What I didn't tell my investors was that I was getting ready to go on the offensive. I was going for the long ball.

Audrey had decided to renovate our co-op on Park Avenue over the summer. When the kids got out of school, we packed up and moved out to the summerhouse in the Hamptons. I played tennis out there with an oily operator who ran another hedge fund. One day he said to me, "So, Motty, whaddya hear about Upjohn?"

"Upjohn?" I said, like I knew something. "Why? What do you hear?"

"I hear that a Swiss company is about to take 'em over. I'm buying."

I called Inside Skinny. Skinny had his ear glued to the Street and if anybody was going after Upjohn, the big pharmaceutical company out in Michigan, Skinny'd know about it.

"Motty," Skinny whispered into the phone, "I was just about to call ya. My Swiss contacts just told me it's a done deal and, ya know, there's a lot of European buying. It's got the smell of the old days, takeover, redux revisited." Skinny had a way with words, and that was all I needed to hear. If I were going for the long ball, Upjohn had to be it. I started to load up on Upjohn. I've always been a glutton for gadgets, and I had finally succumbed to a cellular phone, a big awkward thing that looked like a car battery. I'd sit by the court watching Audrey play team tennis and yell into the phone, "Buy me another ten thousand. Buy me another ten thousand." All through July, Upjohn kept inching up and I kept buying. I'd be at the beach on a Friday afternoon watching the kids build castles in the sand, yelling into my car battery, "Buy me thirty thousand on the bell! Get it!" I was getting longer and longer. I was burying myself in Upjohn. By the beginning of August, I was halfway to China and still digging. I had more than $40 million, over half the funds' money, invested in almost a million shares.

On August 2, Saddam Hussein invaded Kuwait, the market headed south, and oil futures headed north. Upjohn went into the john as the market plunged a quick 10 percent. I started hedging my position by shorting the S&P futures, but it took me another week of getting killed before I realized that the Beta on Upjohn, the correlation of the individual stock's moves with the action of the overall market, was about double the S&P. This basically meant that for every 1 percent the market moved, Upjohn was moving 2 percent. In this case, 2 percent down. I was shorting $40 million in futures, but that wasn't nearly enough; it should have been $80 million.

On a Monday morning in the middle of August, I was short four hundred S&P contracts and the market opened way down. I made $1.8 million in five minutes, but Upjohn dropped another 1⅞ and the funds ended up just breaking even for the day. Meanwhile, thanks to Saddam Hussein, crude oil and lots of other commodities were going crazy and the futures guys like Jones, Kovner, and Bacon, who weren't buried under a million shares of Upjohn, were making fortunes by going long. Because of *Market Wizards*, I had a reputation as a futures player, but I didn't trade many pure commodities. My real expertise was in the S&Ps, which was really the stock market, which was getting hammered. While the top dogs were going long commodities

futures, playing the potential inflation bubble and making millions, I was going short S&P futures to hedge my million shares
of Upjohn and just breaking even.

In mid-September, I had my first big annual review with a
major investor. In addition to Sabrina Partners L.P. and Sabrina
Offshore Fund Ltd., I was managing $5 million for Hausmann
Overseas N.V., which was registered in the Netherlands Antilles.
I'd taken on this private account because Hausmann didn't
want to be part of the pool. They wanted to run their trades
through Neuberger & Berman. Everybody wanted a piece of the
action, but for $5 million, that was all right by me. They could
run their trades through the Dutch Masters for all I cared.

Hausmann's twelve directors would rent a suite at the
Mayfair Regent Hotel on the southwest corner of 65th and
Park, and they'd have their money managers come there to be
grilled. My apartment was just up the street, so all I had to do
was walk a short distance and I was there. I puffed out my
chest, marched into the suite, and said, "Gentlemen, I'm doing
a great job for you. I'm down eight percentage points on
Upjohn and I'm still up twelve percent net for the year. I took
a shot and if it comes through, I'll be up thirty to forty percent
for the year. The only thing that's happened is that it hasn't
happened."

The directors of Hausmann didn't want to hear about
Upjohn. They started comparing my returns with those of
Jones, Kovner, Bacon, and all the other futures stars. "Look," I
said to them, "it's not a futures fund. As I told you when you
came in, preserving capital is my top priority. I'm only putting
twenty-five percent of your money in futures. If I'd put all your
funds into futures, I could have leveraged it fifteen times and
made you one hundred percent, or lost it all and gone to jail."
No sale. They kept comparing me to the futures funds because
I was charging futures fees. And so it went all through October.
After the market closed, I'd lie down on my couch at 750
Lexington Avenue and wait for my foreign investors to arrive.
We'd sit down around my green Carrara marble table in
Audrey's Amelio Ungas designer leather chairs. I'd tell them
what a super job I was doing and they'd tell me how much bet-

ter Jones, and Kovner, and Bacon, and everybody else were doing. It was really discouraging.

The alarm on my night table buzzed. It was seven o'clock. I got up, splashed some water on my face, brushed off my Armani suit, buffed my Bally alligator shoes, straightened my Missoni tie, and headed for Lutèce.

Audrey joined me in the elevator and we headed out to get a cab. "Buzzy, your mother called. She wants to know when we're coming for Thanksgiving."

"Whaddya talking about? We can't go to Florida over Thanksgiving. I've got a business to run."

"Well, what about the holidays? Instead of going skiing, I guess now we'll have to go to Florida."

"Skiing? Who's going skiing?"

"Buzzy, we always take a vacation over the holidays."

"Not this year. Look, Audrey, I can't be taking vacations and going to Florida. I gotta get these results up, or I'm gonna start losing investors."

The dinner at Lutèce was being hosted by Willie the Web, a Swiss middleman who matched wealthy European investors with hot money managers. Willie had sent me some big clients and asked for a seat on the board of directors of Sabrina Offshore Fund Ltd. I didn't know what the board members did other than collect fees and submit expenses, but I acquiesced, because Willie controlled a lot of offshore money. I'd met Willie through my buddy Neil Weisman, but Neil hadn't been invited to Willie's dinner this year. Neil's fund was all in equities and Neil wasn't doing as well as he had the first three years when he averaged more than 75 percent per year. Willie liked his managers hot and Willie thought I was hot. That's why I was looking forward to the dinner. After a tough month of dancing with my investors, I was ready to sniff around with the top dogs for a night.

Willie had reserved one of the private rooms upstairs at Lutèce. When I walked in, I could see that the lineup included some of the fastest-rising stars on the Street. Julian Robertson was talking with Stanley Druckenmiller. Julian was a quiet, unassuming southerner who had left Kidder, Peabody in 1981 when he was forty-seven and started a fund with only $8 million. Now he was managing a billion. Stanley Druckenmiller was George Soros's right-hand man. They were joined by Leon Levy, who was representing Oddysey Partners.

Willie bustled over to greet me. "Martay, Martay, zo good to zee you. Here, come wiz me and meet zee client." The name of the client meant nothing to me. In Sabrina Offshore Fund Ltd., the clients were just numbers on bank accounts in Bermuda, the Bahamas, Guernsey, the Isle of Man, Switzerland, the Cayman Islands, and every other tax-free haven known to man. As we walked over to the other side of the room, Willie explained that the client had started a very innovative business and was making gazillions. "Martay, tell him der fund iss doing ferry vell. Ferry vell, indeed," Willie murmured.

When it came time to sit down, I was placed next to Fiona Biggs Druckenmiller. I was the new guy on the block so I didn't know these people, but during dinner, I learned that Fiona, in addition to being married to Stanley Druckenmiller, was the niece of Barton Biggs, the chief strategist for Morgan Stanley. She and Stanley had met when they were both working for Dreyfus, and it was obvious from our conversation that Fiona knew how to run with the top dogs.

The dinner at Lutèce was better than Commodities Corp's Semi-Annual Trader's Dinner, or even the Sheik's party at King Charles I's country estate. There, I was one of many, here I was one of a few. All through the evening I kept telling myself, "This is where I belong. This is where I want to be. This is why I'm managing other people's money." But the whole time, a nagging little voice kept whispering in my other ear, "Martay, next year you vill be eating at McDonald's wiz Neil unless you fini ze year très bien."

I didn't get back to the apartment until well after midnight. I was dead tired, but I couldn't get to sleep. My mind was racing. I knew that if I was going to keep running with the top dogs, I was going to have to make some big changes. Julian Robertson, Stanley Druckenmiller, Leon Levy, Jones, Kovner, Bacon, Soros—these were the top dogs; I could trade with any or all of them, and my funds could be as big or bigger than theirs. I had to get some numbers, I needed results.

The next morning, I told my trading assistant, Allison Brown, "I want you to sell twenty-five thousand shares of Upjohn every day from now until it's all gone. I want to be completely out by the end of the year." I couldn't post the kind of returns my investors expected with this $40 million gorilla hanging on my back. By easing the stock out at twenty-five thousand shares a day, I figured I wouldn't drive the price down, plus, if the gnomes from Switzerland ever got their act together, I still might have a piece of the action. Inside Skinny kept telling me, "It's gonna happen, Motty. Stick with it. I know it's taken a little longer, because these things always take a little longer."

Next, I sat down and drafted my November 1 letter to my investors. If they wanted a futures fund, I'd give them a futures fund. In my letter, I said:

In planning for 1991, I've decided to make a number of changes in Sabrina. The first and most important will be a change in the investment mix to 50% futures and 50% equities from the previous 25%–75% distribution during 1990. There are several reasons for this—namely we have made all of our profits this year in futures; $10.2 million on a capital base of $16.5 million or a return of 61.8%. The second reason for the change is the feedback from a number of clients who desire greater volatility from their investment and are willing to accept the concomitant risk.

The second important change is that due to the fast changing economic background, investors will be allowed to make a mid-year withdrawal subject to a 1% accounting fee.

The third change will be the introduction of a "knockout" formula whereby the fund would automatically terminate if losses are sustained equal to 35% of beginning of the year capital.

With a plan in place for liquidating the position in Upjohn and altering the investment mix of the funds, I was ready to immerse myself totally in trading for the next two months.

Sorry, Dad, You're Fired

Neil Weisman is one of my best friends. I met Neil back in the spring of '72 when I went to work for the Great Pyramid. Neil was a broker for the Pyramid who liked to collect a lot of information. He was always trying to peek through the Chinese wall, and since I was a new guy covering a hot industry, he made a point of becoming my friend.

Getting to know Neil was about the only good thing that happened to me at the Pyramid. When I was in the unemployment line and nobody would give me a job on the Street, Neil called Gerry Farber, a former analyst at the Pyramid who was the head of research at Edwards and Hanly. Neil told Gerry that I had gotten screwed and that he should hire me. Thanks to Neil, Gerry did hire me and that's how I met Bob Zoellner. It was Neil who plucked me from the depths of despair and got me back in the game.

In the fall of '86, I had a chance to repay the favor. Neil was a great trader and had always wanted to set up his own fund, but he needed a push, so I said to him, "Look, Neil, here's all of my pension money and some of Audrey's. Go manage it."

That was about $750,000. With this base, Neil was able to raise another $12 million, which was enough to start his fund. He was so happy that he decided to take the first week of 1987 off. He went on vacation to some remote island in the Caribbean and was out of touch for the first five trading days of the year. During that time, the market went ripshit and Neil missed the entire move. When we went to dinner in mid-February, Neil's fund was up 9 percent while the market was up 20 percent, so I said to him, "Neil, why the hell did you go on vacation during the first week of the year? You missed the whole rally. I can't believe I gave you my money. If I could take it back right now, I would." That was what I said to Neil, my good friend who'd plucked me from the depths of despair and who'd just started to manage his own fund.

Neil might have said, "Screw you, Marty. I don't need this. Take your money and get out." But he didn't, because he knew the rules. Successful businesspeople, whether they're traders, investors, entrepreneurs, whatever, CANNOT LET FRIEND-SHIPS OR FAMILY RELATIONSHIPS GET IN THE WAY OF MAKING SOUND DECISIONS ABOUT MONEY. What Neil did say was, "Marty, you can beat me up as bad as you want, because nobody can be tougher on me than me." Neil went out and posted a 75 percent return for the year. Over the next three years, he quadrupled my money, and by 1994, his fund had grown to $500 million. I still have money with him, but we both know if I see a better return somewhere else, it's bye-bye, Neil. Nothing personal. That's just the way the game's played.

15

Down the Tubes

I figured that if I could post a really strong November, I'd be able to keep most of my investors. By 3:30 P.M. on Friday, November 2, I couldn't stand up anymore. That week, I'd seen Albert Backward, Bernard Le Buffoon, Helmut Scheisskopf, and Pierre Tete du Merde, some of my best-heeled clients, and some of my most vocal critics. Now, I was bushed. When I was trading on my own, I'd never go out during the week, and the dinner at Lutèce on Monday night, along with all the other meetings I'd had in October, had worn me out. I'd been trading S&P futures all day and had made more than $100,000 for the week, but given the pressure I was under, this was not nearly enough. That morning, I'd gotten a fax from Georges Grenouilles in Geneva. All it said was,

> **Note to redeem on our behalf all shares in Sabrina Offshore Fund Limited, S.V.P. Merci and Rgds.**

A couple of my investors had told me in October that they were going to redeem their shares, but both of them had other reasons why they needed their money. This was the first investor who was getting out because he was dissatisfied with my performance.

I lay down on my couch. I could barely get up to watch the market close. All I wanted to do was go to sleep, but Mike Schmeiss, an old friend, was coming over. Mike was thinking of starting his own fund and was looking for advice. When he arrived at 5:30, I told him how I'd gone about raising the money and showed him my figures for the year, and when he was getting ready to leave I said, "OPM's the only way to go if you want to make the really big money, but there's a trade-off. Everybody's looking over your shoulder and nobody's ever satisfied. They're always calling and asking, 'How's my money doing?' and it doesn't make any difference what you tell them. They always want more."

On Saturday I didn't get up until eleven. Audrey had taken the kids to the Annual Horace Mann Nursery School Book Fair and I was going to join them at noon, but I had no zip. I felt like I was coming down with a cold. I knew I had to fight through it, because I couldn't afford to be sick. I had too much to do. I had to post my charts, calculate my ratios, and set up my strategies for Monday.

By the time I got to the book fair, the temperature had climbed to a balmy seventy-five degrees and I was soaked in sweat. As I walked into the school, I felt dizzy, my head hurt, I could hardly put one foot in front of the other. The fair was packed with teachers and families, there was no air-conditioning, and armies of little kids were running around screaming, yelling, pushing, and shoving. I didn't know if I could make it up the stairs. Over the years, my weight had crept up to 208, twenty-three pounds above my lean and mean Marine Corps days, and now I was feeling every pound.

Audrey and I spent the rest of the day running errands, and that night we went to the 68th Street Playhouse to see the movie *Reversal of Fortune*. The theater was stifling. A sign in the lobby apologized that the air-conditioning had been turned off for the year. As we waited for the movie to start, I was drenched with perspiration. Maybe I should have seen the movie's title as a precursor of things to come, but I was too sick to pick up any innuendos. Audrey wanted to take me home, but I wouldn't hear of it. "Forget it," I said. "We've already paid for the tickets. I'll fight through it. I'm tough. I'm a marine."

Sunday, I lay on the couch studying my charts trying to get ready for Monday. I felt like hell. After October, I should have taken a vacation, but I didn't have the time, not if I wanted to keep my investors. I was sure that if I spent the day on the couch, I'd snap back, but I didn't.

Monday, November 5, I woke up with a sore throat and I hurt all over. "Screw this marine crap," I told Audrey. "Call Hochman. I gotta see a doctor." I got a ten o'clock appointment with our family physician, Dr. Raymond Hochman. He told me that I had a strep infection, gave me a prescription for antibiotics, and ordered me to bed. I took the antibiotics, but I couldn't rest. I had to run Sabrina, I had to have a big month. I was too tired to trade, though, so I lay in bed and watched the Financial News Network.

Tuesday the sixth was another day of lying in bed watching FNN. I tried a few trades, but they didn't work and I lost $30,000. About 5:30 P.M., the pain in my back and chest became unbearable. For the first time in my life, I had this crazy premonition of death. Audrey called Hochman, but it was after five and he was gone for the day. His service got me a 6:30 appointment with Dr. Singh, the physician on call. I struggled out of bed, got dressed, and stumbled into a cab.

Singh didn't show up until 7:15. When he finally saw me, my temperature was 102, my EKG showed an irregularity, and he told me I'd better check into the hospital. Ironically, as the Sphinx and I had predicted eighteen years earlier, thanks to Medicare and Medicaid everyone with a hangnail was hanging out at the emergency room, and even though I was paying millions of dollars in taxes and lived eight blocks away, there was no room for me in New York Hospital. I was shunted off to the emergency room, which did nothing to lift my spirits. The place was packed and the staff was ignoring everyone who wasn't shot, stabbed, OD'd, or psychopathic.

Singh was supposed to be coming right behind us, but again he didn't show. At 9:15, Audrey called his office. His answering service said he'd been delayed, but not to worry, that he was on his way. He wasn't. By 10:00, I was too pissed to be scared. "Let's get the hell out of here," I told Audrey. "I hate this freakin' city." I made it through the night by sleeping upright at the kitchen table with four pillows propped under my arms. I looked like a praying mantis, but that was the only way I could keep the pressure off my lungs.

On Wednesday, I wasn't any better, and after reading two incoming faxes, I felt even worse. One was from Albert Backward in London, the other from Pierre Tete du Merde in Paris. The first was abrupt:

Please accept this fax as notice to redeem my holdings in Sabrina Offshore Fund, Ltd., as of January 1, 1991.

The second began more cheerily:

Good morning. We wish to sell 1,029.855 shares Sabrina Offshore. Please advise by return fax or telex what we have to do. Bonjour. P.T.d.M.

The rats were abandoning my ship. What I felt like saying was, "Good morning to you, take your 1,029.855 shares and shove 'em up your old wazoo, that's what you have to do," but I didn't have the energy.

Later that morning we went to see Hochman again. The bad news was that the strep had progressed to pneumonia and I had fluid in both lungs. The good news was that Hochman had pulled some strings and gotten me a private room in the hospital. We arrived at 1:00 P.M., but it took three more hours to get me admitted. Thanks to Blue Cross, Medicare, and Medicaid, hospitals could require their own set of admissions tests and get paid for them, so I needed a whole new set of EKGs, blood tests, and X rays. By this time my fever was up to 103.3 degrees. I was really sick, but there I was, lying alongside a roomful of nose jobs, tummy tucks, and fanny lifts, waiting my turn for the tests. It was absolutely absurd.

Finally I was able to get into my private room, and Audrey hired round-the-clock private nurses. They cost $780 a day, but by this time, I didn't care. I knew I needed somebody in my corner, somebody who'd be fighting only for me. Normally that would have been Audrey, but Audrey couldn't be with me all of the time. She had to stay home with the kids.

Now that I was checked in and Accounts Receivable knew that I was alive and covered by Blue Cross, waves of doctors and nurses started to flood into my room. Every one of them came armed with a needle. They started taking blood, more blood, and still more blood. They hooked me up to my own IV pole so I could get up if I felt strong enough, but I didn't. I kept asking the doctors what was going on, and they kept ignoring me. They didn't care that I was the Champion Trader. Here I was just another patient. Thank God for Esther Frederiksen, my principal private nurse. Esther wouldn't let them get away with ignoring me. She wouldn't let them touch me until she understood the procedure. She kept peering at my chart, checking the monitors, quizzing the doctors, beating on the nurses, and constantly asking me how I felt.

Doctors and nurses kept hovering around me, probing, poking, prodding, and pricking. Esther told me that the reason they were taking so much blood was that they wanted to determine whether the cause of my infection was bacterial or viral. The head of infectious diseases for New York Hospital was personally monitoring my case. Esther said that he was concerned because he'd seen four similar cases in the hospital the past month, and all of them were viral. "Mr. Schwartz," Esther explained, "if your infection is bacterial, they can find it and kill it with antibiotics, but if it's viral, the odds are that they'll never be able to find it, and hopefully it will just run its course."

"So, what are they going to do?" I said.

"They're going to start intravenous solutions of erythromycin, an antibiotic used to treat respiratory tract infections, and Cefuroxime, a cephalosporin antibiotic used for bronchial and throat infections, and . . ." Wap. Wap. Sure enough, before Esther could finish, they had more tubes in my arms.

The drugs kicked in. All that night and the following morning, they began to beat back the infection. By the afternoon of Friday the ninth, I was feeling a little better. At around 2:45, before Esther wheeled me down to X ray, I phoned Avi Goldfedder, one of my bond brokers in Chicago. I was very bullish on lower interest rates and I'd brought my Metriplex machine with me, which was the size of a beeper and gave me futures updates twenty-four hours a day, so I knew what was going on. "Avi," I snapped, trying to sound like my old self, "buy me four hundred Decembers at the market." I had just bought four hundred U.S. Treasury thirty-year bond futures contracts. According to my Metriplex, I had them at "9224," meaning at $92\frac{24}{32}$, or $92,750 per $100,000 contract.

"Motty, you sure?" Avi said. "You're s'pose to be resting."

"Yeah, I'm sure. In fact, make it six hundred."

"Motty, ya nuts! You're in the hospital, already. What the hell ya doin'? Hey, the last thing ya need is more pressure." Normally, I would have told Avi to shove it and just do what I told him to do, but I was too weak to argue.

"Okay. Just get the four hundred. But get 'em now."

Over the weekend, I kept improving and while my temperature had gone down to 99.8, the bonds had gone up to 9301. When the market opened on Monday the twelfth, I sold the four hundred bonds for a $112,500 profit. I never should've let Avi talk me out of the other two hundred. Still, smacking the bonds put some color back into my cheeks, and I told Hochman I wanted to go home. Two more investors in Sabrina Partners had just notified me that they were pulling out because the new asset allocation (50 percent futures, 50 percent equities) was too volatile for them. I had to start making some real money.

Hochman agreed to let me out and Audrey came to pick me up on the morning of Tuesday the thirteenth. I worked all that afternoon and well into the night updating my charts, calculating my ratios, getting back into control. I went to bed around ten and fell right to sleep, but at 1:30 A.M. on Wednesday, I woke up with a terrific pain in my chest. It was like nothing I'd ever felt before. A vertical white-hot line kept running across my heart. I didn't think I was having a heart attack, but every breath sent a new bolt of pain all the way into my spine. Audrey began massaging my chest, trying to relieve the pressure, but it didn't work. We called Hochman's service. He finally called back about four A.M. and Audrey described my condition to him. "Take two Tylenol for the pain, two Benadryl to help you sleep, put a heating pad on your chest for relief, and I'll call you first thing in the morning." I finally fell asleep and woke up at 7:30 the next morning in a pond of sweat.

At nine, Hochman called. "Marty, I don't want you walking around," he said. "I've scheduled you an echocardiogram at 10:45 with Doctor Christodoulou, who has an office in your apartment building. The four patients with viral infections we've been monitoring have all ended up with pericarditis."

The echocardiogram confirmed our worst fears. I had pericarditis. Fluid was building up in my pericardium, the membranous sac that surrounds the heart, and this fluid was constricting the heart, causing the terrific pain. It was back to the hospital.

Once again, Hochman pulled a few strings and I was able to get a private room. This time I was on a chemo floor. Once again, Audrey hired Esther, and once again, waves of doctors and nurses flooded into my room, all armed with needles to take blood, more blood, and still more blood. Before, I was concerned. Now, I was terrified. Before, it was my lungs. Now, it was my heart.

My temperature kept creeping up all day. 100.3. 100.9. 101.6. Tubes were sticking out from all over me. One was in my right arm administering an intravenous solution of erythromycin. Another was in my left arm administering Cefuroxime. A third tube, a Foley catheter, was stuck in my penis. It was just collecting urine from my bladder, but that was the one I hated the most.

Dr. Gold, the thoracic surgeon, came to see me to explain my options. "Mr. Schwartz," he said, "we're going to try and control this infection with antibiotics, but you know, if that fluid keeps building up around your heart, we're going to have to operate." That was one option I didn't want to exercise.

That evening at seven, Audrey came to see me. After telling me about the kids, she mentioned that Jean-Claude had been calling all day. Jean-Claude was a true parasite, another middleman who matched wealthy Europeans with hot money managers. Unlike Willie the Web, who worked out of Zurich, Jean-Claude worked out of the World Trade Center. That way, he could keep an eye on his stable of managers while his brother Jean-Pierre, a Swiss banker, dug up the clients. For the past ten months, Jean-Claude had been nothing but a pain in the ass. He was always calling, bothering me when I was trading, whining about how the funds should be doing better. "Martay, Martay, pourquoi ze funds, zay are not perform up to standairds. It is necessaire for you to do bettair."

Jean-Claude told Audrey that he had to speak to me immediately. When Audrey told him that I was back in the hospital, Jean-Claude wanted to know which hospital. He said he'd come to see me, but Jean-Claude wasn't worried about me, he was worried about his money. When Audrey wouldn't tell him where I was, he'd become indignant. "If Martay does not respond to me by ze end of ze week, I'm moving my people's monay to zomeone who will."

I told Audrey to go home and to forget about Jean-Claude. I was too looped on drugs to talk with her and too hurting to worry about a little Swiss weasel like Jean-Claude. Audrey left and I tried to sleep, but at about nine P.M., the room started spinning. "Esther, help," I rasped, "I think I'm gonna pass out." The next thing I knew, a "crash cart" came flying into the room. Esther had pushed the button. The drugs hadn't worked; the fluid buildup in my pericardium was strangling my heart. I was code blue, tamponade, blood pressure 50 over 40. Within minutes, a whole team of doctors was hovering all over me. There was an anesthesiologist by my head, a thoracic surgeon leaning over my torso, a cardiologist at the end of my bed reading my chart, even a resident holding the electric paddles. People were crawling all over me calling out numbers and giving orders. "Pressure's 80 over 60 and falling." "Gimme five cc's." "70 over 55." "Pulse 160, very rapid and thready." "50 over 40, we're losing him." Holy shit, losing me? "Save me. Save me. Please don't let me die," I whispered. I saw my little daughter's face, and my little son's. "Please, pleeease, don't let me die." The doctors started to stabilize my blood pressure, but my legs started to shake violently from the cold fluids being pumped into me. I passed out again.

I woke up on a gurney going to the cardiac care unit, tubes coming out of every orifice. A Swan-Ganz catheter was dangling from a hole they'd punched into my neck. Luckily, Dr. Gold was a workaholic. He'd been performing open heart surgery until midnight and was sleeping in the hospital. When he saw me, all he said was, "Let's go."

Gold called Audrey and told her he was going to operate immediately, but she didn't have any help and she couldn't leave the kids. She'd have to call her sister Linda, wake her up, and wait until she could get over to our place. By that time, I'd probably be under the knife. It occurred to me that I might never see her again. Just before I was wheeled into surgery, a very pretty nurse said to me, "Mr. Schwartz, I'm sorry, but we're going to have to remove your wedding ring. You can't wear rings into surgery."

I was a real straitlaced guy and always wore my wedding ring. Even on the rare occasions when I took it off, I still looked like I had it on, because given the weight I'd put on since I'd gotten married, the ring left an imprint on my finger. I tried to slip it off, but I couldn't. I was retaining a lot of fluid and my arms and fingers were swollen from the drugs. The nurse got some soap and water and gently worked the ring off my finger. I started to fight back the tears and said to her, "Please, give my wedding band to my wife and tell her that I hope she gets the chance to put it back on."

At 4:30 A.M., they wheeled me into the operating room. I lay on my back looking up at the stark cold lights, wondering if I'd ever see the sun again. They lifted me from the gurney onto a small stainless-steel operating table. My bulky frame barely fit. They slid another IV into the vein in the back of my left hand. The anesthesiologist started talking into my ear in a low, confident, calming voice. "Marty, we're going to wrap your arms." My right arm was wrapped and pinned in a sheet, and my left arm was wrapped and placed by my side. "Now we're going to slide a wedge under your lower back so that the area of the incision is perfectly aligned for Dr. Gold." The wedge felt hard and cold as it slipped into place. "Now we're going to cover your head with protective drapes. When the anesthesia starts, you'll be out in a few seconds. Now I want you to start counting backward from one hundred. Okay, here we go. Ninety-nine, ninety-eight, ninety-seven . . ." At ninety-six a wild sensation shot through every nerve in my body. I saw white tiles flying past my face, faster and faster. It was like I was on a roller coaster that just kept accelerating.

It was the thirst that woke me up. My mouth was drier than the Mojave and all I could think about was getting a drink. I didn't mind the tubes at all. The tubes and the pain told me that

I was still alive. A nurse was leaning over me. "Good morning, Mr. Schwartz. Nice to have you back. How do you feel?"

"Water," I croaked.

"No, no, not yet. Doctor's going to take a look at you and then we're going to bring you up to the CCU."

"Hurts. Ahhh. Pain."

"That's good. Pain means you're getting better. They'll give you some morphine as soon as we get you to the CCU."

I drifted off again. Pings, rings, and dings were going off all around me; it was like being in a pinball arcade. Then I began to realize that I was lying in the cardiac care unit, that the sounds were coming from banks of machines monitoring fragile hearts all around me. A big clock on the wall read 11:30. Now, I felt pretty good. It must've been the morphine.

I started reconnoitering, checking out the machines that were surrounding me, trying to figure out what all the numbers meant. Even with a tube up my penis, I was trying to regain some control over my life, no matter how small. I focused on a big TV monitor next to my bed. There were five displays. An EKG continuously rippled across the top. Under it were little boxes with green digital displays showing my blood pressure (134/82), my pulse rate (98), my blood oxygen level (97), and my heart pressure (80/10). They reminded me of my Quotron and Metriplex. I started doing breathing exercises to see whether I could control my blood pressure. I kept inhaling and exhaling, holding my breath, peering at my numbers. 130/78. 138/86.

"Buzzy! Stop that!" I was so focused on my monitor that I hadn't seen Audrey walk in. She turned to the nurse who'd come in with her. "What are you people doing! Reading screens is what he does for a living. You want to get his blood pressure down, turn those damn monitors around!" The nurse did.

Time passes slowly when you're lying on your back watching the clock, and that was about all I could do for the next five days. When I was trading, I never seemed to have enough time and I was always willing the clock to stop. Now, I kept urging it to keep moving because I knew that the more it moved, the better I'd be. My goal was to get the fever down and be home for Thanksgiving. I made it. On Thursday the twenty-second,

Thanksgiving Day, Audrey came to get me. I didn't have the strength to sit and eat at the table, and I was still groggy from the medication, but I was out of the hospital and home with my family. That was a great trade.

Over the weekend, I went through the previous week's mail. Zurich: "As requested, we hereby instruct to redeem the total of Sabrina shares . . ." Rakesh Bhargava, c/o Kidder, Peabody & Co., New York: "We hereby instruct to sell from our account . . ." Cayman Islands: "Refer to my telephone call of the 13 November and confirm that shares will be sold . . ." Grand Bahamas: "This letter serves to inform you that we wish to redeem our total holdings . . ." Channel Islands: "We hereby request redemption of *all* shares 'as soon as possible,' latest December 31, 1990 . . ." Rasulgarh, India: "Will be drawing out my capital as of the end of the year, I am uncomfortable personally with the increased risk . . ." And finally, from Curaçao: "Please accept this letter as official notification that Hausmann Overseas N.V., has decided to redeem its entire account (terminate its agreement) . . ." Like I was too stupid to figure it out for myself. Seven more investors, including Hausmann, my $5 million private account, were bailing out. You would've thought that at least one of them would have said, "P.S.: Hope you're feeling better." But all they cared about was their money.

I was hoping that this was the end of my investors' exodus. Wrong. Monday morning, the twenty-sixth, a new batch of faxes, letters, and couriers arrived at 750 Lexington Avenue, all with bad news. The Pakistani clients had bailed out. My Panamanian investors had told me "hasta luego," my Channel Islanders had said "ta ta," my Luxembourgers, "au revoir," and my Zürichers, "auf Wiedersehen." My Italians probably would've said "arrivederci" if I'd had any Italians. My capital had plummeted from $70 million to $45 million in a month, and I still had to get through December. I needed to MAKE SOME MONEY.

But first, I had to see Dr. Gold. He was removing my staples on Monday. The thought of going back to the hospital put me in a panic. I was sure that once I got inside, they'd recapture me and the whole ordeal would start all over again. It didn't.

"Marty, the incision's healing nicely," Gold said, "but you're not out of the woods. Go home, relax, and don't put yourself under any stress."

I kept trading all that week, but on Friday the thirtieth, the market opened lower and I could feel a knot growing in the pit of my stomach. I was physically drained and just wanted to get out of all my positions. I held on until the market ticked up and dumped everything. Then the bond market really started to take off. I was totally exhausted, almost too weak to take advantage, but I couldn't be left at the station watching the train pull away. The hell with Dr. Gold. I had to show all those bastards who'd sold me short that I was still the Champion Trader. I called Goldfedder and put on a six hundred contract bond futures position.

Saturday, December 1, I could barely get out of bed. As I worked up my month-end figures, my temperature crept up to 100.5. By Sunday afternoon, it was 101.2 and I knew I was back in trouble. Audrey called Hochman and he told me to get over to the ER. My temperature was up to 102.8 by the time we checked in. Fortunately, Dr. Gold, the other workaholic, was there. I begged him to make me well. I asked him if there was anything he wanted. I told him to just name it and it was his. He thought that I was kidding, that I was delirious. "JUST NAME IT!" I shouted at him. Maybe I was delirious.

"Well, er, now that you mention it, I could use a new stereo," he said in jest.

"AUDREY! Get Dr. Gold a new stereo!" I yelled. "Spare no expense! Now SAVE MY LIFE!"

Dr. Gold immediately started an echocardiogram. The problem was that my pericardial sac was starting to fill up with fluid again. He reviewed my situation with us. "We're going to take you back up to the cardiac care unit and observe your coronary functions. We don't want to operate again, but we might have to. If we can't beat this thing with drugs, we can take out your pericardial sac and you can live safely without it."

The Chicago Board of Trade had a Sunday-night session where the bond futures traded. On my way to the hospital, I'd put a call in to Avi Goldfedder and left a message for him to get back to me immediately. I might be able to live without my peri-cardial sac, but I wasn't sure that my body could withstand another major operation. I had to get out of that bond position. When those avaricious schmucks called and wanted to know "how's my money doing?" Audrey could tell them that it was fine, even if I were dead.

I lay on my bed, listening to the pings and rings and dings, wondering what was going on with my bonds. Then a nurse came up with a phone. "Mr. Schwartz. It's your personal physician, Dr. Goldfedder from Chicago. We've read him your charts, but he insists on talking with you." Dr. Goldfedder?

"So Motty, they wouldn't put me through. No phone calls to the CCU. So I told them I was your personal physician and that you'd called me in for a second opinion."

"Uh. You're a good doctor, Avi," I whispered. "What's my prognosis?"

"You're up ten ticks, just about two hundred thousand dollars. Whaddya wanna do? Sell?"

"That seems like good advice. Thanks, Dr. Goldfedder."

The next morning, my real doctors put me on steroids and, thank God, they worked. My fever went down dramatically and my pulse rate fell back to 90 from 140. I finally left the hospital for good on December 14. Since November 7, I'd been in the hospital on three separate occasions for a total of twenty-six days. Sure I'd made more than $500,000 for my investors, but at what cost? My hospital bills alone were over $100,000, but that was just money. What really hurt was the realization that for a year, I'd been putting clients, none of whom cared enough about me to so much as send a get-well card, ahead of my family and my health.

I thought back to my meeting with Mike Schmeiss on the night this whole nightmare had started. What would I tell him now about starting his own fund? I'd tell him that OPM isn't worth the aggravation. I'd tell him that no amount of money is worth working for people who don't care anything about you.

I'd wanted to prove that I could run with the top dogs, and I did for a while, and it almost killed me. Big funds might be okay for Tudor Jones, Soros, Druckenmiller, Robertson, Bacon, and Kovner, but they weren't okay for me. I'd found out that I was a pure trader. I didn't like people looking over my shoulder, and I didn't want to be responsible to people whom I didn't like. I just wanted my freedom, and my health.

Even so, I wanted to continue on, still being naive enough to believe that I could run a major fund by finding investors who appreciated me and my abilities.

December 14, 1990 (the same day I was released from my third stay in the hospital)

Dear Partners:

I'm terribly sorry for the delay in reporting our November results, but as some of you know, I was stricken with a mystery virus that began as pneumonia and traveled to my pericardial sac, which necessitated emergency life-saving surgery in the early morning hours of November 16th. . . .

I look forward to a far more productive 1991. The funds will be downsized in 1991 to a total of $45 to $50 million, which should enable you remaining clients to get a higher return on your investment. The people who remain are now part of a family who will get a much more focused effort from me in 1991, particularly after what I've lived through.

Two Lessons for Life

I. Break the Pressure Before It Breaks You

Ray Gura was a stocky, white-haired, crew-cut options trader who sat in the bullpen, a bunch of desks packed together that were filled with small-time traders trying to grind out a living. I met Ray in the early eighties soon after I started spending more time off the floor of the American Stock Exchange. Bear Stearns, my clearing broker, had given me a small private office on the ninth floor of 86 Trinity Place, the building next door to the Exchange. The bullpen was right outside my door.

One day I was building a large position in S&P futures and the pressure was really starting to get to me. The market was dropping and I kept adding to my already substantial position. Buying on the way down was something I almost never did, but my indicators kept telling me that the market was oversold and due to rally. Plus, Audrey had taken the day off and wasn't around to tell me that I was violating my first and best rule: never let your ego take over your trading.

As the sweat began dripping from my brow, I started looking for some way to break the pressure. I fumbled through my desk, found a paper bag, put it over my head, and ran out into the bullpen. I jumped up on Ray's desk and began dancing from desktop to desktop across the bullpen screaming through the bag, "I'm long! I'm long! I'm too fuckin' long!"

WHEN YOU'RE IN A LOSING POSITION AND YOU'RE BRAINLOCKED, DO WHATEVER'S NECESSARY TO HELP CLEAR YOUR HEAD. Whether you're a pro or an amateur, you cannot lose your objectivity.

I went desktop dancing to break the pressure because I was afraid I might freeze, like I had when I sold the Republicans short. Then I was able to come back to my chair, sit down, and rethink my strategy. I came up with the same conclusion—being long was right—but this time I also put in a stop loss on my position. Not too long afterward the market began to turn, and by the end of the day I was up $100,000.

The next morning, Ray Gura came into my office. He was holding a baseball. It was autographed by the 1960 New York Yankees, the team that had won the American League pennant. "Here," he said offering me the ball, "I want you to have this, because you're such a big Yankee fan."

I looked at the ball. Mickey Mantle, Roger Maris, Yogi Berra, Elston Howard, Whitey Ford, all of my heroes when I was a kid growing up in New Haven, had signed it. "Ray," I said, "I can't take your ball. And why would you want to give it to me?"

"'Cause you made me and my family a lot of money, that's why," Ray answered. "Yesterday when you were dancing over the desktops with that bag over your head screamin' about how long you were, I called my son and son-in-law down on the floor and told them that if you were long, we'd better start buying, too. Marty, yesterday was the best day we've had in a long time, and we want you to have the ball as a present from us."

I still didn't want to take Ray's twenty-three-year-old memento, but after he continued to insist that I accept the baseball as a token of his appreciation, what could I say? I didn't want to be rude, and I was truly touched by the gift. Today, that ball sits proudly in a plastic case in my son's bedroom, right on his desktop.

II. Nobody Ever Lay on Their Deathbed Wishing They'd Worked Harder

In 1992, a bond broker from Chicago named Ken Kush called me and asked if I wanted to go in on a racehorse with him. I was trying to wean myself away from the market and develop some new interests, and ever since my first day at Aqueduct, I'd dreamt of owning a racehorse, so I said, "Sure, let's do it."

Ken got us a four-year-old filly named Prebend, and Prebend was a loser right out of the gate. She had all kinds of allergies and spent most of her time wheezing along at the back of the pack. Ken used to fly around going to all her races and he was always calling me and telling me, "Marty, don't worry, she's a great horse. The trainer just can't get her medication right," or "Marty, the trainer thinks he's found this new drug that he's sure is gonna make her a winner," or "Marty, she just missed third place. It was so exciting, you've gotta come see her."

I wasn't about to fly around to watch Prebend run out of the money, but one day Ken called and said, "Marty, good news. We've entered Prebend in a race at Pimlico next Wednesday, and she's got a real good shot. The trainer's got her on a new drug that's just been approved by the Maryland Racing Commission and she's running like Secretariat's sister. Her training times are awesome. You've gotta go down and see her."

I figured what the heck's the use of owning a horse if you never get to watch it run and Pimlico was in Baltimore, so it wasn't a bad trip from New York. "Okay," I told Ken, "I'll take the Metroliner down and make a day of it."

I was going to catch a 10:30 train, but when the market opened, I got into a couple of interesting positions and when it came time to leave I figured, why go all the way down to Maryland to see Prebend? If she didn't win, I'd be disappointed that I wasted the whole day, and besides, I didn't have to go to Maryland. I could just walk over to the nearest OTB and make a bet.

So I don't go, and it turned out the Prebend won the race. To make matters worse, I'd bet $2,000 at OTB, but I was so much of the pool that I only got back $5,500. At the track, Prebend went off at better than 12–1, which meant I would have gotten $25,200 back on a $2,000 bet. When I didn't meet Ken at the track, he couldn't believe it. "Marty," he said, "you've got to get your priorities straight."

Prebend's asthma got worse, and we eventually sold her for a pittance compared to what we could have gotten if we'd sold right after her only winning race. I've never bought into another racehorse, but I might someday. If I do, I'm going to get my priorities straight. A lot of people get so enmeshed in the markets that they lose their perspective. Working longer does not necessarily equate with working smarter. In fact, sometimes it's the other way around.

I've learned through the years that after a good run of profits in the markets, it's very important to take a few days off as a reward. The natural tendency is to keep pushing until the streak ends. But experience has taught me that a rest in the middle of the streak can often extend it.

KEEP YOUR BALANCE. When your horse runs, be there. Sit in the owner's box, bet your buns off, have a great time, and forget about the market.

16

Night Fighting

"Because I am tough, you will not like me. But the more you hate me, the more you will learn. I am tough, but I am fair. There is no racial bigotry here. I do not look down on niggers, kikes, wops, spics, or micks. Here you are all equally worthless. And my orders are to weed out all slackers who don't pack the gear to serve in my beloved Corps. From now on you will speak only when spoken to. And the first and last words out of your filthy sewers will be Sir. Do you maggots understand that?"

"Sir, yes Sir."

"Bullshit, I caaaan't heeeeear you. Sound off like you got a pair!"

"Sir, yes SIR!"

"I still caaaaan't heeeeear you!"

"SIR, YES SIR!!"

On February 5, 1968, I arrived at the U.S. Marine Corps base in Quantico, Virginia, to start my training at Officer's Candidate School. I'd signed up for the USMC Reserves after my first semester at Columbia Business School because the rumors floating around academia had it that the Pentagon was going to do away with graduate school deferments, and I didn't want to get drafted and go to Vietnam.

The marines owned you for ten weeks, and during that time, they controlled every move you made. Their objective was to break you down and rebuild you in their own image. They kept you busy from 5:30 A.M., when they got you up by rolling a metal garbage can down the concrete floor of the squad bay, until 10:00 P.M., when they said "good night, ladies" and cut the lights, leaving you prone, but still at attention, stretched out, scared and exhausted on your bunk. But I survived. *"Congratulations, Lieutenant Schwartz, you are now a marine."*

* * *

On November 7, 1990, I'd started my six-week battle with viral pericarditis and I didn't get out of the hospital for good until December 14. Since then, I'd been working from my office at home, trying to recuperate. During the lunch hour, Rob LeVine, one of my assistants, would come up from my office at 750 Lexington Avenue and walk me around the block. Dr. Hochman insisted that I get out and take walks in the fresh air even though it was twenty-five degrees outside. I'd bundle up in the Revillon cashmere coat that I'd gotten for an art trip Audrey and I took to Russia in 1987 with my dear friend Al Fresco, wrap an Armani scarf around my neck, turn up the fur collar on the Revillon coat, put on the sable hat I'd bought at Gum's in Moscow, and march out with Rob into the cold New York winter.

We'd started this routine at the first of the year because when a new year comes, a new bell goes off in my head and a new race begins. Even though I'd almost died and half of my investors had deserted me while I was in the hospital, I was still Captain Schwartz of Sabrina Partners. Investors were depending on me and I had a good chunk of my own money tied up in the funds, so getting back to work was as much self-preservation as it was duty. I had to start fighting for some big numbers.

> *I love working for Uncle Sam.*
> *I love working for Uncle Sam.*
> *Let's me know just who I am.*
> *Let's me know just who I am.*
> *One, Two, Three, Four, United States Marine Corps.*
> *One, Two, Three, Four, United States Marine Corps.*
> *One, Two, Three, Four, I love the Marine Corps.*
> *One, Two, Three, Four, I love the Marine Corps.*
> *My Corps. Your Corps. Our Corps. Marine Corps.*
> *My Corps. Your Corps. Our Corps. Marine Corps.*

On January 2, I could hardly make it around the block. I had no energy, no stamina. My chest hurt from where they'd cut me open and spread my ribs, and I was still on Prednisone, a corticosteroid. Prednisone was not a good drug for traders because one of its side effects was psychological derangements. According to my medical encyclopedia, they "range from euphoria to mood swings, personality changes, and severe depression. Prednisone may also aggravate existing emotional instability." Hochman was trying to wean me off the drug, and to do that I had to build up my physical strength.

I'd come back from my walks with Rob sweaty and dog tired, but improving a little bit every day. Four blocks, eight blocks, twelve blocks. As my distances went up, my dosages went down, 30 milligrams, 25 milligrams, 20 milligrams.

Ever since August 2, 1990, when Saddam Hussein invaded Kuwait, the markets had been gyrating wildly. Stock prices generally had been sinking, while commodities, especially oil, had been gushing upward. But every time the Iraqis punched out a SCUD missile toward Israel, the program traders in New York would hit their buy and sell buttons, and the markets would be projected into chaos.

On January 9, 1991, Secretary of State Baker met in Geneva with the Iraqis to try to reach some kind of political accommodation. The market expected an agreement, but when Baker came out of the meeting and stepped in front of the cameras, the first word out of his mouth was "regrettably." The S&Ps dropped ten points before he could finish the sentence as a wave of selling broke loose in the market. I dove into my bunker and started firing live rounds. I was going short, selling S&P futures that I didn't own and would have to buy back later, hopefully at a lower price. Cover up, cover up.

The following Wednesday I told Audrey, "You know, the market can only discount this potential war so many times, and I think it's bottomed out. All my indicators say it's oversold. Something's going to happen and I think I should be buying stock before it happens." Getting Audrey's opinion was more important now than ever; I was never sure whether my feelings were due to the markets or to the Prednisone.

"Buzzy. If you like it, get it."

I started buying. Amgen. Bristol-Myers Squibb. Compaq. Delta Airlines. Fannie Mae. The Gap. Gillette. Home Depot. Johnson & Johnson. The Limited. Merck. Microsoft. Nike.

Novell. Philip Morris. Texas Instruments. United Airlines. Wal-Mart. Waste Management. I was convinced that the United States was going to have to take some action to resolve the crisis in the Gulf, and that when it did, the market was going to react positively. On Monday and Tuesday, I'd gone long 160 S&P contracts, so in three days, I'd spent $12 million starting to position my funds for any potential up move.

That evening, Wednesday, January 16, I lay down on the couch in my library to watch *NBC Nightly News* with Tom Brokaw. I was drained. It was just five weeks to the day that I'd gotten out of the hospital for the third and last time, and that afternoon, I'd had my best walk yet, one New York mile, twenty short blocks. I hit the remote control and Tom Brokaw came onto the screen. He was even more full of himself than usual, the way newscasters get when they've got something really big on their plates. Just moments ago, speaking from the Oval Office, President Bush had announced that U.S. forces had launched an all-out attack on Iraq. Operation Desert Storm had erupted.

Once a marine, always a marine. I didn't pray for war, I was not a minister of death, and I was still weak from my near-death experience, but when war came on January 16, 1991, I was still a marine, and I was ready. It was time for me to go to war. I pulled myself up from the couch, went back into my office, eased into my chair, put on my phone headset, and looked at the clock. It was 1840 eastern daylight time. I was in no condition to trade, but I was tough, I was a marine. What did it matter that half of my investors had deserted me? I was still determined to do my duty as a responsible officer.

"Candidate Schwartz. Lemme see your war face."

"Sir?"

"You got a war face? This is a war face. AAARRRRGGGHH!"

"Aaarrrrggghhh!"

"Bullshit, you didn't convince me, lemme see your real war face."

"AAAAAAAAARRRRRGGGGHHHHH!!!!"

"You don't scare me. You'd better work on it or I'll really jump in your shit!"

"SIR, YES SIR!"

The United States was attacking with F-15s that were capable of delivering smart bombs and laser-guided missiles with surgical precision. There was no question that we were going to annihilate this camel driver and bury his so-called elite Republican Guard deep in the desert sands. And we were going to do it fast, so I had to move even faster.

"There will be a magic show at 0900. Chaplain Charlie will tell you how the free world will conquer all with the aid of God and a few marines. God has a hard-on for marines because we kill everything we see. He plays his game, we play ours. To show our appreciation for so much power, we keep Heaven packed with fresh souls. God was here before the Marine Corps so you can give your heart to God, but your ass belongs to the Corps. Do you ladies understand that?"

"SIR, YES SIR!"

Now that America had joined in battle, all of the fear and uncertainty that had been driving the oil and gold markets higher for the past four months would evaporate overnight. I had to find a market that was open. I wanted to sell oil and gold contracts short and buy them back later when the prices had dropped. Why, you might ask, would anybody in their right mind want to short crude oil when the Persian Gulf was about to blow up, and why short gold when gold was the one thing everybody ran to in a crisis? The reason was that crude oil and gold had been overbought since the invasion of Kuwait, and once the markets realized that Saddam was no longer a threat to the Gulf and its oil supplies, crude oil and gold would drop like a couple of overripe coconuts. I had to short gold and oil immediately. I leaned forward in my chair and punched in the number for the Kidder, Peabody night desk.

"Marty Schwartz here. I've got an account with you guys. Sabrina Partners L.P. . . . What do you mean you can't find it? . . . S-A-B-R-I-N-A, Sabrina, Sabrina! I want to short gold and oil! Find me a market! Fast!"

Pause.

"My mother's maiden name? Snyder, dammit. S-N-Y-D-E-R, Snyder, Snyder!"

Pause. I checked my watch. 1842. The markets were going

to get away from me. I didn't have time for this. I switched to the Board of Trade in Chicago. The Chicago Board of Trade had an after-hours session where bonds were traded from 1820 to 2105. I had direct lines to two clearing firms, Discount Corp. and LIT Futures. Sergeants Kush and Goldfedder came on the lines. Ken Kush at Discount and Avi Goldfedder at LIT (now known as "Doc," thanks to his timely second opinion when I was in the cardiac care unit) were my two main bond brokers. Immediately upon hearing the news of Desert Storm, these two battle-tested professionals had jumped into cabs and sped back to their positions on the front line at the CBOT. Excellent. Now that I had established radio contact with my two key forward observers, it was time to engage the enemy.

For the last three days I'd been sensing a green light on bonds. On my daily blotter, I keep handwritten notes of every trade, and on the edge, I scribble down my thoughts for later reference. My notes during that week kept saying, "Look to go long bonds." "Watch for int rate break, buy big." "Could be major bottom in US Treas." I had the contacts and the accounts all set up where I could buy as many bonds as I wanted. During the day session, I'd sent out a reconnaissance force into what I was confident would be excellent buying territory by going long 80 March bonds at 9315. ("9315" meant 93$^{15}/_{32}$, or about 93.47 cents on the dollar. Bond prices were quoted in thirty-seconds of a dollar.) If gold and oil were "shorts" based on these uncertainties being resolved, that meant that other commodities and interest rates would tend to drop. That in turn meant that bond prices would soar. A drop in interest rates corresponds to a rise in bond prices, and vice versa.

"Ken! Gimme a quote on USH!" USH was the symbol for the March 1991 thirty-year Treasury bond futures contract. One CBOT bond futures contract had a face value at maturity of $100,000.

"9318, Marty."

"Buy me twenty bonds at 9318!" I ordered.

Pause. "You got 'em at 9318, Marty." I had just purchased twenty contracts, entitling me to $2 million face value of thirty-year Treasury bonds, for delivery in March 1991. At a price of

9318 (93.5625 cents on the dollar), my total cost was $1,871,250. I didn't have to put up any cash up front, however, because I had enough funds on deposit with my clearing firm to cover the margin requirement.

I checked the quotes on my screens. "USH, 9320." It had ticked up to 93²⁰⁄₃₂. My intelligence was correct. The bonds were on the move. It was time to attack in force.

"Hello, Mr. Schwartz, Kidder, Peabody here. Sorry to keep you waiting." It was 1844. Two minutes on hold, an eternity by a trader's clock. "We've checked your account status. Neither Sabrina Partners L.P. nor Sabrina Offshore Fund Limited is set up to trade gold or oil anywhere but the U.S."

Fuck! "Get 'em set up, now!"

"I'm sorry, Mr. Schwartz, the only markets trading gold and oil contracts are in the Far East. Hong Kong, Japan, Singapore. And their contracts aren't fungible into U.S. contracts."

Doublefuck. "Well, open up a foreign account and let's go!"

"Let me see what I can do."

"In the meantime, find me something that is fungible, and make it quick." I switched back to Chicago to make sure the bonds didn't get away from me. "Doc! Doc! You there?" This time I was on the LIT line. When you can, always have at least two of everything and spread your business around. You don't want to be sole-sourced, or they'll take you for granted. You get the best deals and the best service by having more than one broker and playing them off against each other.

"Yeah, Marty."

I checked my screens. "USH, 9324." "Doc, buy me twenty March T-bonds at 9324!"

Pause. "Done, twenty at 93 and 24." It was 1848.

Beep. It was the Kidder, Peabody night desk.

"Good news, Mr. Schwartz. I can get you Eurodollars in Singapore because they're U.S. currency and could be swept into your domestic account at the opening."

Shit. Tell me something I don't know, you maggot! "I can get those on the SIMEX any time I want 'em. Keep working on getting me accounts so I can trade gold and oil."

"What makes the grass grow?"

"Blood, blood, blood."

"What do we do for a living, ladies?"

"Kill, kill, kill."

"Bullshit, I can't hear you."

"KILL! KILL! KILL!"

Beep. Sergeant Kush. "Yeah!"

"Lookin' strong, Marty. The bonds are galloping. They're up to 9403."

"Get me forty more USH at 9403!"

Pause. "We got 'em, Marty, forty at 9403." It was 1905.

My bond position was now long 160 contracts, 80 from the day session at 9315 and 80 more just in the last twenty minutes. Since each bond futures contract had a face value at maturity of $100,000, I now had $16 million face value of USH with a paper profit of $67,500. Things were going great. My left flank, the bonds, anchored by Sergeant Kush from his command post in the upper booth of the CBOT, was solid. It was time to send Sergeant Goldfedder over to beef up my right flank.

"Doc! Doc! Do you read me?"

"Roger, Motty." Interestingly, Goldfedder in his other life was a member of the Israeli Air Force Reserves. For two weeks every summer, I couldn't trade with him because he was back in the Middle East on active duty. I wondered what his thoughts were about Desert Storm, but I didn't have time to talk about it, not with $16 million bonds flying around.

"Doc! Get me one hundred March Eurodollar contracts! Buy them on the SIMEX in Singapore." (The SIMEX was the Singapore Mercantile Exchange. Eurodollars were U.S. dollars on deposit in overseas banks, predominantly in Europe.) I wanted to touch all of the bases. By going long Eurodollars I was making a bet that short-term interest rates were going to fall, just as I'd made my bet in bonds that long-term rates would drop.

Pause.

"One hundred March Euros secured for you at 9265."

It was 1918. Back to my left flank. "Ken, twenty more at 9407." As the bonds kept going up, my confidence rose with them. I became more and more convinced that my battle plan was working. I was long two hundred bonds, large, but not nearly large enough in this market. I had to press the offensive. I was starting to perspire. Audrey came in to refill my canteen with a nice cup of tea. She wiped my brow with a napkin. "Buzzy, are you all right?"

"I'm smackin' 'em, Audrey! I feel great!"

"Are you sure it's not the Prednisone?"

"I hope not, I'm long up to my eyeballs, and I'm goin' longer."

Audrey studied my blotter. "Buzzy. You look good. If you like it, go for it."

1958: "Doc, twenty more at 9422!"

2006: "Ken, twenty more at 9425!"

2019: "Ken, fuck it, it's time to take the hill, get me seventy at 9428!" I was long 350 USH, $35 million in bonds, and the market was still rising.

Mama and Papa were layin' in bed.
Mama rolled over, this is what she said.
Oh give me some
(Oh give me some)
Oh give me some
(Oh give me some)
P.T.
(P.T.)
P.T.
(P.T.)
Good for you
(Good for you)
Good for me
(Good for me)

"Ken, buy me fifty at 9506."

Pause. "Can't get 'em, Marty. They've gone through 9506."

"The hell with it. Not Held, NOT HELD!" "Not held" meant pay whatever you have to pay. Sergeant Kush got twenty at 9509 and thirty more at 9510.

"Doc, thirty more, NOT HELD!"

"Motty, ya gotta slow down. Remember, you're still sick."

"Don't tell me what to do! You just buy the fuckin' bonds, NOW!" My Israeli commando nailed them at 9512.

By 2105 when the CBOT evening session closed, I'd been trading for two and a half hours straight and was long five hundred bond futures. I clicked on the news. Our technology was working to perfection. We were killing Iraqis as easily as I was killing the bonds. This war was going to be over before it began.

Audrey came in with a sandwich and more tea. "Buzzy, how are you doing?"

"Great. I think I've got it figured out perfectly. I don't have an account to short gold or oil overseas, but I'm working on it. And I'm killin' the bonds."

"Well, you've done all you can do for today. You should go to bed. You need your rest. You don't want to have a relapse."

Audrey was right. I was running on adrenaline and 20 milligrams of Prednisone. I'd forgotten that I was still recuperating. "Yeah, you're right. Just let me finish checking my positions and setting up my strategy for tomorrow."

Audrey left. I dismissed Sergeants Kush and Goldfedder for the night and checked in with Kidder, Peabody. They hadn't been able to set up an overseas account, but assured me that they were working on it. With one eye on CNN and the other on my blotter, I began my calculations. I was long 500 USHs at costs ranging from 9315 to 9512, long 100 Eurodollars at 9265, long 160 S&P futures, and long $12 million in stocks. The stocks and the S&Ps wouldn't start moving until the market opened tomorrow. My paper profits on the bonds were close to $400,000. Not bad for two and a half hours of work, and I was sure that the best was yet to come. If only I could short some oil and gold. . . .

I still had to do all my regular paperwork, computing the moving averages and put-call ratios, jotting down ideas for the next day on five-by-eight cards, checking my hot-line services, going through twenty pages of incoming faxes, charting my new $12 million worth of stocks, all the work I normally did right after supper. It was 2330 by the time I closed the books.

I struggled out of my chair and went into the guest bedroom

to lie down. I was sleeping in a hospital bed by myself in the guest bedroom because the Prednisone made me sweat and I'd have to get up two and three times a night to change my johnny. I wasn't wearing pajamas; I had a supply of hospital gowns that were easier to get in and out of, because my chest was still sore where they'd cut me open. My heart was racing, and that was not what I wanted after suffering viral pericarditis. I lay there sweating, thinking about my positions.

"Candidate Schwartz, you run like old people fuck. Do you know that, Schwartz? Get moving, you bag of shit. Move it, move it! Whatever you do, don't stop, that would break my fucking heart. Keep moving, moving! Well, what in the fuck are you waiting for, Candidate Schwartz? Move it, move it! Are you quitting on me? Well, are you? If you do, I'm gonna rip your balls off so you cannot contaminate the rest of the world. I WILL motivate you, Candidate Schwartz. DO YOU UNDERSTAND ME?"

"SIR, YES SIR!"

What the hell was I doing lying in bed? Sergeants like Kush and Goldfedder and camp followers like Audrey could sleep, but there was no rest for the captains until the battle was won. Still dressed in my johnny, I went back into the office and turned on CNN. CNN was interviewing pilots who had returned to their bases in Saudi Arabia after bombing the shit out of the Iraqis. It was now 0200 in the United States. The sun was high over the desert. Even though they were all trying to sound like Chuck Yeager with his folksy aw-shucks, down-home, understated West Virginia drawl, they couldn't hide their excitement. Desert Storm was going better than anybody could have expected. We'd pounded the parliament buildings, knocked out an oil refinery, shut down the Baghdad International Airport, and delivered bombs literally to the front steps of Saddam's presidential palace. It was a picture-perfect operation. Damn. I had to short oil and gold.

I called the Kidder, Peabody night desk again. Still no luck setting up my account. Gold and oil futures were plummeting on the Far East markets. London was getting ready to open, could Sabrina trade there? He didn't know. I called Kidder, Peabody in London. Sorry, old chap, not fungible. I called

Kidder, Peabody in Sydney. G'dye, mate, no listing in Sydney, try Melbourne. Shit. It was 0345. Gold and oil were starting to stabilize. I'd missed it. I couldn't keep my eyes open.

"Pray!"

"This is my rifle. There are many like it but this one is mine. My rifle is my best friend. It is my life. I must master it as I must master my life. Without me, my rifle is useless. Without my rifle, I am useless. I must fire my rifle true. I must shoot straighter than my enemy who is trying to kill me. I must shoot him before he shoots me. I will. Before God I swear this creed. My rifle and myself are defenders of my country. We are the masters of our enemy. We are the saviors of my life. So be it, until there is no enemy. But peace. Amen."

"At ease, good night, ladies."

"Buzzy. Buzzy. Wake up. It's after five o'clock. What are you doing sitting here in your chair in a johnny? You've gotta go to bed."

All I wanted to do was sleep, but not today. I could sleep anytime. Great trading opportunities like this only came along three or four times a decade, and I wasn't going to miss this one. I took a shower, changed into a clean johnny, got some breakfast, and was back at my command post by 0630. The fax machine had been humming all night, spitting out account information. I reconciled all my trades from the previous day, because today, more than ever, it was essential to have everything in order before the markets opened. They were going to be so volatile that an error could cost hundreds of thousands of dollars. I scanned the *Times* and the *Journal* and my newsletters and services. The headline of the *New York Post*, founded by Alexander Hamilton in 1801, screamed WAR!

At 0730, General "Stormin' Norman" Schwarzkopf gave a briefing. It was the most massive air strike in history. Baghdad was the center of hell. The Republican Guard had been "eliminated" and most of the Iraqi Air Force had been "decimated without getting off the ground." Saddam Hussein was in hiding someplace. Not a single American plane had been lost, and not a single casualty suffered.

Everything was telling me to go long stocks and S&Ps and get out of the bonds. I called London. Gold and oil futures were continuing to stabilize, and that meant that bonds and Eurodollars should follow suit. It was time to hear the cash register ring. I decided to start selling my bonds and Eurodollars at the opening. At 0800, I got Sergeants Kush and Goldfedder on the line. The Chicago bond futures market would open in twenty minutes.

"Candidate Schwartz, why did you join my beloved Corps?"

"Sir, to kill, sir!"

"So you're a killer."

"SIR, YES SIR."

"Then get out there and kick ass, you sorry maggot!"

"Doc, let's nail the Euros. What are they?"

"Motty. The Euros are 92.89."

"Sell 'em all."

"Done, Motty." That was a quick $60,000.

"Good work. How are the USH? 9612? Sell fifty. Doc! Sell fifty USH. Ken, sell fifty more." Bing, bang, boom. A ray of morning sun peeped through my window as the last bond bit the dust at 9619.

"The deadliest weapon in the world is a marine and his rifle. It is your killer instincts which must be harnessed if you expect to survive in combat. Your rifle is only a tool. It is a hard heart that kills. If your killer instincts are not clean and strong, you will hesitate at the moment of truth. You will not kill. You will become a dead marine. And then you will be in a world of shit because marines are not allowed to die without permission. Do you maggots understand?"

"SIR, YES SIR!"

I had not hesitated at the moment of truth. My instincts had been clean and strong. I had killed the stocks and bonds to the tune of $1.2 million. I had done my duty as a good marine and a good officer. Semper fi.

Money Talks, Bullshit Walks (aka Early in the Day, Early in the Week)

In the late seventies, when I was in the early stages of trying to build my grubstake, Audrey and I would drive out to our group house in Westhampton Beach to escape from the City. When we were in Westhampton Beach, I used to hang out at Robb & Robb, a small brokerage firm on Main Street. Robb & Robb was owned by a group of Big Board specialists who'd check in at the office on summer afternoons after a round of golf, lunch, and a few pops at the Westhampton Country Club.

Robb & Robb felt more like a clubhouse for wayward speculators than a place of business. The office was just one room with half a dozen desks in the main area and a bench along the west side under the windows. High up on the east side, dominating the room, was a big Trans Lux ticker tape with the latest quotes marching along it from wall to wall. Anyone who wanted to could wander in and make himself at home on the bench and there was always a group of old-timers watching the tape and swapping stock tips. Whenever one of them sold a winner, he'd strut proudly over to an empty desk and shout the sell order into the phone. A loser, on the other hand, was whispered into the phone in the farthest corner, out of presumed earshot. I loved sitting on the bench, watching the tape with the old-timers and listening to the boys bullshit each other. The egos were so thick you could hardly breathe.

I pretty much kept to myself, but one day I struck up a conversation with John, a guy in his midseventies who came into the office once in a while. Like me, John carried a stack of dog-eared charts. He'd come in, find a spot on the bench, start to watch the ticker, and begin collecting data for his indicators. In between scribbles, John told me that he was retired, but that he'd spent years on Wall Street and was now supplementing his income by consulting for some of the specialist books on the

New York Stock Exchange. Then he taught me something I'd never heard of before or since, but I've found to be true.

In those days, the markets were different. There tended to be a more even distribution of bull and bear phases. It wasn't like the bull run we've been experiencing since 1982. What John told me was that during bear phases, there was a tendency for the markets to try to rally early in the day and early in the week, but to sell off later in the day and later in the week. The reason, John said, was because if a day trader is losing money and the market weakens, he wants to close out his position before the end of the session and start again the next day with a clean slate. And, as the week goes on, a slightly longer-term trader often wants to close out his losing position before the weekend. That way, he doesn't have to carry a debit balance on his margin account for two days when the market is closed and he has no chance of getting any price movement. But in a bull market, said John, a trader is absorbed with making money and is driven by greed rather than fear, so rather than bail out, he'll ride the bull overnight or over the weekend.

What John was saying made sense to me. Knowing this tendency for traders to buy early in the day and early in the week and to sell late in the day and late in the week in a bear market helped me use a down-trending tape to make money many times.

How did I know that John's take on the market was any better than that of the other old boys who sat around Robb & Robb bullshitting each other? At first, I didn't. You never do. There's a lot of bullshit flying around any brokerage firm. You just have to keep an open mind, be a good listener, respect experience, keep trying, and keep testing. This tip worked for me. Thanks, John.

17

The Best Trade

On January 26, 1991, ten days after Desert Storm, I was lying on the hospital bed in my guest room with a temperature of 101. I was suffering my third relapse from viral pericarditis. Once more I'd pushed myself too hard; I was sure that the virus was going to recapture me and send me back to the hospital. Esther Frederiksen, my private nurse, was giving me alcohol baths, and Dr. Christodoulou had upped my Prednisone to 40 milligrams a day. All that walking in the cold with Rob LeVine had been wiped out by Desert Storm.

The treatments worked, and the fever broke, but I was weak, I was totally dependent on Prednisone, and I was scared. Every time I tried to trade like my old self, my temperature would start to climb and I was sure I'd be heading back to the hospital. I wasn't getting any better, and I was afraid I never would. I kept having mood swings, and Dr. Hochman was trying to get me off the drugs, and I was trying to trade, but I never knew which feelings were real and which were chemically induced. I was tired, grouchy, and more impossible to live with than ever. I don't know how Audrey and the kids put up with me.

Hochman recommended that I start seeing a stress management consultant. He said that I had to find somebody who could teach me how to relax. I went to see Dr. Bernard Landis. The first thing Landis did was hook me up to a monitor to check my breathing pattern. He wanted to see how many breaths I took in one minute. He told me to start counting back from 600 by subtracting 13: 587, 574, 561, 548, 535, 522 . . . I kept counting backward as fast as I could until Landis finally stopped me at 67. He said that he'd never seen anybody go so far back in one minute.

"Whaddya mean?" I protested. "You cut me short. You didn't give me the full minute. I could've done it. Let me try again."

"Marty. I don't care about the counting. I was just trying to gauge your breathing pattern when you were concentrating. Most people take twelve breaths a minute when they're concentrating. But you were taking twenty."

"Yeah, so what, I wanted to win the contest. I still think I can do it. Come on, let's go again."

That was the start of a long relationship with Dr. Landis. All that winter and the following spring, he kept working on me, teaching me different techniques to get me to relax and get healthy. It took until June to wean me completely away from the Prednisone, and Landis recommended that I take a vacation as a reward. Audrey and I decided to go back to Aspen for two weeks. We hadn't been there since two years earlier, when I decided to start Sabrina Partners L.P.

It was supposed to be a peaceful, stress-free rest in the crisp, cool mountain air two thousand miles away from New York and the markets. Once again, we rented a three-bedroom condominium at the base of Snowmass. But once again, I couldn't stop trading. I'd brought my laptop computer and a fax machine with me and I was making trades from phone booths all over Aspen. I couldn't take a vacation, I still had my funds to run.

But as I thought about it, it became obvious to me that regaining my health was the most important thing I had to do. And if running the funds meant this would hurt my peace of mind, I decided that they had to go.

Part of me already knew that. I thought back to the summer of 1989 and my meeting with Porky from the Bronx, right after my first trip to Aspen and my decision to start Sabrina Partners L.P.

I'd been waiting an hour outside his office, and I wasn't very happy about it. I wanted to get back to my trading. But when you're starting your own fund, one of the things you have to do is call other members of the club to see if they can get you introductions to big hitters with money to invest.

A few days earlier, I'd called A. N. Alyzer, the head of research for the firm that was going to clear trades for Sabrina

Partners L.P., and Sabrina Offshore Fund Ltd. A.N. had committed some of his own money to my funds, so I figured that he'd be a good reference. "Sure, Marty," Alyzer told me, "I'm good friends with Porky, and Porky's always looking for hot traders that can make him money. I'll give him a call and set up an appointment for you." Now I was sitting outside Porky's office cooling my heels.

I knew all about Porky. Everyone on the Street knew all about Porky. He was a real top dog, a big swinging dick. His fund ran several billion dollars, and Porky took great pleasure at pissing on everyone else's hydrant. I'd never met him before, but I didn't like him. He had a reputation for being gruff and abrasive and he thought that he was a great practical joker. He liked to brag about how he would tweak brokers. Brokers were always calling Porky looking for business, so what he'd do was call them back when there were just a few minutes left before the market closed and say, "Okay, you want some of my business, buy me five hundred thousand shares of Urmigblmsblurg." Then he'd hang up.

The broker, having missed the name of the stock, would immediately call back, but Porky would tell his secretary to say that he was in the can and couldn't be disturbed. The broker would be going crazy, screaming at his secretary to look up every stock starting with "Urm" or "Erm," and pleading with Porky's secretary. "Honey, please! Just stick your head in the can and ask him the name of the stock!" At the average commission, that would be 6 cents a share, or $30,000, and the broker would get to keep 20 percent, so he was looking at missing out on a $6,000 paycheck. What the hell was the name of that stock? The market would close and the broker would be devastated. Not only had he lost a big commission, he'd blown his only chance to do a deal with Porky. Porky loved it. Some joke, huh?

I got up and started pacing around. Finally, the receptionist told me to go on in. Walking into Porky's office was like walking into the showroom at Circuit City. The place was packed with screens, Telerates, Quotrons, faxes, phones, copiers, and a dozen other gizmos. Porky had three times as many gadgets as I had. A nervous young assistant was standing on the Oriental carpet being dressed down for some infraction. Porky himself was wallowing around in a custom leather swivel armchair with a back about nine feet high. The chair was set behind a ponderous mahogany desk that was as big as a lunch counter and had just as much food spread on it. Bagels, bialys, knishes, Krispy Kremes, and half-consumed celery sodas were scattered among PCs, cell phones, and piles of paper.

Porky's bowling ball head jutted straight out of his shoulders. If he had a neck, it was well hidden under his Jabba the Hutt jowls. His florid, moonlike face looked bloated with blintzes and lots of sour cream. "Rumph," he said to me, waving a fat hairy hand in the direction of a distant couch. I sat down while Porky continued to dress down the young assistant. "I don't give a shit about your sources on the Street! You have to do your own thinking!" I was sure that in his own mind, Porky thought that he was doing the kid a great service by training him how to think, but it was obvious he was enjoying it, a lot. Porky was a carnivore. Like Jabba, he had to have a certain amount of meat each day, and today was this poor guy's turn to be devoured. I was embarrassed to watch it.

This harangue went on for another twenty minutes before Porky spit out what was left of his assistant and turned to me. "Hggrlgnh. So Schwartz, whaddaya want?" he said.

I told him that I had an incredible track record, that I was setting up a fund, that I'd sent him the documents regarding the offering, that I wanted to know if I could manage some of his money.

"Whaddaya charge?"

"Four and twenty," I said. Porky's face turned even redder and his eyeballs started to pop even further out of his head.

"Rrrrrrrrgh! Four and twenty!" he growled, rising in his chair. "That's more than I charge! How dare you charge more than me? I only charge one and twenty, and I'm the best. Who the hell do you think you are? Get out of here! Grrgghhh!" He rummaged around his desk until he found a blintz and shoved it into his mouth. The sour cream trickled down his chins.

I was dumbstruck. How could he act this way? The appointment had been set up by a mutual friend, he'd kept me waiting for over an hour, and now he was throwing me out after less than a minute. If he didn't like my fees, all he had to say was "I'm sorry" or "Let me think about it." I wasn't one of his flunkies. They were paid to be kicked around. I wanted to jump over his lunch counter and pound his arrogant fat head into his rude nonexistent neck, but I restrained myself. If I popped Porky, he'd undoubtedly sue me, and I was just starting a new business. I didn't need any problems with Porky.

I got up and left, but as I rode down in the elevator, I kept getting hotter and hotter. When I got back to my office, I was steaming. I had to trade, but I couldn't concentrate because I couldn't get Porky out of my mind. I just sat there thinking to myself, "How can I get this rude arrogant fat fuck back?"

The phone rang. It was Tommy Collins, my clerk on the Merc. Collins had been a going away present from Debbie Horn. Right after the October 22, 1987, trade where we climbed on for a free ride while the boys in the pit took George Soros to the cleaners, Debbie had decided that she'd had enough. That trade had sent her over the edge. She'd finally come to the conclusion that there had to be an easier way to make a living than listening to me rant and rave all day.

When she told me that she was leaving she recommended that I hire Collins as my clerk. "Marty, you'll like this guy. He's big, he's strong, he's smart, and most important, he's tough. He'll get in there and fight for you." Debbie had been right. I still ranted and raved about getting screwed all the time, but I knew that Collins was in there doing his best, fighting for me.

"Tommy," I said, "you ever run into this fat fuck, Porky from the Bronx?"

"Porky, yeah, I've talked to him a couple of times and he always says to me, 'Listen, Collins, you ever come across something that can make me some money, gimme a call. Ya know something, give itta me, ya know, first and I'll make it worth ya while.'"

"Tommy, here's what I want you to do," I said. "I want you to call Porky just before the market closes and tell him that you've got something real hot for him, and then when he asks you what it is, you say 'Marty Schwartz says, Urmigblmsblurg' and then hang up."

"Say what?"

"Urmigblmsblurg. Don't worry, Porky will know. And he's gonna call you right back, and he's gonna be bullshit."

So at 3:59, Tommy called Porky's office. He said that Mr. Porky had told him to call if he ever had anything that could make Mr. Porky some money. Porky hopped right on the line.

"Yeah, Collins, ya got something good for me?"

"Yeah, Marty Schwartz says ya oughtta go get some Urmigblmsblurg." And Collins hung up.

Sure enough, Porky called him right back. "Collins, you fuckin' jerk, whose phone lines you using? I'm gonna get you! I'm gonna get you thrown out of there. Whose phone lines? I'm very important. You can't do this to me. I'm gonna get you! I'm gonna get you good! Rgghpfrgh!" The veins in his forehead were exploding through the phone. The receiver was melting in his sweaty palm. Porky had lost his sense of humor.

Jamming Porky's mind, if even only for a minute, made me feel so good that right then and there, I decided that my goal was to make my fund bigger than Porky's. I was going to beat him, I was going to beat them all. I was gonna be the top dog, even if it killed me.

Now it almost had killed me.

I finally admitted to myself that managing other people's money was not for me. I didn't like reporting to anybody or having people looking over my shoulder, comparing my results to everyone else's. I was a market timer, a scalper. I liked to jump in and jump out, and that was tough to do when you were managing big money. And what about my freedom? That's why I'd gone out on my own in the first place.

But as I hopped into my Jeep Wrangler, put the canvas top down, and drove past the Aspen airport, the other part of me was reminded of what I'd be giving up. I'd never have one of those Cessnas, Lears, or Gulfstreams that were sitting on the tarmac. I'd never be part of the jet set; I wouldn't be running with the top dogs.

I needed to go to the bookstore at the Little Nell Hotel to get a copy of *Market Wizards* for the tennis pro at the Snowmass

Club. He had patiently been hitting hundreds of balls to me while I tried to regain my stamina. He was interested in the market and I thought that he'd enjoy reading *Market Wizards*, especially since I was in it.

I picked up a book and got in line behind a well-coiffed woman in her sixties. Out of the blue, she turned and said, "So you want to be a Market Wizard?"

I didn't know what to say. I just stared at the woman. She was immaculately dressed, and somebody in her family must have come over on the *Mayflower*. She was probably in her mid-sixties and looked like she had been collecting dividends and clipping coupons for as long as I'd been alive. She was comfortable, relaxed, serene, and healthy, obviously without a worry in the world. Suddenly it all became clear. I didn't want to be a Market Wizard. I wanted to be like her.

"No, ma'am," I said, "I'm already a Market Wizard. And believe me, it ain't what it's cracked up to be." At that moment I resigned myself to the fact that I was not going to beat Porky at the money management game. Aspen was where I'd decided to open the funds and Aspen was where I'd decided to close them down. In my heart, and in my mind, I knew that I'd just made a good trade.

SABRINA PARTNERS L.P.
750 Lexington Avenue
New York, N.Y. 10022

31 July 1991

Dear Partners:

I'm writing this letter to notify you that I've decided to liquidate the partnership as of the end of July 1991. I'm returning your starting capital for 1991 now and the remainder will follow after the audit is completed.

My doctors have advised me that the best way to fully recover from the life-threatening illness that I experienced last November requires that I be in a less stressful environment and that I need time to relax and enjoy life. The pressure of managing an aggressive pool of money full time does not afford me the necessary tranquillity I need to fully regain my health. My recuperation has taken longer than I ever expected and I don't want to have any setbacks. I just last month completed seven months on Prednisone and I don't want to go back on it if I can possibly avoid it.

The past eight months have been the most difficult of my life. And in order to be most fair to myself and my family I intend to take a sabbatical from trading and enjoy some of the simpler things in life that I have neglected for too long in the pursuit of fame and fortune. I want to thank all of you for your confidence and support you have shown in me and for that I am grateful.

During the month of June we lost 1.36%, reducing our gain for the year to 9.39%. In July we are down slightly. We will do our utmost to get the audit completed quickly and get your final payment out to you.

Sincerely,
Martin Schwartz
General Partner

In August 1991, I was back at the beach house in the Hamptons under my towel, trading for myself, and it felt good. Landis had convinced me to take up golf and Audrey and I had joined a golf club out there. Golf was not a game that I would have taken up on my own. It required too much practice to be good and too much time to play. A round of golf shoots a whole day. But that's what Landis advised, for me to shoot a whole day.

We'd only been in the club for a little while when Audrey set up a match with a banker and his wife. Now that I was going to take it easy, she wanted to expand our social circle. We were set to tee off at 10:30 A.M., but just before we left the house, I saw that the S&Ps had broken through one of my channels. I knew that the market was overbought so I called Tommy Collins and sold fifty contracts short. I tucked my Metriplex and my little cellular phone into the ball pocket of my bag and off we went to the country club.

We were whacking the balls around and talking about nothing important with the banker and his wife, supposedly having a good time, but all I could think about was my fifty contracts and how I was going to cover them when the market turned. At every tee, I'd stick my head into my bag pretending to be looking for a new ball and punch up a quote on my Metriplex. On the sixth tee it happened. The market turned. I had to call Collins and cover my fifty contracts, and I had to do it right away. I couldn't wait until we took a break at the ninth hole. By then, it would be too late. But I couldn't let anybody see me. Conducting business on the course would be rude, and I wasn't supposed to be trading.

Audrey and the banker's wife had gone to the ladies' tee way over on the left, so it was just me and the banker. "You're up, Marty," he said.

I stood on the tee and addressed my ball. This would be my biggest shot of the day. I had to hit it just right. I thought about what the pro had been telling me during my lessons. "Set the ball on your left shoulder. Keep your head down. Bring the club back slowly. Don't break your left arm. Swing through the ball." I put the ball on my right shoulder, picked my head up, jerked the club back, bent my left elbow, and lunged at the ball. Whack.

I looked up as the ball sailed deep into the woods. Perfect. What a shot. "Gee, too bad," the banker said. "You'll be lucky to find that one, Marty. Do you want me to come over and help you look?"

"No, no, don't bother. I think I know right where it went and if I have any trouble, I'll just drop another ball. What's another stroke on a score like mine?"

I dashed into the woods, ducked behind a big tree, pulled out my phone, and punched in Collins's number. "Tommy, cover those fifty contracts, NOW!"

I made $60,000 on that trade and nobody was the wiser, at

least until Landis pried it out of me. "Marty," he said, "I don't have to tell you that your behavior's not normal."

"Normal?" I said. "Who wants to be normal? Doc, what you've got to understand is that ever since I was five, I've tried to be abnormal or supernormal. Get ahead, get ahead, get ahead. I'm a trader. No trader's normal. If I wanted to be normal, I'd put my money in an index fund and be an analyst. The only thing I want normal is my temperature."

"Marty, you're like an alcoholic. You're addicted to your own adrenaline. You get so high, so manic on the action that comes with trading, that you can't stay away from it. Then you get so exhausted, so run down, that it's like a hangover, and you're so depressed that the only way you can feel better is to start trading again, until you make yourself sick. You have to figure out what you really want."

Therapists are like backboards. You just keep bouncing things off of them until you feel like you've finally found your groove. And that's what I did with Landis for the next six months. I kept bouncing things off of him until I started to see what I really wanted. When I was lying on the operating table fighting for my life, I'd made a pact with myself that if I ever got out of the hospital alive, I was going to spend less time trading and more time with Audrey and the kids.

I had enough money for now and if I ever needed more, I knew that I could earn it. That was my gift. I had the knowledge to wake up in the morning with a clean slate and go into the war room and make $20,000, $40,000, $80,000 that day. So what if I'd never beat the Porkys of the world at managing money? I could beat them in other ways. After my own near-death experience, the loss of a child, and Audrey's battle with breast cancer, it was time for me to stop sniffing fire hydrants and start smelling the roses. I decided that, like Sandy Koufax, I was going to walk away at the top of my game.

But where would I go? I had to get out of New York because Landis was right, I was addicted to trading. If I stayed in New York with my old friends and my old lifestyle, I'd keep falling off the wagon and sliding back into Porkyism. Besides, I was tired of the cold and the gray. I wanted to go someplace where it was warm and blue. I decided that to save myself, I'd move us all to Florida.

Changing my lifestyle and cutting our ties to New York took great courage. Audrey and the kids didn't want to go. Their lives were geared to the City. What did they know about Florida? What did I know about Florida? Florida was a place you went to retire, and I was only forty-eight. A big part of me didn't want to go. It would be such a hassle: selling the apartment, moving my business, moving twelve rooms of furniture, buying a new house, redecorating it, trading in the old car, buying a couple of new cars, schools for the kids, insurance, bank accounts, and a hundred other things. And I'd really miss New York, the galleries, the museums, the beach house, being close to the heartbeat of the Street, seeing Inside Skinny and my other buddies.

On the other hand, in New York, I'd go outside to try and hail a cab, and if it wasn't raining, I'd get one, but it would take forever. There was noise, and garbage, and someone cutting you off trying to make the light, there was a panhandler on every corner, the sirens were wailing, and there was nothing to look at but bricks and asphalt. Bricks and asphalt, that was New York.

In June of 1993, we sold the apartment and moved to south Florida. It was quiet, and clean. The other drivers meandered politely along, probably because they were mostly octogenarians. There were no muggers, no panhandlers, no bricks, no garbage, and nothing to look at but old guys in sans-a-belt slacks, old ladies in tennis shoes, green palms and blue water. I couldn't adjust to this environment. Audrey had a new house to work on, the kids had a new school to go to, I had nothing but my work. Once we got organized, I went into my nice new bright, clean, office overlooking the ocean, pulled all the drapes so I could see my screens, and called Collins at the Merc.

This wasn't right. I called Landis. "Doc, all I've done is exchange a dark office in New York for a dark office in Florida."

Landis gave me the name of a therapist who he thought could help me. I made an appointment with my new Florida doc. After a few sessions, he said, "Marty, you're too serious, your wife's too serious, and you're raising your kids to be too serious. You're in Florida now. Go play golf, sit on the beach, read a book, relax."

"Of course, we're serious," I said. "Life is serious. You know, you either win or lose, and winning is much better than losing. After you win, you can pay a therapist to get fixed up."

For the past few years, I've been paying, and paying, and paying, bouncing more and more balls off of the backboard. What I've discovered is that there isn't enough time in the day to be a good son, a good brother, a good husband, a good father, and still be a good trader. I'm a perfectionist and I want to do everything right, but to trade the way I have to trade takes fourteen hours a day. As I've gotten older, I've tried to take shortcuts like having an assistant to post my charts, transcribe my hot lines, and reconcile my sheets, but the shortcuts don't work. I had a plan, and I built a machine just the way I wanted it, and I tuned it to perfection, and now it owns me.

I've tried to set my goals lower, play smaller, and be an investor as well as a trader. I play on the Battling Barristers, a softball team dominated by superannuated lawyers. I spend at least two afternoons a week on the golf course. Sometimes I go down to the beach and just sit there, watching the waves roll in. Often, I wonder if this is where I want to be, if I made the right decision, but then I think of Manhattan in February, and how I'd be running around sniffing the hydrants, and I know that I was right to get out of New York.

Inside Skinny called me after he went to Dan Dorfman's wedding a while back and he told me that Porky from the Bronx was there. "The guy musta weighed three hundred and fifty pounds," Skinny said. "He parked himself at the buffet table and didn't move the whole time. All the other guests hadda squeeze around him if they wanted something to eat, and all he could talk about was this takeover, and that merger, and this leveraged buyout, and that IPO, and how he'd made a fortune on all of them. Dorfman was afraid that Porky was going to blow a hole in the back of his heart and croak on the spot." It was the same old story, *ubi est mea.*

That same day, I'd played golf in the morning with my son, had lunch with my mother, gone swimming in the afternoon with my daughter, and had a candlelight dinner with my wife. I didn't even think about trading. Well, maybe just once or twice. In that sense, maybe I had beaten Porky. If I'd kept running my funds and stayed in New York, I would've been right there next to him. All the top dogs would've been at Dorfman's wedding.

Despite all my best efforts, I'm still addicted to trading. A little over a year ago, when everyone else was making money, I was in a prolonged losing streak and feeling depressed. I was sure that I was right and the market was wrong, but as usual, the market didn't give a shit. My Florida therapist told me that I had to go cold turkey and give up trading entirely for one week. I agreed, but just before my next appointment, I saw that the move I'd been waiting for for months was just about to happen. I called Collins, bought forty S&P contracts, and told him to call me just as soon as the market turned. I slipped my vibrating cell phone, the one I'd gotten for golf, into the breast pocket of my jacket and went to my session.

As we were talking, I felt the phone vibrate. It had to be Collins. "Excuse me," I said to my Florida therapist, "I have to go to the can."

I ran in, locked the door, and called Collins back. As I'd predicted, the S&Ps were up and the market was turning. "Sell," I whispered into the phone. I'd just made $30,000. Now I felt like Sandy Koufax.

"See," my therapist said as I walked back into his office all smiles, "you seem much better. Taking a week off is just what you needed."

Hey, what could I say? I'm a trader.

The Pit Bull's Guide to Successful Trading

The reason a lot of people do not recognize opportunity is because it usually goes around wearing overalls looking like hard work.

—Thomas A. Edison

Hard work is the primary reason why I've become so successful, but hard work's just part of the equation. By nature, I'm a **gambler with a good feel for numbers,** and, as I've mentioned before, Amherst taught me **how to think,** Columbia Business School taught me **what to think about,** the Marine Corps taught me **how to perform under fire,** and Audrey taught me the importance of **money management.** These are the five blocks that must serve as the foundation for constructing a trading methodology.

Methodology

After nine years as a securities analyst, I decided to make a complete transition from fundamental analysis, the use of economic data to forecast individual stock prices, to technical analysis, the study of price and volume independent of the underlying economic data. Your trading methodology has to fit your personality. You have to understand your strengths and your weaknesses. It took me nine years to figure myself out.

My strengths are dedication to hard work, dogged persistence, ability to concentrate for prolonged periods, and a hatred of losing. My weaknesses are insecurity, fear of losing, and a need for constant reinforcement and frequent gratification. A trader, like a chain, is only as strong as his weakest link, and it's your weaknesses that must dictate your trading style.

I'm a scalper. By that I mean that I'm in and out quickly, always, *always,* **ALWAYS!** I'm often in and out in five minutes or less, never more than a couple of hours. Initially, I adopted a short-term trading system because I had limited resources and needed a consistent string of small winners to build up my capital base, but as I became more successful, I discovered that short-term trading was what gave me the most reinforcement and gratification. I just love to hear the cash register ring. It's the sound of the market telling me that I'm a winner, again and again and again.

Most books on trading say that you only have to be right three or four times out of ten if you cut your losses quickly and let your profits ride. That doesn't work for me. I cut my losses quickly, but I take my winners just as quickly. I need to be right seven or eight times out of ten.

I'm a boxer-counterpuncher. I spot an opening, jump in, score, and jump back out. In and out, in and out, a point here, a point there. I'm not going for the knockout, but at the same time, I'm making damn sure that I don't get knocked out. That's my style, and I tailored my technical analysis and my methodology to fit it.

Before you step into the ring, know exactly how you want to fight. Take my buddy Inside Skinny. While I'm at my desk crunching numbers, he's out schmoozing it up over martinis, fishing for hot tips. Hard work is not one of Skinny's strengths. And Skinny's no boxer-counterpuncher; he goes for the knockout, all of the time, every time. He'll go into ten trades, and be wrong on eight of them, and he won't care, because he makes enough on the other two to end up way ahead. Or take Porky from the Bronx. He's so huge, he's got so much talent on the payroll, he's ready for anything that comes along. His strengths are his size, his organization, and his appetite for any deal that will make him money. I tried to compete with Porky, and it nearly killed me.

Tools of the Trade

I'm a scalper and a market timer, and I've developed my tools accordingly. Here they are.

- The **Dow Jones Industrial Average** (**DJIA** on the Quotron) is the most widely quoted measure of stock market price movement. Changes in it provide me with a quick snapshot of the direction of the market.
- The **New York Stock Exchange Net Ticks (TICK)** shows me how many stocks on the NYSE had a last tick that was up netted out against those that were down. My friend Mark Cook has developed several strategies using net ticks that are very helpful during this new era of continual computer trading programs. For example, a strongly negative number like –1000 is often a time to go countertrend to the decline; a strong sell-off has been too rapid (it's either news induced or program generated) and the market is likely to rebound.

The opposite is true when the TICK is +1000, which is usually caused by a computer buy program. When the buy program ends, the market usually drops back down over the short term. Another short-term trading trick is when the DJIA opens up and the TICK is –200, for example; this usually means that there is more selling pressure in the broad market and the DJIA is being held up by only a few stocks, so you can usually go short.

- The **Short-Term Trading Index (TRIN)** is primarily a short-term trading tool that shows me whether volume is flowing into advancing or declining stocks. It is calculated by taking the ratio of (up issues/down issues) divided by the ratio of (up volume/down volume). If more volume is flowing into advancing stocks than declining stocks, the TRIN will be less than 1.0; if more volume is flowing into declining stocks, the TRIN will be greater than 1.0. A TRIN less than 0.80 is an indication of stronger buying bias; above 1.20 is an indication of greater selling pressure. It can help key you in to strong or excessive buying or selling pressure.

- The **Dow Jones Net Ticks (TIKI)** is the net number of the thirty Dow Jones Industrial stocks ticking up or down. A value of +26 to +30 or –26 to –30 often suggests that a buy or sell program has just gone off, because it is unusual for all the DJ stocks to be ticking up unless a buy program was buying all of them at the same time, for example.

- The **Standard & Poor's 500 Stock Index (SPX)** is important because it is the underlying index on which the S&P 500 futures price is based. It is an inclusive index made up of 500 stock prices including 400 industrials, 40 utilities, 20 transportation, and 40 financial issues. The SPX is constructed using market weights (stock price × shares outstanding) to provide a broad indicator of stock price movement.

- The **New York Composite Index (NYA)** is an index made up of all the stocks listed on the New York Stock Exchange and weighted according to the market value (stock price × shares outstanding) of each security.

- The **QCHA** (rhymes with "gotcha") is the average percentage movement for all exchange-listed stocks on an unweighted basis. This market-breadth indicator helps me identify divergences. For example, if the Dow is down twenty points, but the QCHA is +0.12 percent, this shows that the broader market is acting firm and it's a fake-out trade. You can usually go long for a quick profit when the Dow Jones starts to turn back up.

Feel free to use my tools, but don't think that you can just pick them up and start making money. To make yourself into a skilled craftsman, you'll have to find the tools that feel right to you, and use them over and over until you learn how they work, what they can do, and how to get the most out of them.

Market Analysis

Listening to what the market is saying takes extreme concentration. Like a doctor monitoring the health of a patient, I take the pulse of the market by keeping charts on my indicators and checking them every ten minutes during the trading day.

I record the pulse reading on the exact half hour by drawing a box around the indicators. Then I overlay a red or green arrow between each boxed set to reflect whether the New York Composite was up or down from the previous half hour and by how much (see Exhibit I).

This exercise forces me to focus on how the market is trying to move. This is critical when the market is making a major move and I may be positioned incorrectly. Without this information, I might freeze and not react in time.

I'm a synthesizer. I like to bombard my brain with lots of opinions from various sources. I reread faxes that came in during the week and I try and put my own unique stamp on other people's ideas, incorporating them into my own thoughts about where a particular stock, an industry, or the market as a whole is heading. Here are some of the services that I use. There are many more, and everyone has to find the ones that best match his or her time horizons, trading philosophies, goals, and work ethics.

Exhibit I

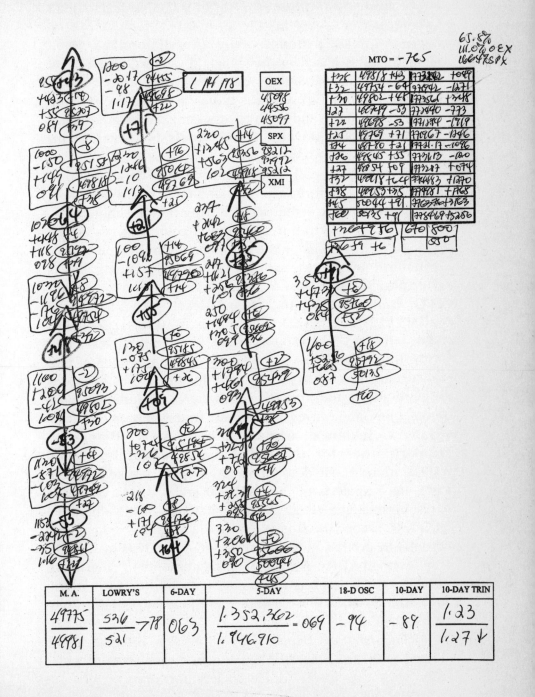

- **Amshar Management Report** by Terry Laundry (Nantucket, MA); amshar@worldnet.att.net; http://www.amshar.com; 1-888-228-2995.

  Terry does a longer-term overall outlook (i.e., months–years) based on his Magic T Theory—the notion that superior investment periods can only last as long as the prior cash buildup phase. His indicators have become the cornerstone of my approach to analyzing various markets.

- **Lowry's NYSE Market Trend Analysis** (North Palm Beach, FL); 561-842-3514.

  Lowry's does a daily update of each day's breadth action and changes to short-term and long-term buy-sell signals. The quotes are a calculation of buying power, selling pressure, and short-term buying power. Weekly, Lowry's writes up their observations on the week's action from an intermediate-term perspective with short-term adjustments, based on historical patterns of the three indexes.

- **P. Q. Wall Forecast, Inc.** (New Orleans, LA); 1-900-SUN-LIGHT ($2 per minute) for updates at 10:10, 12:30, 3:00, 5:00, intraday; call 1-800-259-0088 for monthly newsletter with interim bulletins and/or daily telephone update. For day traders as well as longer-term investors. Uses a variety of both short- and long-term techniques, including cycles, projections, and ranges on the Dow. Trades only on the Dow.

- **Stan Weinstein's Global Trend Alert—Detecting Opportunities for the Individual Investor;** 1-800-868-STKS; monthly. He does an overview of the market, as well as a stage analysis of the S&P 500 and secondary stocks, most promising S&P 500/secondary stocks, most vulnerable S&P 500/secondary stocks, group stage rating scan, most promising groups, global analysis, stage analysis of foreign fund/foreign ADRs. A stage analysis attempts to determine which stage a stock is in: basing, uptrend, top formation, downtrend—and splits each of these four stages into three substages.

- ***The Chartist*** (Seal Beach, CA); editor: Dan Sullivan; published every three weeks. Has an actual cash account, current market comments, and a trader's portfolio.

- **Crawford Perspective.** Telephone update on Monday, Wednesday, and Friday and special updates on the other days if there is a move of one hundred points on the Dow. Newsletter published monthly focuses on gold, S&P 500, and bond futures.
- ***Dick Davis Digest—Investment Ideas from the Best Minds on Wall Street*** (Fort Lauderdale, FL); biweekly; 954-467-8500. Publishes comments from leading thinkers in the investment community about individual stocks, mutual funds, and market direction.
- **Daily faxes:**

    Schaffer on Sentiment; Investment Research Institute; 1-800-448-2080; http://www.options-iri.com

    Cowen Morning Call

    Bear Stearns Morning Comments

    Mark Cook; 8333 Maplehurst Avenue, East Sparta, OH 44626; 330-484-0331

    Dick West's Morning Comment

Red Light, Green Light: Allowing the Trend to Be Your Friend

The ten-day exponential moving average (EMA) is my favorite indicator to determine the major trend. I first learned about this valuable tool from Terry Laundry (see www.amshar.com). I prefer the EMA over a straight ten-day moving average, or any other arithmetic average, because it emphasizes the most recent events, giving me a faster signal of when to buy or sell. With a straight ten-day moving average, each day is weighted equally, at 0.10. You start by taking the most recent ten days' data, adding them up, and dividing by 10. Then on the eleventh day, add that day's data, subtract the first day's data, add them up, and divide by ten. Day after day, repeat the same process.

The exponential moving average (EMA) that I use weights the most recent data point at 0.18, and the previous day's EMA 0.82. So it is much more sensitive to the last data point, crucial for a short-term trader. I call this "red light, green light" because it is imperative in trading to remain on the correct side of the moving average to give yourself the best probability of success.

On the floor of my office are two huge charts, four feet wide by ten feet long and growing. The first is a record of the Dow at hourly intervals. I keep another chart of the New York Composite on a closing basis and the ten-day EMA, with the MTO (Magic T Oscillator) charted below it (see Exhibit II). The ten-day EMA bounces along the page in dotted black. Whenever the New York Composite is above the ten-day exponential moving average, I draw it in as a solid green line. When it dips below, the line turns solid red. When you're trading above the ten-day, you have the green light; the market is in a positive mode and you should be thinking buy. Conversely, trading below the average is a red light. The market is in a negative mode and you should be thinking sell. That doesn't mean you should never buy when you have a red light, but if you do, it is critical that you have an extremely good intellectual reason for taking that position.

The hardest point to make a trade is when the price of the issue is hovering at the value of the moving average. This is the point that offers the maximum profit potential, but also has the greatest risk. Even though you can experience whipsaws, the profit potential in a trend move can be enormous. For instance, the market could be trading for several days below the EMA and then start heading back up, getting closer to the EMA. If it is able to close over it, this is often the beginning of a trend change and you are one of the first people to ride the young, new, and powerful positive trend. But often, the EMA is a repellent and the price action will turn back down once it has kissed the EMA from below. It is the spot where things are hanging in the balance.

I use this approach when trading futures and stocks. Every day after the close I write down that day's ten-day EMAs for the S&P 500, New York Composite, OEX, XMI, bond, Eurodollar, and S&P futures. I get these numbers off my FutureSource machine, which calculates and graphs the EMA for me.

So my moving averages are the key to being on the right side of the trade: going long when the market is in positive mode. The next step is picking an entry point and risk amount. What I

Exhibit II

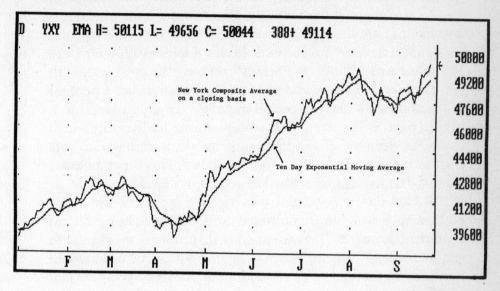

Courtesy of FutureSource

am usually looking for is a turn, an inflection point—and it is at this point where your moneymaking opportunity is greatest, because you're one of the first traders to identify the change in trend. I use channel lines and oscillators to help me pick levels and identify these situations. FutureSource does the calculations, and I have set up the parameters. I look at 120-, 60-, and 30-minute time frames. Pictorially, you have the price bars with one channel line above and one below; the bands are 1 percent above and below the ten-period moving average. I liken it to a rubber band being stretched too far—it eventually has to snap back. For example, if I'm in positive mode, and the price gets close to the lower band, I am looking to buy. This is not an exact science, but the channels provide good entry levels.

The ten-day exponential moving average gives the latest event a 0.18 weighting compared to a 0.10 weighting for an arithmetic average. The way to start this moving average is to add up the last ten price closes, which will produce what would normally be thought of as an arithmetic moving average. Then weight this total with a multiplier of 0.82. Then take the eleventh result and give it a weighting of 0.18 and add the two together. You have now started a ten-unit exponential moving average. To move forward, take your new calculated exponential moving average and again weight it at 0.82 and take the twelfth result and weight it at 0.18 and sum the two. For example:

Date	New York Exchange Composite Close
9/2/97	482.90
9/3/97	483.71
9/4/97	485.11
9/5/97	484.64
9/8/97	485.78
9/9/97	486.69
9/10/97	480.63
9/11/97	477.06
9/12/97	483.30
9/15/97	482.60
9/16/97	493.69

9/17/97	493.21
9/18/97	495.41
9/19/97	496.56

Step 1: Calculate the ten-day moving average. Sum 9/2/97–9/15/97 and divide by 10.

$$4832.42 / 10 = 483.242$$

Step 2: Multiply this value by 0.82.

$$483.242 \times 0.82 = 396.25844$$

Step 3: Take the eleventh day's (9/16/97) result and give it a weighting of 0.18.

$$493.69 \times 0.18 = 88.8642$$

Step 4: Add the values from steps 2 and 3 together.

$$396.25844 + 88.8642 = 485.12264, \text{ rounded to } \textbf{485.12}$$

This is the ten-day exponential average for 9/16/97.

To get the ten-day EMA for 9/17/97:
Step 5: multiply the previous day's EMA by 0.82.

$$485.12 \times 0.82 = 397.7984$$

Step 6: Take the newest value (9/17/97) and multiply that by 0.18.

$$493.21 \times 0.18 = 88.7778$$

Step 7: Add the values from steps 5 and 6 together.

$$397.7984 + 88.7778 = 486.5762, \text{ rounded to } \textbf{486.58.}$$

This is the ten-day EMA for 9/17/97.

This process is repeated after each day, so the ten-day EMA for 9/18/97 =

$$(486.58 \times 0.82) + (495.41 \times 0.18) = \textbf{488.17}$$

It will take about ten days of calculations to smooth the results to the ongoing existing true ten-day exponential moving average. In order to make it more useful, I would recommend going back at least twenty days when the data are available to get the proper smoothing. This will produce a more reliable tool to utilize immediately in your trading.

How I Play Stocks

I've developed a routine over the years. I'm a get-your-hands-dirty type of guy in my approach to preparation; I absolutely have to see and feel the numbers—charting the price action of seventy stocks daily and keeping large graphs of my daily indicators updated by hand, after calculating several mathematical ratios. The trade-off is time.

Each weekend, I get two chartbooks sent to my house by express mail. The first is *Standard and Poor's Trendline Daily Action Stock Charts* (212-208-8000). *S&P Trendline* has the daily charts for more than 700 companies, each going back 1½ years. I draw in trend lines and support areas for over 150 of those companies that catch my eye. I do this to get a feel for what industries and companies are doing well. On the front cover of the chartbook I make notes like "oils strong," "large cap techs weak." While many traders have computers that run industry analysis, I have to do it by hand to really feel changes in institutional money flow. I also make a one-page compilation of the companies that I drew trend lines for, listing the support area beside its ticker symbol.

Then I go through my second chartbook, which is custom-made for me and provided by Security Market Research (SMR; 303-494-8035). The chartbook has the daily price action and proprietary oscillators for seventy large-cap companies that I watch, plus indexes like Dow Jones Industrial Average (DJIA), Dow Jones Transportation Average (DJIT), S&P 500 (SPX), New York Composite (NYA), and NASDAQ Composite. Every three months, I change a few names that appear more interesting, but the list contains an excellent representation of all the major industries—mainly large-capitalization household names with high liquidity like Compaq, Coca-Cola, Merck, and Chase Manhattan.

On each page, I draw several support and resistance lines for that company and look at the oscillators at the bottom. The support lines connect important lows, and will indicate a price level where a fall in a stock's price could slow down and/or reverse. Resistance lines connect important highs and indicate areas where the price is likely to fall back down. Because I am a short-term trader, I use the highs and lows from the previous week or two to draw in aggressive trend lines as well. I circle the major nearby area of support on the price axis and write that level on a one-page sheet alongside its ticker symbol and the direction of the short-term oscillator. I fax this sheet to my assistant, who then enters the support levels on her computer. When these levels are touched during the trading day I make a decision if I want to take the trade. This preparation allows me to react quickly when prices are moving fast.

I play the OEX and SPX options when I want to play a little longer-term strategy. Longer term for me might be a few days to a week. The options are less liquid and slower moving than the futures. I will buy way out of the money puts with an expiration three months into the future (for example, December 900 SPX puts when the SPX is currently trading at 910). Often I turn to options when I am frustrated with the stress and volatility of the futures. If I have a longer-term idea, buying the options allows me to sit with it and let things play out a little longer. When I go long puts or calls at least I have a defined risk (the cost of the options) whereas in futures the risks can be more extreme due to the high leverage. Sometimes I like to trade the bond futures when I have a strong technical setup.

In terms of buying and selling stocks: above all else, I'm a trader, not an investor. My SMR chartbook of seventy large-cap names reflect the companies I focus on. I need the liquidity and volatility that these names provide. Because my scope is so short term, I'm in and out for a point or two on a 10,000 to 20,000 share position. If an idea isn't panning out in a day or two, I jump ship. Because I play large, I don't want the risk of riding a stock down $3, and because I am playing the larger, more volatile names, $3 is oftentimes less than the daily range. I also don't pick the weak and downtrodden. I look for tempo-rary weakness in strong stocks to buy, which is the same idea as the rubber band having to snap back and why drawing all my trend lines and writing the support levels out are so important. My assistant sets alarms on the computer with the support list I give her; if the price dips into the support area, she notifies me and I look to buy if I have a green light and like the looks of the chart. If a company is trading below a major trend line, I stay away. With the strength of the market over the past several years, I use the futures to go short, rather than shorting indi-vidual stocks.

How I Play Futures

Since they were first introduced, the S&P futures have been my meat and potatoes. I trade them day in and day out. To moni-tor the futures action, I go through two sets of charts printed out from my FutureSource machines. I get all my futures data from FutureSource (1-800-678-6333). I have four monitors stacked up two on top of the other and have twenty "pages" that are preprogrammed to display the charts that I like to look at. My assistant prints out the pages each weekend featuring dif-ferent studies over different time periods (2-, 30-, 60-, and 120-minute, daily, weekly, and monthly) for different futures con-tracts (S&P 500, Eurodollar, currencies, bond, U.S. dollar index, CRB index, and crude oil). I draw trend lines on these to help refine my sense of how the individual futures markets are doing. Also by checking the exponential moving averages I try to determine whether the different futures markets are in a pos-

Exhibit III

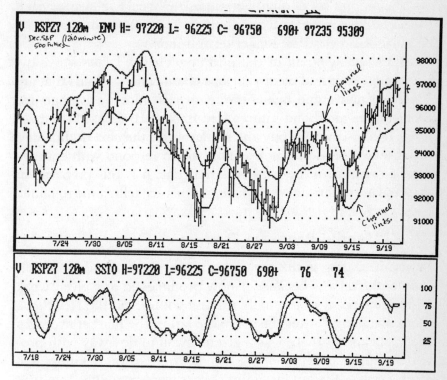

Courtesy of FutureSource

itive or negative mode. The old axiom about the trend being your friend is best acted upon by owning futures above the exponential moving average and shorting those below.

The second set of charts contains the weekly chart for each of the futures markets that I look at. This allows me to take a step back and view the longer-term trends.

After reviewing all of these futures charts, I take a five-by-eight index card and record various channel lines, bands that are 1 percent above and below the ten-period moving average, for S&P futures and bond futures (see Exhibit III). Based on these levels I record average buy and sell levels for the next trading day. All of these "pregame" notes allow me to respond with courage during the heat of the battle the next day. It is this preparation that makes me strong when my emotions are telling me to panic.

How I Handle Program Trading

Program trading is the scourge of the common trader. I call it "Nintendo Vegas," because it now produces in any given week 15 to 20 percent of the daily trading volume on the New York Stock Exchange. After the dramatic fall in the market averages in October 1987 there was a groundswell to do away with program trading because of its mindless effect on a vulnerable stock market. Eventually, point collars were introduced to limit the destruction that can be done on any given day. The large wire houses (brokerage firms) that participated that October day in 1987 vowed not to participate in these heinous activities again. But as time has passed and greed has returned to the arena, most of the players have crept back into the casino. Fifteen to 20 percent of the Big Board's daily volume is big business, and money and power always prevail on Wall Street.

Still, there are ways to survive and prosper even in the face of all this might. You must know the trend of the market and wait and wait for these technocrats to drive the market averages deep into your channel lines. In addition to using Mark Cook's extremes with TIKI and TICK, you counterattack by taking a contrary position to the mechanically driven direction of the market, hoping you are at an artificial extreme that will lead to a profitable trade. Like any good warrior, you lie in wait until these people conduct their mindless malevolence and you counterattack with a contrary position, always using a well-disciplined stop loss.

This is the way I've been able to adapt. While I dislike having to use these guerrilla trading tactics, the great challenge is to continually adjust my skills to ever-changing market conditions. I have done this successfully by adding new tools to my methodology and continuing the stern discipline of stop losses, channel lines, and moving averages.

Tricks of the Trade

When I was in the first grade, the teacher asked each of us what we wanted to be when we grew up. I said, "a detective." This investigative nature has carried through into adulthood. I love searching for clues, synthesizing tons of unrelated data, and arriving at a logical conclusion. While these observations are not entirely scientific, they are things that I've seen repeatedly over the years. I do not usually use these observations independent of my other tools and analysis, but I definitely factor them into my decision-making process when they occur.

Technical indicators that show me low-risk entry points for high probability trades are at the core of my methodology. But I am always intensely searching for patterns, setups, recurring themes, no matter how small, to help further swing the odds in my favor on a given trade.

Gaps in Charts

These are important tools that I use to trade stocks in particular and futures, too, when they happen. Gaps are instances when an issue opens significantly higher or lower than the previous day's price and maintains that level throughout the day (see Exhibit IV). This usually happens on a news announcement or an event that catches investors off guard. On a price chart this shows up as a gap. If the gap is not filled in two or

Exhibit IV

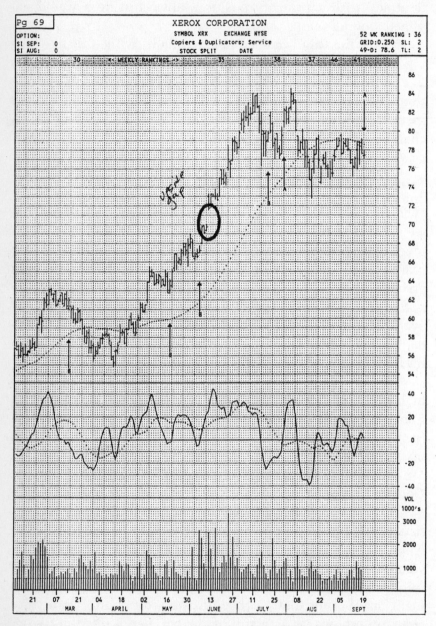

Courtesy of FutureSource Security Market Research

three days, it's a strong signal to take a position in the direction of the gap. The change in perception can sometimes last for a long time and be a very good source of trading ideas.

There are basically three types of gaps. The first is the breakaway gap. This occurs when a stock or futures contract gaps out of a base. It is usually very bullish. The second is a continuation gap, which happens after a stock has already made a move up. The third is the exhaustion gap. It shows up at the end of a move and usually the price action reverses trend shortly thereafter.

Cash Infusions from Mutual Funds

Another interesting pattern is due to automatic investments into mutual funds. The market often is stronger the last day of the old month and the first four of the new, as new money flowing into mutual funds are invested into stocks. This pattern also appears around midmonth, when new cash is often invested in index funds. I note things like "midmonth buying" on my blotter to remind me of this phenomenon. It will be interesting to see how outflows affect the market averages when we enter a bear market.

Three-Day Rule

Whenever a stock like a Microsoft or an Intel has had a large three-day move in one direction, you do not want to be buying on the third day or selling on the third day of a down move. That's a sucker play. Usually stocks will have big moves in three days. The first day the smart people are moving, the second day the semismart people are moving, and by the third day, the dunces have finally figured it out. This is an important rule. If the stock has bad news and it sells down, by the third day you may want to start looking to buy it because the bad news probably has been fully discounted.

Put/Call Ratios

My friend Marty Zweig was one of the first to identify a contrarian indicator that gauges market sentiment by computing the relationship between the number of puts to calls traded on the Chicago Board Options Exchange. His theory is that market tops and bottoms are often signaled by the actions of small unsophisticated investors who are attracted to the options market by the potential for a big score with a limited risk. The put/call ratio indicates the bullish or bearish expectations of these ineffective investors. When extreme readings take place, the market usually corrects in the opposite direction. Theoretically, an extremely high reading usually means that fear is at a peak and selling will soon stop so the market should rebound. For example, a reading greater than 1.00 shows an extreme bearish sentiment (buy signal), while a reading less than 0.45 shows high call volume and extreme bullish expectations (sell signal). Like all other indicators, this must be used in conjunction with other data to assess an entry point for a successful trade.

How the Market Reacts to News

Bob Zoellner taught me a very important indicator about how the market reacts to news. If the market gets negative news and the market shrugs it off and it continues to go up, this is a bullish reaction because it means the market has already discounted the news. On the other hand, a sign of a fully priced market is one that reacts poorly to good news. In terms of stocks, some investors are puzzled when good news causes a decline in stock price. Investors should understand that this "good news" had already been priced into the issue. My favorite lesson that Bob Zoellner taught me is that when the stress gets so great that you think you might vomit, you should probably double your position, but only if you are then willing to use a tight stop loss on the entire position.

New Highs/New Lows

Financial newspapers have a new-high and new-low list for stocks. Based on the first law of physics, an object in motion will continue in motion until an outside force affects it. A stock that's going down will continue to go down until it stops going down. A stock that's going up will continue to go up until it stops going up. So the new-high and new-low list is many times a good place to look for new ideas.

Up Mondays

What I've noticed in the past few years is that as the influx of money into index funds has increased dramatically, Mondays are no longer the dull day that they formerly were. Mutual fund managers will put money into the market that may have flowed in over the weekend because they have a responsibility to put that money to work. Since the volume is usually lower than that of other days of the week, this recently has exacerbated the move to the upside.

Market Probability Calendar

Every day I acknowledge and make a mental note of how the markets have done historically on that date. While this might not cause me to take a position, it might make me more cautious of fighting a historical pattern. I keep a copy of *Stock Trader's Almanac*'s Market Probability Calendar (1-800-477-3400) on my desk, which gives the probability of the market rising on any trading day of the year, and I have circled the highest and lowest readings. So if we're in a positive mode and you have a 75 percent chance historically that the day will be up, you might consider going with it.

Option Expirations

I am very cautious of expiration strategies: options and futures have an expiration date, and I've noticed that the market will often have a severe drop into the Thursday or Friday the week before expiration, only to then turn up and rally into the following week's option expiration. If I see this pattern set up, I'm leery of getting caught on the short side because I've seen this pattern before. Many times during option expiration, buy and sell programs will hit and shake you out of your position and fool you into leaning the wrong way.

Something else that I've observed is that program traders oftentimes will close the market very strongly in the last half hour, and I've noticed they go the opposite way the last hour of the following day. I've named it the Schwartz Rule of Alternation. I find expiration day very hard to trade and try to stay out because there are many fake-out moves due to the unwinding of options positions.

Trading on the Half Hour

I've noticed lately that for some unknown reason, program trading often occurs at half-hour marks: some bozo's watch reminds him that it's 11:00 and he pushes a button that starts a buy program; another program trader's watch is set for 1:30. I've also noticed a rising market right around noon that I've nicknamed the "noontime rally," probably so that everyone can attend their martini lunches without too much stress on their minds. The last half-hour of the trading day has been particularly volatile of late, because institutional daylong strategies are completed then.

Take Out the Highs, Take Out the Lows

In nontrending days where the market is trading back and forth in a range, the locals in the futures pits will make money trying to take out the stops, which are oftentimes concentrated around the highs and lows of the day. In a nontrending day, since the locals know where the stops are, they will accommodate both sides and blow out the stops on the highs. No sooner will they do that then they will start heading south and take out the stops on the lows. The way to counteract this is to put bids in below the low and offers above the highs to participate with the locals.

First Trade Back

After taking some time off, make certain you take the first day back to work very slowly to adjust your eyes to the rhythm of the markets. When I have rushed back into the fray, I have invariably gotten myself into trouble before I knew what hit me. Make your first trade upon returning an intellectual one and not an emotional one.

Worst Fears Not Realized

I have stated before that whenever your worst fears are not realized about a trade and the market is letting you out better than you expected, it is not just good luck. Rather, your position is most likely correct and should not only be held but perhaps added to.

Ego

We have met the enemy, and they are us.

—Pogo

I've said it before, and I'm going to say it again, because it cannot be overemphasized: ***the most important change in my trading career occurred when I learned to DIVORCE MY EGO FROM THE TRADE.*** Trading is a psychological game. Most people think that they're playing against the market, but the market doesn't care. You're really playing against yourself. You have to stop trying to will things to happen in order to prove that you're right. Listen only to what the market is telling you now. Forget what you thought it was telling you five minutes ago. The sole objective of trading is not to prove you're right, but to hear the cash register ring.

My Typical Day

*Baseball is 90 percent mental. The other half is
physical.*

                                 —Yogi Berra

6:45 A.M.

Alarm goes off. I get up begrudgingly. As a kid, I could sleep twelve hours a day. Now, I'm lucky if I can get eight. Anything under eight and I'm not ready for work, I feel like I've shorted myself.

6:45–7:20 A.M.

Shower and shave. I used to have a little pager that gave me market prices twenty-four hours a day, and I'd put it next to the mirror so I could watch the prices while I was shaving. But after three years in Florida, my new shrink made me get it out of the house. He wanted me to get all of my machines out of the house. He wanted me to turn my home into a refuge from trading. We compromised by removing the pager, and I must admit that it's good not having a razor in your hand when you're watching a position go down the toilet.

7:20–7:30 A.M.

Clean out the plumbing I. My grandfather Pappy Snyder always maintained that you were not ready to start the day until you'd cleaned out your plumbing twice. "When I was a boy your age," he once told me when we were walking together through New Haven on a cold winter day, "we lived just outside of Kiev and we had to go to an outhouse at thirty below. Try taking a crap in an outhouse in the dead of winter and you'll always appreciate indoor plumbing." I do, twice a day.

7:30–7:40 A.M.

Breakfast, a bowl of Kellogg's Oat Bran, a glass of Blood's fresh-squeezed grapefruit juice, and two pieces of Pepperidge

Farm whole wheat toast. I eat to loosen up, not to fill up. While I'm eating, I look at the *New York Times,* especially the sports section. I still like to see how my Yankees are doing and what Steinbrenner's done this time to tighten them up.

7:40 A.M.

I'm at my desk collating all the sheets that have been faxed in overnight. I get a thirty-page report from Bear Stearns, my clearing firm, listing the P&L of all of my accounts and all of my trades from the previous day. I also get sheets from my different commodity brokers. If the sheets aren't right, I'm on the phone ripping somebody a new asshole, because everything has to be reconciled before the market opens. The market's so volatile these days that if my accounts aren't reconciled before it opens, I could lose tens of thousands of dollars at the bell. That's why I record all of my trades. You can't trade if you're emotionally upset, and I want all of my accounts right by 8:00. I start each day with a clean slate. I don't bring any emotional baggage from the previous day. Each day stands on its own merit, and once it's over, it's over. My exhaustive evening work ritual helps put yesterday behind me so I can focus on today. Not doing this is dangerous for me. My biggest losses have always followed my largest profits because overconfidence has led to complacency and careless trading. Trading S&P futures is conducive to this psychological approach because futures are marked-to-market by the clearing firms—all open positions are credited or debited to your account at the end of the day based on their increases or decreases in value. So everyone starts with a clean slate each and every morning. I try to make money every day. I also keep track of my profits and losses for each week, each month, and each year.

8:00–8:10 A.M.

This is when I fly through the *Wall Street Journal.*

8:10–8:15 A.M.

Clean out the plumbing II. According to Pappy Snyder, I'm now ready to start the day.

8:15 A.M.

I call my bond brokers and get their support and resistance levels on bonds for the day. I write these down on my blotter. I have every ratio calculated: Terry Laundry's Magic T oscillator, the eighteen-day oscillator from the previous day, the high/low/close on various indexes: the OEX, the S&P, and the XMI.

8:20–8:30 A.M.

Round 1. The bonds open. I have to see if I want to trade bonds. I usually do because bonds are a good way to loosen up. Unless the government is about to release some numbers, they move a lot slower than stocks, options, and some other futures and they're easier for me to hit. Sparring with the bonds gives me a chance to get a feel for the markets and to work on my timing. Unfortunately, the government has wrecked the bond market. For some perverse reason, their most important releases always seem to come on Friday morning at 8:30. When you're over fifty, by Friday morning you have a hard time climbing into the ring. You'd think that the government would have the courtesy to make their important announcements earlier in the week so that we senior citizens would still be semifresh.

8:30–8:45 A.M.

During this time I might trade bonds, unless some announcement's come out. When a news item comes out, the futures exchanges have this thing they call "a fast market" and an F will go up on the machine to let you know that it's "fast." That means all the normal rules for trading are suspended and you're at the mercy of the boys in the pits. I don't trade bonds when the F sign's up because you never know what's happening and it's too easy to get screwed.

8:45–9:27 A.M.

A lot of different faxes roll in: Cowen and Co., Bear Stearns, various gurus, my friend Mark Cook out in Ohio, Dick West's daily market comments. I match all of this information with the opinions I've written on five-by-eight cards that I've taped to my quote machine the night before, and then I check the buy and sell levels I have for the S&P futures based upon 1 percent bands I've drawn around my channel lines. There is no excuse for not being prepared. Preparation is simply doing the work. If you have a game plan prepared ahead of time, it can help you find courage in the heat of the battle.

9:28 A.M.

I review my checklist. It's a handwritten sheet, laminated in plastic and taped to the right-hand corner of my desk where I can't overlook it. It summarizes my checkpoints for taking positions and contains general strategy reminders.

Check charts and moving averages prior to making a trade—the moving averages work better than any tool that I have. Don't go against them.

- Are we above or below my moving averages, i.e., in positive or negative mode?
- Are we above or below a dominant trend line?
- Has recent price action taken out previous highs or lows?
- Is the MTO (Magic T oscillator) in positive or negative mode?

Always ask before taking a position: do I really want to have this position?

Always know the amount I'm willing to lose before taking a position. Know the uncle point and honor it.

After a very profitable run of trading, reduce the position size.

After a successful period, take a day off as a reward.

9:29 A.M.

I'm on the phone to the S&P pit. The first minute and the last minute of the S&Ps are the most furious of the fight. Anybody who calls me during those times is going to get their head ripped off. I need total concentration. I cannot be disturbed. My adrenaline is pumping, and this can be a problem. When we were in New York, one of my friends' wives called at 9:29 on my business line one morning looking for Audrey. All of my brokers knew never to call me at 9:29 or 4:14 so I picked up the phone and shouted, "You asshole. I've told you never to call me at this time. Who the fuck do you think you are! . . . Oops, sorry, Molly. Molly?" I sent her a dozen roses, but Molly's been cool to me ever since. I've lost a few friends who've called me at 9:29 or 4:14.

9:30–12:30 P.M.

Rounds 2 through 7. The stock market is open. The Merc S&Ps are open. I write all of my orders on my blotter and when a trade is completed, I circle it. If it's not completed, I either leave it open or cancel it. If I cancel it, I write C-A-N-C-E-L next to it. That way, I have a running log of everything I've done and attempted to do during the day. I P&L the blotter every half hour while the market's open. I like to know exactly how much I'm up or down all of the time and I find it emotionally upsetting if my accounts aren't right. I have a grid with thirteen different squares, one for each half-hour bracket at the Merc, and I do incremental rates of change on the NYSE Composite. I'm always looking for patterns. Pattern recognition is my karma.

12:30 P.M.

Lunch. "Seaside Superette, this is Marty Schwartz. I want a number four to go." The market used to be an old-boy's club that went from 10:00 until 12:30, and then the old boys would go out for a two-martini lunch, come back and work from 2:00 until 3:00. It was very civilized. Since I'm not a drinker, that's when I'd get a sandwich and go to post my charts. Not anymore. Now I post charts at my desk.

1:00–4:00 P.M.

Rounds 8 through 14. More of the same. Keep on punching.

4:00–4:15 P.M.

Round 15. There's a fifteen-minute flurry when the stock market's closed, but the S&Ps are still trading. This is when you can really get clobbered. The premium level will rise or fall based on the orders for the close and the psychological setup for the next day's trading.

4:15–6:00 P.M.

Cool down. A little postfight analysis. Work on the P&Ls, get the blotter squared away, go for a workout or a run.

6:00–6:30 P.M.

Dinner.

6:30–7:00 P.M.

Charts. I have my own custom chart book produced by Security Market Research (SMR), a stock-charting service in Boulder, Colorado. I chart about seventy stocks, and I post the oscillators when they are faxed in from SMR.

7:00–8:30 P.M.

Data collection and review. I listen to all my hot lines, transcribe them, work on my moving averages, etc., etc.

8:30–10:30 P.M.

Preparation for tomorrow. Big picture work. five-by-eight cards, strategies, plot inflection points, channel bands, review hot lines, spot trends.

Any time between 4:15 and 10:30 P.M.

After-hours trading. Today, the fight never stops. Markets move around the globe like the sun. The main ones in the United States are open from 9:30 A.M. to 4:00 P.M., but there are after-hours markets for just about everything; bonds, stocks, futures. The S&Ps, which are my bread and butter, trade forever. The S&P pit on the Merc closes at 4:15, but then it reopens on a computer system called GLOBEX at 4:45.

GLOBEX trades all through the night until 9:15 the next morning, and then the Merc pit opens up at 9:30. That means that there are only forty-five minutes a day when you can't trade the S&P futures. To help produce more volume, GLOBEX now opens at 6:30 Sunday night. Today the exchanges are just like casinos. They want you playing around the clock. These extended hours can make you old in a hurry

10:30 P.M.

Lights out. Pillow talk.

Audrey: Buzzy, how'd you do today?
    Me: Okay, but I should've done better.
Audrey: All traders are the same. You want to buy at the low, sell at the high, do it three times as large, and quit at the top.
    Me: Yeah, absolutely.

Index

Aesthete, The (painting; La Farge), 151

After-hours trading, 91–93, 103, 238–43, 245, 293–94

Agents, 128

Alyzer, A. N., 250–51

American Impressionism (Gerdts), 144–45

American Impressionists, 145–55

American Medical International, 57–58, 59, 60, 61, 63–64

American Medicorp, 51

American Paper Institute, 18, 91

American Stock Exchange, 229
  buying seat on, 4, 11, 27
  as Curb Exchange, 2
  described, 2
  first trades by Schwartz on, 1, 3–5, 7–13
  members' lounge, 1–2
  minimum trading increments, 8
  opening of, 2–3

Amgen, 235

Amherst, Jeffrey, 35

Amherst College, 7, 9, 35–36, 58, 69–70, 99–100, 142

Amshar Management Report, 270

Analogs, 181

Appel, Uranus J., 60, 62, 63

Applebaum, Allen, 10

Aqueduct, 35, 43–44

Arbitrage, 85

Art collecting, 143–55
  American Impressionists, 145–55
  auction houses and, 146–53
  Impressionists, 144

ASA, 74–76, 97

Aspen Institute, 180

Asset Management, 137

At the Crest of the Tidal Wave (Prechter), 173–74

Avon, 64

Bacon, Louis, 181–82, 203, 207–9, 210, 227–28

Bally Entertainment, 26

Barron's, 114, 117, 120, 121, 171, 177, 193, 195–96, 197–98, 200

Baseball cards, 33–34

Basketball bets, 41–42

Bay Networks, 122

Bear markets, 247

Bear Stearns, 4, 10, 75–76, 101, 138, 160, 229, 289

Bear Stearns Morning Comments, 271

Berra, Yogi, 230, 288

Bertelli, Rich and Susan, 17–18, 19

Beta, 207

Bevill, Bresler & Schulman, 135–39

Bhargava, Rakesh, 194, 195, 197, 198–99, 225

Bhutto, Benazir, 199–200

Big Board. *See* New York Stock Exchange

Biggs, Barton, 210

Blue-chip companies, 145, 168. *See also names of specific companies*

Blue Cross, 218

Bond futures, 195–96, 226–27

Bookies, 40–42

Brant, Kevin, 194, 195, 197, 198
Breakaway gap, 282
Bristol-Myers, 235
Brokaw, Tom, 236
Brokers
  dishonest, 128–30
  front running by, 128–30, 169
  scale trading and, 129–30
Bronchtein, Abe, 50–51, 53, 58–59, 65
Brooks, John, 186
Brown, Allison, 211
Brown, Harry, 73–74
Bucketing trades, 116
Bull markets, 247
Bunker Ramo, 27–28
Burr, Aaron, 9
Bush, George, 163, 236

Cantor Fitzgerald, 90
Carew, Rod, 98
Carmine (bookie), 40–42, 164
Casey, Doug, 73–74
Cash bonds
  after-hours trading of, 91–93, 103
  S&P 500 futures and, 91–95, 100–101, 105
Cash settlement, 132, 133
Cassatt, Mary, 145, 154
Cayne, Jimmy, 138
Chartist, The, 271
Chase, William Merritt, 147, 152
Chase Manhattan, 277
Cherry, Wendell, 41, 51
Chicago Board of Trade (CBT), 81–86, 178, 226–27, 238–43, 245
Chicago Board Options Exchange, 26, 284
Chicago Mercantile Exchange (Merc), 65, 81–86, 128–40, 178
  brackets on, 115
  Crash of 1987 and, 167–71

front running and, 128–30, 169
Index Options Membership (IOM), 132–40
legal department, 131, 138, 139
open outcry system, 130, 157, 168
pit committee, 130–31
scale trading and, 129–30
Schwartz visits floor of, 156–58
slippage, 131–32, 170–71
Third LaSalle Services and, 133–40
whistling out trades, 130–31
Christie's, 146, 154
Clark, Jack, 50–51
Clearing firms, 4, 86
  Bear Stearns, 4, 10, 75–76, 101, 138, 160, 229, 289
  Discount Corp., 238
  LIT Futures, 238, 239
  Saul Stone & Co., 139–40, 156–58, 160, 167, 168, 169, 170
  Spear, Leeds & Kellogg, 86, 92–94, 132, 133
  Third LaSalle Services, 133–40
Closing the book, 168
CNN, 242, 243
Coca-Cola, 277
Coe-Kerr Gallery, 147–48
Cohen, Eddie, 34, 143
Coins
  gold, 71–73, 76, 77–79, 164
  silver, 73
Collins, Tommy, 253, 257, 259, 261
Columbia Business School, 7, 36, 49, 142, 233
Coming Currency Collapse, The (Smith), 73–74
Commissions, 129, 132, 133
  slippage and, 131–32, 170–71
  transfer fees, 27

Commodities Corporation, 175–84, 189
  negotiations with, 178–80
  origins of, 176, 178
  Semi-Annual Trader's Dinner, 175–77, 180–84, 190, 210
Commodity Futures Trading Commission (CFTC), 133–34, 136, 139
Compaq, 235, 277
Concept stocks, 50–52
Contests. *See* United States Stock, Option & Commodity Trading Championship
Continuation gap, 282
Cook, Mark, 141–42, 266, 271, 281, 290
Cost of capital, 86, 134–35
Cowen Morning Call, 271
Craps, 37–38, 47–48, 110
Crash of 1987, 159–71, 181, 186, 195–96
  gold and, 163–67, 171
  Merc and, 167–71
  program trading and, 279–80
  S&P 500 futures and, 161–62, 168–71
Crawford Perspective, 271
Crisis Investing (Casey), 73–74
Crocker, Elaine, 178
Curb Exchange. *See* American Stock Exchange

D'Agostino, Leon, 96–97
Daley, Richard, 128
Davis, Dick, 271
Davis and Gilbert, 60
Dean Witter, 193
Dee, Joey, 1, 10
Defined contribution retirement plans, 177–78
Defined risk, 278
Delta Airlines, 235
Denny, Harry, 177, 181, 184

Deutsche marks futures, 86
Dick Davis Digest, 271
Dick West's Morning Comment, 271
Digital Equipment, 14, 96–97
Discount Corp., 238
Diversification, 12
Dorfman, Dan, 62, 64, 260, 261
Double Eagles, 71–72, 73
Dow Jones & Company, 185
Dow Jones Industrial Average (DJIA), 159–62, 266, 277
Dow Jones Net Ticks (TIKI), 267, 281
Dow Jones Transportation Average (DJIT), 277
Dow Theory Letters, 206
Drexel Burnham, 195
Druckenmiller, Fiona Biggs, 210
Druckenmiller, Stanley, 209, 210, 227–28

E. F. Hutton, 11, 18, 22, 27–28, 100
East New York Savings Bank, 163, 171
Easton, Bob, 176, 178–79, 181, 182, 183
Economic Recovery Tax Act of 1981, 85
Edison, Thomas A., 263
Edwards and Hanly, 7, 24–25, 186, 212
Efficient market theory, 114–15
Ego, dangers of, 47–48, 156–58, 287
Elders Futures Inc., 189–90
Elliott, Ralph Nelson, 172
Elliott Wave Hotline, 169
Elliott Wave Principle (Prechter and Frost), 172
Elliott Wave Theorist, The (newsletter), 169, 172
Escape to the Futures (Melamed and Tamarkin), 82–83, 131

Estes, Billy Sol, 113
Eurodollar futures, 86, 239, 240, 242, 245
Exhaustion gap, 282
Exponential moving average (EMA), 270–76
Extendacare, 41

Fannie Mae, 235
Farber, Gerry, 212
Fast markets, 290
Fat Mike, 75, 96–97
Favia, Jack, 50, 53, 58–59, 65
Financial News Network, 217
Financial Traders Association, 114
Fine, Ellen, 69–70
First trade back, 286–87
Football bets, 40–41, 42
Ford, Whitey, 230
Four Seasons Nursing Centers, 50–51
Frederiksen, Esther, 219, 221, 222, 249
Fresco, Al, 144–54, 156, 191, 193, 194, 234
Fresco-Pallette Gallery, 144–54, 191
Friedman, Bob, 26
Friedman, Milton, 163
Frieseke, Frederick, 145, 147, 153, 154
Frist, Tom, 51
Front running, 128–30, 169
Frost, A. J., 172
Fundamental analysis, 23, 265
Futures contracts, 82–98
  Eurodollar, 86, 239, 240, 242, 245
  fast markets, 290
  gold, 86, 237–39, 243–44, 245
  oil, 182–84, 207, 237–39, 243–44, 245
  short sales, 84, 104–8, 207–8, 235
  Standard & Poor's 500 Stock Index Futures, 88–95

taxes and, 84–86
tax straddles, 84–85
trading methodology, 278–79
Treasury bond, 83–84, 86, 89–92, 238–39
See also S&P 500 futures
Futures magazine, 117
FutureSource, 274, 278–79

Gambling, 33–48
  on baseball, 41–42
  baseball cards and, 33–34
  bookies and, 40–42, 164
  craps and, 37–38, 47–48, 110
  European trip and, 36–37
  on football, 40–41, 42
  horses and, 35–36, 43–44, 231
  in Las Vegas, 39–40, 47–48
  in Paradise Island, 44–45
  planning and, 38–40, 45–46, 47–48
  poker and, 34–35, 114
  priorities in, 45–46
  roulette and, 36–37
  rules of, 34–46, 47–48
Gambling Times, 114
Gap, The, 235
Garden, The (painting; Prendergast), 147–48, 152–53
Gee, Donnie, 10, 97
General partners, 192
Georgia Gulf, 204
Gerdts, William, 144, 145
Germany, 161
Gillette, 235
Ginnie Mae, 83
Glackens, William, 154
GLOBEX, 293–94
Goals
  planning and, 18–19, 21–22
Godfather, The (film), 42, 164
Gold, 70–79
  coins, 71–73, 76, 77–79, 164
  Crash of 1987 and, 163–67, 171

gold standard, 71, 82–83
  gold stocks, 74–76, 97
  as investment, 73
  rumors concerning, 77–79
Gold, Dr., 222–23, 225–26
Goldfedder, Avi, 219–20, 226–27,
    238, 240, 241, 242, 243, 245
Goldfinger (film), 69–70
Gold futures, 86, 237–39, 243–44,
    245
Goldsamt, Bob, 51
Goldstein, Paul, 65, 87
Golf, 256–57, 260
Granville, Joe, 122
Great Depression, 6, 7, 71, 102
Great Pyramid, 52–64, 118, 212
Greenspan, Alan, 167
Grubstake, 21–22, 25, 26, 30–31,
    246
Gura, Ray, 106–7, 229–30

H. Hentz & Co., 42–43, 44
Hamilton, Alexander, 9, 13, 244
Hassam, Childe, 147, 151–52, 154
Hausmann Overseas N.V., 208, 225
Hedge funds, 190–228
  annual reviews, 208–9
  fee structure, 203–4
  formation of, 190–201
  managing large sums and, 204–5
  redemptions, 215, 217–18, 220,
    225
  Sabrina Offshore Fund Ltd., 192,
    193–201, 203, 208–10, 215,
    239, 251
  Sabrina Partners L.P., 192–93,
    203, 208, 237–39, 250–51,
    255–56
  Upjohn and, 206–7, 211
Hershkowitz, David, 86
Hirsch, Neil, 90
Hochman, Raymond, 20, 217–18,
    220–21, 226, 234, 235, 249
Home Depot, 235

Homer, Winslow, 145, 154
Honeywell, 25
Hoover, Herbert, 163
Horn, Debbie
  leaves trading, 253
  at Saul Stone & Co., 139–40,
    156–58, 160, 167, 168, 169
  at Spear, Leeds & Kellogg, 77,
    78, 86, 92–94, 101, 104–5, 132,
    133
  at Third LaSalle Services,
    133–40
Horse racing, 35–36, 43–44,
    230–31
Hospital Corporation of America,
    51, 57–58, 59, 61
Hospital management, 51–66
House Ways and Means
    Committee, 84–85
Howard, Elston, 230
*How to Profit from the Coming
    Devaluation* (Browne), 73–74
*How to Prosper from the Coming
    Bad Years* (Ruff), 73–74
Hunt brothers, 113
Hussein, Saddam, 207, 235, 237,
    243, 244

IBM, 25
Impressionists, 144
Index funds, 285
Index Options Membership (IOM),
    132–33
India, 194
Inflation, 97, 178
Inside Skinny, 67–68, 77–79, 118,
    167, 171, 186, 206–7, 259, 260,
    266
Intel, 282
Interest rates, 91, 108
Internal Revenue Service, 84
International Monetary Market
    (IMM), 83
Investment banking, 49, 52

Investment Research Institute, 271

Investor's Daily, 117

Jardin de paysanne (*Peasant Garden*) (painting; Vonnoh), 144, 153–54

Jarrett, Dennis, 160

Jean-Claude (middleman), 221–22

Joe, Frankie, 117, 118–19

Johnson, George, 63

Johnson & Johnson, 235

Jones, David, 51

Jones, Paul Tudor. *See* Tudor Jones, Paul

Keynes, John Maynard, 193

Khayyam, Kamran, 198–200

Khayyam, Omar, 197, 198–99

Kidder, Peabody, 160, 194, 237, 239, 242, 243–44

Kissinger, Henry, 163

Kodak, 64

Kohl, Helmut, 163

Korman, Bernie, 51

Kornstein, Dan, 178–80

Koufax, Sandy, 258

Kovner, Bruce, 176–77, 179, 180–81, 184, 190, 203, 207–9, 210, 227–28

Kuhn Loeb, 39, 44, 50–52, 53, 58–59, 65

Kush, Ken, 230–31, 238, 240–41, 242, 243, 245

Kuwait, 207, 235, 237

La Farge, John, 151

Landis, Bernard, 249–50, 256–60

La Salle, Sieur de, 133

Las Vegas, Nevada, 39–40, 47–48

Laundry, Terry, 23–24, 141, 172–73, 270, 290

Lawson, Ernest, 144, 154

Leverage, 22, 85, 86, 88, 89

LeVine, Rob, 234, 235, 249

Levy, Leon, 210

Lewis, Michael, 113

Liar's Poker (Lewis), 113

Limited, The, 235

Limited partners, 192

Lin Broadcasting, 204

Lincoln, Larry, 36

Lincoln, Steve, 36

Liquidity, 25

Liscio, John, 114, 120, 121, 193, 195–96

LIT Futures, 238, 239

Locked limits, 105–7

London Metal Exchange, 178

London School of Economics, 194

Long-term capital gains, 85

Losses
  losing streaks and, 48, 110–11
  taking, 122–23

Lowry's NYSE Market Trend Analysis, 270

MacMaster, R. E., 23

Magic T Theory (Laundry), 23–25, 172–73

Mantle, Mickey, 98, 230

Marcucci, Jackie, 133, 135, 136, 137, 138, 140

Marcucci, Johnny, 135, 136, 138, 140

Marcus, Michael, 22, 176, 179, 184, 190

Margin calls, 136, 167

Margin requirements, 86, 88, 93, 239

Margolis, Mike, 138

Marine Corps, 17, 39, 58, 142, 149, 162, 233, 234, 236, 237, 239–40

Marion, John, 150–53

Maris, Roger, 230

Market analysis, 268–70

Market Probability Calendar, 285

Market Technicians Association, 173

Market Wizards (Schwager), 31, 193, 197, 203, 207, 254–55

Marking to the market, 132

Massey, Jack, 51

Medicaid, 51, 55, 56, 57, 59, 217, 218

Medicare, 51, 55, 56, 57, 59, 217, 218

Melamed, Leo, 82–83, 84–85, 88, 131, 138, 167, 168

Merck, 235, 277

Merrill Lynch, 76, 84, 172

Mesa Petroleum, 1, 3–5, 7–13, 74, 75, 96, 97

Metriplex, 219, 257

Mexico, 77–79, 89, 159

Miceli, Louis "Chickie," 3–5, 8–14, 74, 75, 96

Microsoft, 235, 282

Midmonth buying, 282

Mondays, up, 285

Monet, Claude, 144

Money Game, The (Smith), 23

Montgomery Securities, 26

Morgan Guaranty, 165–66

Morgan Stanley, 167, 210

Moynihan, Daniel Patrick, 84–85

Muldoon, Jerry, 10, 96–98

Murphy, Dan, 28–29

Mutual funds, 177–78
    cash infusions from, 282
    index funds, 285
    up Mondays, 285

NASDAQ Composite, 277

National Association of Securities Dealers, 27

Nature's Law (Elliott), 172

NBC Nightly News, 236

ND (nothing done) orders, 129

Neuberger & Berman, 208

New highs and lows, 186, 285

Newton, Wayne, 143

New York Commodity Exchange (COMEX), 74

New York Composite Index (NYA), 204, 267, 272, 277, 292

New York Futures Exchange (knife), 86, 105–9

New York Hospital, 217, 218–20, 221–24, 227

New York Post, 244

New York Society of Security Analysts, 63

New York Stock Exchange (Big Board), 2, 3, 10, 117, 168
    gold stocks on, 74
    highs/lows, 186
    special investigation of hospital management stocks, 60–61, 62
    Stock Watch program, 62

New York Stock Exchange Index, 105

New York Stock Exchange Net Ticks (TICK), 266–67, 281

New York Times, 118

NH (not held orders), 241

Nike, 235

Nixon, Richard, 82–83, 163

Noel, Hayes, 10, 11, 15, 26–27, 97, 156

Nontrending days, 286

Noontime rally, 286

Not held (NH) orders, 241

Nothing done (ND) orders, 129

Novell, 236

Nursing homes, 50–51

Odyssey Partners, 210

Oil futures, 182–84, 207, 237–39, 243–44, 245

On the River (painting; Frieseke), 147, 153

Open outcry system, 130, 157, 168

Operation Desert Storm, 236–45
Options, 85
    defined, 3
    expirations of, 285–86
    first trades by Schwartz in, 1,
        3–5
    put/call ratios, 186, 284
Outcry system, 130, 157, 168

Pakistan, 194
Palette, Cliff, 144–54, 156, 191,
    193, 194
Paper trading models, 11
Paradise Island, Bahamas, 44–45,
    159–60
Performance bond, 134–35
Peter the Mustache, 74–76
Philip Morris, 236
Physicals, 89–94, 94
Pickens, Boone, 8
Pit committee, 130–31
Planning
    gambling and, 38–40, 45–46,
        47–48
    goals and, 18–19, 21–22
    trading and, 17–23, 31
Poker, 34–35, 114
Polaroid, 25, 54, 64
Polokoff, Audrey. *See* Schwartz,
    Audrey Polokoff (wife)
Polokoff, Mac (father-in-law), 11
Polokoff, Sally (mother-in-law), 11,
    103, 106
Porky, 251–54, 260, 261, 266
P.Q. Wall Forecast, Inc., 270
Prebend (horse), 230–31
Prechter, Bob, 169, 172–74
Prednisone, 234–35, 241, 242, 243,
    249, 250
Prendergast, Maurice Brazil, 147,
    152–53, 154
Principals, 128
Program trading, 279–80, 286
Put/call ratios, 186, 284

QCHA, 267–68
Quantum B.V.I. Mutual Fund, 171
Quotron machines, 87–88, 92,
    96–97, 101, 104, 106

Reagan, Ronald, 76
Reaganomics, 102
Red Book, *A Guide Book of United
    States Coins*, 72–73
Regulated accounts, 134–35, 136,
    137, 139
Repurchase agreements (repos),
    134, 137, 139
Reserve requirements, 134
Retirement plans, 177–78, 212–13
Reversal of Fortune (film), 216
Reverse repos, 137
Road to the Sea (painting;
    Hassam), 147, 151–52
Robb & Robb, 246–47
Robertson, Julian, 192, 209–10,
    227–28
Robinson, Theodore, 145, 147,
    152
Rockefeller, David, 163–64, 165
Roosevelt, Franklin D., 71–72, 99
Rosenthal, Les, 84
Rostenkowski, Dan, 84–85, 89
Roulette, 36–37
Round turns, 132
Royko, Mike, 128
Ruff, Howard J., 73–74
Rukeyser, Louis, 160
Rumors. *See* Inside Skinny
Russell, Richard, 23, 206

Sabrina Offshore Fund Ltd., 192,
    193–201, 203, 208–10, 215,
    239, 251
Sabrina Partners L.P., 192–93, 203,
    208, 237–39, 250–51, 255–56
Saint-Gaudens, Augustus, 72
Sandner, Jack, 168
Sandor, Richard, 83, 89

Santangelo, Frannie, 14, 96–97, 151
Saul Stone & Co., 139–40, 156–58, 160, 167, 168, 169, 170
Saunders, Paul, 194, 195, 197, 198
Scale trading, 129–30
Schaffer on Sentiment, 271
Schmeiss, Mike, 215, 227
Schwager, Jack D., 31, 193, 203
Schwartz, Audrey Polokoff (wife)
  at American Paper Institute, 18, 91
  art collecting and, 143–55
  breast cancer, 143
  in business with husband, 91–94, 99, 101–9, 189–91, 229
  Crash of 1987 and, 162–63, 165, 171
  engagement and marriage, 20–21, 45
  gold rumors and, 78–79
  hospitalization of husband and, 217, 218–20, 221–24, 227
  initial relationship with Schwartz, 19–20
  move to Florida, 259–61
  planning and, 17–23, 31
  pregnancies, 87, 103, 126, 127
  Schwartz's career as trader and, 4, 5, 7, 9, 10
Schwartz, Gerry (brother), 43–44, 60, 78–79, 166
Schwartz, Martin "Buzzy"
  art collecting and, 143–55
  in Aspen, 191, 250, 254–55
  beach house, 77–79, 87–88, 126, 206, 256
  buys seat on American Stock Exchange, 4, 11
  children, 127–28, 216, 259
  Crash of 1987 and, 159–71
  education, 7, 9, 35–36, 49, 58, 142, 233, 265

engagement and marriage, 20–21, 45
family background, 6–7
first trades, 1, 3–5
and the Great Pyramid, 52–64, 118, 212
grubstake of, 21–22, 25, 26, 30–31, 246
hedge funds. *See* Hedge funds
hospitalization, 217, 218–20, 221–24, 227
at Kuhn Loeb, 39, 44, 50–52, 53, 58–59, 65
managing other people's money and, 120, 177, 180, 189–228
in the Marines, 17, 39, 58, 142, 149, 162, 233, 234, 236, 237, 239–40
move to Florida, 259–61
Park Avenue apartment, 125–28, 135, 143, 154–55, 206, 259
personal retirement funds, 212–13
recovery from illness, 234–47
as securities analyst, 4–6, 7, 11, 18, 19, 21, 27–29, 39–40, 44, 49–66, 94, 100, 107
trading methodology of. *See* Trading methodology
trading rules. *See* Trading rules
trips to Europe, 36–38, 196–201
unemployment and, 64–66, 212
Schwartz, Sam (grandfather), 71–72
Schwarzkopf, Norman, 244
Scudder, Stevens & Clark, 59, 62–63
Securities and Exchange Commission (SEC), 120–21, 137, 192
Security Market Research (SMA), 277–78, 293
Selling climax, 160
Seward & Kissel, 190

Seykota, Ed, 22

Sharp, Dee Dee, 15

Shearson, 169–71, 177, 181, 184

Shinnecock Landscape (painting; Chase), 147, 152

"Shoot dying quails" rule, 11, 12

Short sales, 7, 84, 97–98, 103, 104–8, 158

Short-Term Trading Index (TRIN), 267

Shultz, George, 163

Silver coins, 73

SIMEX (Singapore Mercantile Exchange), 239, 240

Slippage, 131–32, 170–71

Smith, Adam, 23, 193

Smith, Jerome F., 73–74

Snyder, Pappy (grandfather), 6, 34–35, 36, 70, 87, 289

Softball, 260

Solomon, Jack, 160

Soros, George, 171, 192, 210, 227–28, 253

Sotheby's, 145–54

  auction at, 150–54

  "by appointment only" evenings, 148

Spear, Leeds & Kellogg, 77, 78, 86, 92–94, 101, 104–5, 132, 133

Specialists, 3–5, 101, 168, 246–47

S&P 500 futures, 99, 242

  cash bonds and, 91–95, 100–101, 105

  cash settlement, 132, 133

  Crash of 1987 and, 161–62, 168–71

  Schwartz on floor of Merc and, 156–58

  shorting, 104–8, 207–8, 235

  trading methodology for, 278–79

Squibb, 235

Standard and Poor's Trendline Daily Action Stock Charts, 276–77

Standard & Poor's 500 Stock Index Futures, 88–95

Standard & Poor's 500 Stock Index (SPX), 267, 277

Standish, Paul, 59, 62–63, 64

Stan Weinstein's Global Trend Alert, 270

Steinbrenner, George, 143

Steinhardt, Michael, 192

Stengel, Casey, 96

Stern, Eddie, 10

Stock buyback programs, 168

Stocks and Commodities magazine, 117

Stock Trader's Almanac, 285

Stop losses, 122–23, 161, 284, 286

Stress management, 249–50, 256–60

Strike price, 1

Sullivan, Dan, 271

Summary of Top Managers, 120

Summer Hillside, Giverny (painting; Robinson), 147, 152

Sunspot theory, 106

Swiss francs futures, 86

Syntex, 20–21, 25

Tamarkin, Bob, 82–83

Tavss, John, 190

Taxes

  futures and, 84–86

  long-term capital gains, 85

  rates, 99

  tax straddles, 84–85

Technical analysis, 23–26, 27, 265–87

  cash infusions from mutual funds, 282

  computer modeling and, 178, 181, 182

  ego and, 47–48, 156–58, 287

  Elliott Wave theory, 172–74

  exponential moving average (EMA) in, 270–76

first trade back, 286–87
gaps in charts, 281–82
market analysis in, 268–70
Market Probability Calendar, 285
market reaction to news, 284
new highs and lows in, 186, 285
nontrending days, 286
option expirations, 285–86
put/call ratios, 186, 284
three-day rule, 282–83
tools of the trade in, 266–68
trading on half hour, 286
tricks of the trade, 281–87
up Mondays, 285
worst fears not realized, 287
Teledyne, 25
Telerate, 89–92, 94, 95, 100, 101, 103, 105, 114
Tenneco, 159
Texaco, 10, 96
Texas Instruments, 236
Thatcher, Margaret, 163
Third LaSalle Services, 133–40
Three-day rule, 282–83
Tips. *See* Inside Skinny
Trade deficit, 161
Trading increments, minimum, 8
Trading methodology
in bull and bear markets, 247
development of, 21, 23–26, 116, 156, 265–66
effectiveness of, 132
ego and, 47–48, 156–58, 287
for futures, 278–79
Magic T theory and, 23–25, 88, 92, 169, 172–73, 179–80, 270, 290
market analysis and, 268–70
other people's money and, 192–93
planning in, 17–23, 31
program trading and, 279–80, 286
rounds in, 115

rules for successful traders, 141–42, 149
for stocks, 276–78
typical day, 288–94
Trading rules, 11–12
amount at risk, 11–12
lessons for life and, 229–32
losing streaks and, 110–11
"shoot dying quails," 11, 12
take losses, 123
Transfer fees, 27
Treasury bills, 86, 134–35, 137
Treasury bond futures contracts, 83–84, 86, 89–92, 238–39, 242, 245
Triple M's (market-maker-margins), 22
Trump, Donald, 198
Tudor Jones, Paul, 22, 173, 179, 181–82, 184, 190, 197, 203, 207–9, 210, 227–28
Tullis, Eli, 22
Turner, Ted, 143
Twachtman, John H., 144

Ultimate contract, 88
Uncle point, 122, 161
Unemployment, 102, 212
United Airlines, 194–95, 236
United States Stock, Option & Commodity Trading Championship, 113–21, 173, 177
divisions of, 115, 120
entry fees, 116
first contest, 116–17
minimum investment, 115–16
origins of, 114–15
other uses of, 119–21
second contest, 117
suspension of, 120–21
third contest, 118
University of California at Los Angeles (UCLA), 114–15

Upjohn, 206–7, 211
Up Mondays, 285

Van Pelt, Kimberly, 165–66
Volcker, Paul, 79, 89, 159
Vonnoh, Robert, 144, 145, 153–54

Wall Street Journal, 62, 102, 119,
    120–21, 191, 244, 289
  Bevill, Bresler & Schulman
    incident, 136, 137, 139, 140
  Crash of 1987 and, 160
  tips for reading, 185–87
Wall Street Letter, 117
Wall Street Week, 160, 161
WalMart, 236
Wash sales, 84
Waste Management, 236
Weinstein, Stan, 270
Weiskopf, Danny, 26–27
Weisman, Neil, 209, 212–13
West, Dick, 271, 290
Weymar, Helmut, 178, 179–80,
    181, 182, 183, 191

Whistling out trades, 130–31
Willie the Web, 209–10, 221
Wilson, Eugene S., 100
Windy City Museum (Chicago),
    156, 158
Winning Poker Systems (Zadeh),
    114
Winter Reflections (painting;
    Lawson), 144

Xerox, 25

Yeoman, R. S., 72–73

Zadeh, Norm, 114–21, 173, 177
Zoellner, Bob, 66, 85, 101, 107–8,
    109, 173, 212
  becomes mentor, 22, 24, 29
  Crash of 1987 and, 166, 167,
    171
  first trades by Schwartz and,
    7–8, 9–11, 12, 13
Zweig, Marty, 160–61, 284